Programming VAX-BASIC

E. Joseph Guay
BRYANT COLLEGE

ADDISON-WESLEY PUBLISHING COMPANY

READING, MASSACHUSETTS
MENLO PARK, CALIFORNIA
DON MILLS, ONTARIO
WOKINGHAM, ENGLAND
AMSTERDAM ■ SYDNEY
SINGAPORE ■ TOKYO ■ MEXICO CITY
BOGOTÁ ■ SANTIAGO ■ SAN JUAN

This book is in the ADDISON-WESLEY SERIES IN COMPUTER SCIENCE

James T. DeWolf/Sponsoring Editor

Hugh J. Crawford/Manufacturing Supervisor
Mel Erickson Art Services/Illustrator
Robert C. Forget/Art Coordinator
Richard Hannus, Hannus Design Associates/Cover Designer
Marion E. Howe/Production Editor
Martha K. Morong/Production Manager
Martha Stearns/Managing Editor
Patti Williams/Text Designer

Photos courtesy of Digital Equipment Corporation
VAX is a trademark of Digital Equipment Corporation
DEC is a tradement of Digital Equipment Corporation.

Library of Congress Cataloging in Publication Data

Guay, E. Joseph.
    Programming in VAX-BASIC.

    Bibliography: p.
    Includes index.
    1. VAX-11 (Computer)—Programming.   2. Basic (Computer
program language)   I. Title.   II. Title: Programming in
V.A.X.-B.A.S.I.C.
QA76.8.V37G83   1986   001.64'2   84-14602
ISBN 0-201-11566-2

Reprinted with corrections November, 1985
Copyright © 1986 by Addison-Wesley Publishing Company, Inc.

All rights reserved. No part of this publication may be reproduced, stored in a retrieval system, or transmitted, in any form or by any means, electronic, mechanical, photocopying, recording, or otherwise, without the prior written permission of the publisher. Printed in the United States of America. Published simultaneously in Canada.

BCDEFGHIJ-HA-89876

Preface

Programming in VAX-BASIC evolved from course notes used in conjunction with a BASIC programming course that I taught for several years at Northeastern University. My experience showed that beginning students were easily confused and frustrated by a discussion of the many variations of the language and that there was a need for an introductory text that focused on the particular version of BASIC used on the VAX computer.

This specific approach has a number of advantages. Perhaps the most direct advantage is that it makes things easier for both the student and the instructor by eliminating details that do not apply or need not be of concern. In addition, this approach allows more time to focus on the more important topics that involve program planning and algorithm development.

Chapter 1 is a detailed introduction to the procedures for using BASIC on the VAX computer. The instructions and procedures include "screens" that show the computer display in order to provide immediate feedback and encouragement to the student. This chapter is the longest and most detailed part of the book. It has gone through several revisions in an effort to help the student become comfortable with the computer with a minimum of frustration.

At the other end of the learning spectrum, the book covers a number of advanced programming topics and tools that are of interest only to the more experienced programmer. Even if this text is used for a one term course that does not cover these topics, I feel that it is valuable to include sections that deal with them. If the student continues to use the computer, the text will provide a valuable reference when there is a need for one of these features. In addition, many of the programs from the later chapters can be used as examples to illustrate the capabilities of VAX-BASIC.

The text can be used for a one- or two-term course on VAX-BASIC. The core material is contained in Sections 1.1 through 9.4 and can provide the basis for a 12-week introductory course. Additional topics can be selected from the remaining chapters based on the interests of the audience. A continuation with Sections 9.5–9.8, 11.1–11.3, and Chapters 12, 13, and 15 would provide a more numerical emphasis, while a continuation with Chapters 10, 11, 12, and 14 would provide a more business oriented emphasis.

Many of the most useful and powerful features of VAX-BASIC are discussed in Chapter 12. A glance through the book will reveal a radical difference in the appearance of the programs beginning with that chapter. In general, the programs are longer, more structured, and tend to do more useful things. There is a program that students can use to get an accurate evaluation of exercise activity, a word processing program, programs to solve linear equations, a "game of life" simulation, and programs to create and maintain database files (including some that are indexed with multiple keys). A tape containing most of these programs is available to instructors who adopt this text. Contact the publisher for details.

Acknowledgement

I would like to extend my sincere appreciation to all of the people who have contributed in some way to the production of this book. In particular, I would like to thank my former colleagues at Northeastern University who used the Northeastern Custom Text version of these notes and contributed helpful suggestions. Special thanks to Dean Richard Astro and Pete Gilmore for their encouragement and support, and to John Casey, Paul Holly, and Victor Staknis for helpful suggestions and sample exercises. My sincere thanks to the reviewers: Ann T. Goodman of the University of Massachusetts (Amherst), Randy M. Kaplan, Cynthia E. Johnson of Bryant College, Glenn Pavlicek of Northeastern University, and Brad Wilson of Western Kentucky University who all provided additional suggestions for improvement. Finally, I would like to thank the entire production staff at Addison-Wesley for their patience and fine work in bringing this project to completion. Special thanks to Jim DeWolfe, Marion Howe, and Patti Williams.

Providence, Rhode Island   E.J.G.

Contents

1

Introduction 1

- 1.1 **Why VAX-BASIC?** 1
- 1.2 **The Computer Program** 2
- 1.3 **The Programming Process** 4
  - Review: The Programming Process 5
- 1.4 **The VAX Computer** 5
- 1.5 **Using the Terminal** 8
  - Some Common Mistakes 8
- 1.6 **Getting Started** 11
  - Review: Getting Started 15
- 1.7 **Correcting Errors** 15
  - Review: Correcting Errors 21
- 1.8 **Displaying and Retrieving Your Programs** 21
  - Review: Retrieving Programs from Disk Memory 26
- 1.9 **Renaming and Deleting Programs** 26
  - Review: Renaming and Deleting Files 29
- 1.10 **Using DCL Commands in BASIC Mode** 29
  - Review: Entering System Commands from BASIC Mode 31
- 1.11 **Obtaining Copies of Your Programs** 31
  - Using the High-Speed Printer 32

Review: Obtaining Copies Using the
High-Speed Printer   33
Using a Printing Terminal   33
Review: Using a Printing Terminal   35
Using the DOPRINT Command   35
1.12 **Other BASIC Commands**   35
The SEQUENCE Command   35
The EDIT Command   36
The HELP Command   37
1.13 **Exercises**   38

2

Elementary Grammar   41

2.1 **Variables**   42
Naming Variables   42
2.2 **The LET Statement**   43
Review: The LET Statement   45
2.3 **The Print Statement**   46
Tabbing Over   48
Review: The PRINT Statement   49
The TAB Function   49
Review: The TAB Function   50
2.4 **The READ and DATA Statements**   50
Review: The READ/DATA Statement Pair   52
2.5 **The INPUT Statement**   53
Review: The INPUT Statement   56
2.6 **The REMARK Statement**   56
Review: REMARK and !   57
2.7 **The GOTO Statement**   58
2.8 **The END Statement**   58
2.9 **Using These Statements**   59

　　　　　An Age Graph　　59
　　　　　A Retirement Table　　60
　2.10　**Exercises**　　62

3

Working with Data　　65

　3.1　**More about the LET and the PRINT Statements**　　65
　3.2　**Algebraic Operations**　　66
　　　　　Example: Present-Worth Factor　　70
　3.3　**Exponential Notation**　　70
　3.4　**Built-in Functions**　　71
　　　　　Example: Root of a Quadratic Equation　　74
　　　　　Example: Game Simulations Using RND　　74
　　　　　Review: Using Functions　　75
　3.5　**Exercises**　　75

4

Decision-Making Methods　　79

　4.1　**Conditional Execution (IF-THEN)**　　80
　4.2　**Logical Conditions**　　80
　4.3　**The Multiline IF-THEN Statement**　　82
　　　　　Line Continuations Using the Sequencer　　83
　4.4　**The IF-THEN-ELSE Statement**　　84
　　　　　Example: Roots of a Quadratic Equation　　86
　　　　　Example: Calculating the Exercise Value
　　　　　　　of a Run　　88
　　　　　Review: The IF-THEN-ELSE Construct　　90

4.5 **Multiple Alternatives Using the SELECT Statement** 91
4.6 ★ **Nested IF-THEN-ELSE Statements** 93
4.7 **Exercises** 94

Loops 97

5.1 **Situations in Which Loops Are Useful** 97
5.2 **The FOR Loop** 98
   Example: Sums and Averages 100
   Example: Retirement Fund Table 102
   Review: FOR Loops 102
5.3 **Nested FOR Loops** 104
5.4 **The Use of the FOR Loop** 106
   Bar Graphs 106
   Geometric Patterns 109
   Time Delays and SLEEP 110
5.5 **WHILE and UNTIL Loops** 111
5.6 **Exercises** 114

String Variables 117

6.1 **Assigning a Value to a String Variable** 119
   The LET and PRINT Statements 119
   The READ, DATA, and INPUT Statements 120

The LINPUT Statement   122
Review: Assigning the Value of a String Variable   123
6.2 **String Comparisons**   124
6.3 **Example: Obtaining a Word at Random from a List**   124
6.4 **Exercises**   125

7

Building Programs   127

7.1 **Planning the Program: The First Outline**   127
7.2 **Refine the Algorithm**   128
7.3 **Writing the Program**   129
7.4 **Getting the Bugs Out**   131
    Finding Logical Errors   132
7.5 **The Final Draft**   132
    Example: The Number Game   133
7.6 **Exercises**   139

8

Program Structure   141

8.1 **Subroutines**   141
    Review: Using Subroutines   143
8.2 **The ON-GOSUB Statement and Menus**   145
8.3 **User-Defined Functions**   148
    Example: Swimming Exercise Value   149

8.4 **Building a Program with Subroutines**   150
         Using the APPEND Command To
         Combine Programs   153
  8.5 **Exercises**   160

9

Arrays and Sorting   163

   9.1 **Subscripted Variables**   163
        Review: Subscripted Variables   164
   9.2 **The Dimension Statement**   165
   9.3 **Using Arrays with Lists**   166
   9.4 **Finding the Largest Number in a List**   166
       The Selection Sort   169
       The Bubble Sort   172
       ★ Using a "Boolean" Variable to Test for
          a Sorted List   175
       Tandem Sort   178
       ★ Index Arrays   179
   9.5 **Exercises**   183

10

More Operations with Strings   185

   10.1 **Built-In String Functions and Constants**   185
        The CHR$ Function   185
        The DATE$ Function   187
        The EDIT$ Function   187
   10.2 **Building Strings Up**   188

- 10.3 **Taking Strings Apart**   **190**
  - The SEG$ Function   191
  - The LEN Function   192
  - The POS Function   194
  - Example: Obtaining the First Word of a Sentence   195
- 10.4 **Converting Numbers to Strings**   **197**
  - The NUM$ and STR$ Functions   197
  - The FORMAT$ Function   198
  - Review: Converting Numbers to Strings   199
- 10.5 **Converting a String to a Number**   **200**
  - Example: Rounding a Number   201
- 10.6 **The PRINT USING Statement**   **202**
  - More about the PRINT USING Statement   203
  - Example: Calculating Compound Interest   207
  - Example: A Julian Date Conversion Function   210
  - Example: The Hangman Game   211
- 10.7 **Exercises**   **216**

11

Using Standard Data Files   219

- 11.1 **Writing Output to a Data File**   **220**
  - Review: Writing Data to a File   222
- 11.2 **Obtaining a Copy of a Program and the Output**   **222**
- 11.3 **Getting Data from a File**   **223**
  - LINPUT from a File   224
  - Review: Getting Data from a File   225
  - Creating the Data File Used for Input   225
- 11.4 **Testing for the End of a File**   **226**
- 11.5 **Adding to a Data File**   **227**
  - Example: Displaying the Contents of a File   227
  - Example: Text Analysis   228

11.6 **The RESTORE Statement for a File**   230
   Example: Cryptograms   230
   The XLATE Function   232
11.7 **Exercises**   235

12

Block-Structured Programming Methods   239

12.1 **Omitting Line Numbers**   239
12.2 **Using Labels**   240
   Example: The ECOUNT Program   240
   Example: The Aerobic Exercise Program   242
   Example: FORMTXT—A Word Processing Program   247
12.3 **Exercises**   258

13

Matrices   261

13.1 **The MAT Statements**   263
   Assigning Values Using MAT   264
   The MAT PRINT Statement   265
   The MAT READ Statement   265
   The MAT INPUT Statement   266
13.2 **Matrix Calculations**   268
   Advanced Matrix Operations   268
13.3 **Examples**   270
   The BUSINESS Program   270

★ The Game of Life   278
★ Solution of a Linear System of Equations   286
13.4 **Exercises**   291

14

Mapped and Indexed Files   295

14.1 **The MAP Statement**   295
14.2 **The OPEN Statement for a Mapped File**   297
14.3 **The PUT and GET Statements**   298
14.4 **Adding to, Updating, and Creating Files**   299
   Example: Improving Data Entry   300
14.5 **Indexed Files**   307
14.6 **Using Compound Keys and Alternate Keys**   312
   ★ Example: Birthday List and Reminder Program   312
14.7 **Exercises**   317

15

Other Features of VAX-BASIC   319

15.1 **Standard Representation of Real Numbers**   320
   The DECLARE Statement   321
   Data Types in the DIMENSION Statement   322
   The OPTION Statement   322
   DECIMAL DATA Type   325

xiii

15.2 **Compiling Programs in DCL Mode** 326
15.3 **External Function Programs** 327
15.4 **External Subprograms** 330
15.5 **Exercises** 331

Appendix A **DEC Command Language Summary** 333

Appendix B **Summary of BASIC Commands** 337

Appendix C **Summary of BASIC Statements** 339

Appendix D **Numeric Functions and Constants** 351

Appendix E **String Functions and Constants** 353

Appendix F **Table of ASCII Values** 357

Appendix G **Program Template** 359

Appendix H **The Text Editor** 361

    H.1 **Entering and Leaving EDIT Mode** 361
        Review: Entering and Leaving EDIT Mode   363
    H.2 **Entering and Leaving CHANGE Mode** 363
        Review: Entering and Leaving CHANGE Mode   364
    H.3 **EDIT/CHANGE Command Keys** 364
    H.4 **An Easy Way to Make Changes** 365
        Review: Quick Corrections   367
    H.5 **Splitting and Joining Lines** 367
        Review: Splitting and Joining Lines   367
    H.6 **Some Additional Features of EDT** 368
    H.7 **Cut-and-Paste Operations** 369

Appendix I   **Effective Use of the Video Terminal**   371

         I.1   **Communications**   371
         I.2   **Double-Size Displays**   374
         I.3   **Moving the Cursor**   374

Index   377

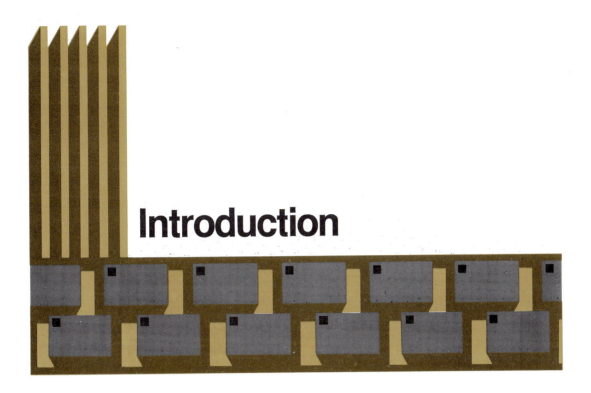

Introduction

The best method of learning to use the computer is through practice. This chapter is both an information source and a guide that is designed to allow you to begin writing programs almost immediately. You will soon realize that a mistake will not result in disaster and that the BASIC programming language is quick and easy to learn.

1.1 Why VAX-BASIC?

The BASIC programming language is one of the most popular languages in use today. However, the language may vary slightly from one computer to another. VAX-BASIC, the version in use on the VAX-11 computer, is a powerful extension of the ANSI standard "minimal" BASIC found on many small computers.

It is unfortunate that there are variations in the different versions of the BASIC language, but if we are to be learning BASIC on the VAX computer it makes sense to have a text that is tailored to that environment. This approach will enable you to write programs for the VAX computer with a minimum of concern for the variations that might be present from one computer to another. In addition, the more advanced features of VAX-BASIC can and should be used to learn structured programming methods.

VAX-BASIC is a good learning tool. It is possible to write very poor programs as well as very clear, well-structured programs. This makes it possible to illustrate vividly the differences between good and bad programming style. This can also help to illustrate the rationale behind more structured programming languages such as Pascal.

BASIC is a versatile and popular language. Besides its well-known popularity for microcomputers, a significant number of larger minicomputers used for business applications have BASIC as a primary language. Indeed, BASIC is the language of choice for certain applications. Matrix algebra, string manipulations, and file-handling operations are all easier to accomplish in BASIC than in Fortran, Pascal, or COBOL.

All of these factors combine to make VAX-BASIC an excellent choice for an introductory programming course.

1.2 The Computer Program

A *program* is a series of instructions for the computer to carry out. As a simple analogy, we can think of a computer program as a special kind of board game consisting of a playing board with data cards, a memory scoreboard, and an output pad (Fig. 1.1). When instructed to play the game (RUN the program), the computer moves around the board one square at a time and carries out the instruction on each square. The instructions may cause the computer to record values of variables in its memory scoreboard, to read a data card, to carry out a calculation, to write information on the output pad, or to go to a different square. Some of the instructions might be conditional: If you have enough money, pay the rent; if not, go to jail.

A programmer is like the "banker" who sets up the game for the computer. He may decide to get out an old game, or he can create a new game by using a blank board and writing instructions in the squares.

Of course, the computer can do much more than we have indicated here. The board game example provides a simple way to think of how the computer carries out a program. A more accurate picture of the process is depicted in Fig. 1.2.

The program is contained in a *"program list"* section of main memory and consists of a number of different program steps. Each step has a number to identify it. Steps are listed in consecutive order, and the computer uses a program-list pointer to keep track of the step currently being carried out.

1.2 THE COMPUTER PROGRAM

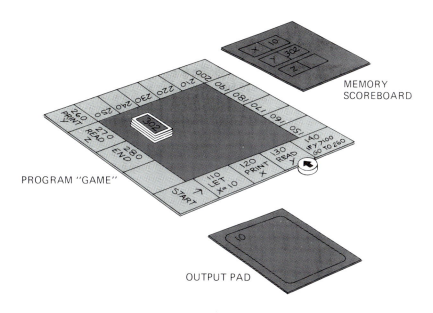

FIGURE 1.1 The main elements of a computer program are depicted using a board game. Each square on the board contains an instruction.

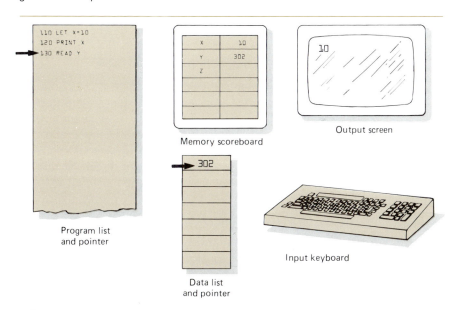

FIGURE 1.2 A program is a list of instructions, which the computer is to carry out one after the other. The pointer arrow indicates which step the computer is on. The data cards are represented as another list with an arrow indicating the next value to be read. The memory scoreboard shows the variables that the computer is keeping track of. A television screen is used as an output pad, and a typewriter keyboard is used for input.

Another section of main memory contains the *data list*, which consists of numbers or other information that may be needed in a program. Data items are listed in a particular order and read in sequence, just as the data cards would be turned over one at a time in the game analogy. A data-list pointer is used to keep track of the next data item to be read.

The computer may need to keep track of numbers that are used in various calculations in a program. For example, a particular program may compute the sum or average of the numbers given in the data list. These numbers are stored in the "memory scoreboard" section of main memory. Each number is identified by a variable name, like X or Y.

1.3 The Programming Process

Programming is more than simply giving the computer instructions to carry out. Usually, we have a task in mind. For example, we may wish to have the computer figure out the average of two numbers or the next winning lottery number. The computer is a tool to help us in the process of completing the task. The computer is good at doing calculations, but not so good at thinking.

It would be nice if we could sit at the computer and type in the instruction:

```
DETERMINE THE NEXT WINNING LOTTERY NUMBER
```

but things are not that simple. We have to figure out a way to carry out the task and give the computer precise step-by-step instructions. This step-by-step procedure is called an *algorithm*. In some respects, finding an algorithm is the most important step in the programming process, despite the fact that no actual programming is involved.

To illustrate these points, consider the simple task of finding the average of the first two numbers in a data list. The algorithm to do this might be outlined as follows:

> Read the first number; call it X
> Read the next number; call it Y
> Compute the sum of X and Y, call it Z
> Divide Z by 2 and print the result

All of the steps involved in the programming process are important, but at first we will be concerned mainly with the mechanics of entering and checking programs. Later, as we learn more programming tools, we will be able to discuss the planning process in more detail.

Review: The Programming Process

The programming process can be broken down into the following steps:

1. *Understand the problem.* Make sure that there is a clear understanding of what task is to be done by the program.
2. *Devise an algorithm.* Work out a step-by-step "game plan" to solve the problem or accomplish the task.
3. *Enter the program.* In some ways this is the easiest part of the process, but it does require some careful typing.
4. *Check the program.* Ensure that the program contains no typing or grammatical errors or errors of logic. In some cases the computer can and will point out errors.
5. *Run the program.* This is where the computer is asked to carry out the steps of the algorithm.

1.4 The VAX Computer

The main components of the VAX-11 computer, depicted in Figs. 1.3 and 1.4, may be divided into three categories:

- *Input and output devices* are used to communicate with the computer. This may include a two-way communication device, like the terminal, or a one-way communication device, like the high-speed printer or a device that reads punched cards.
- *The central processor* executes programs and carries out calculations under the control of the operating system. The central processor includes an Arithmetic Logic Unit (ALU), which carries out calculations, and a storage area called main memory. When the operating system is ready to run your program, it uses a section of main memory to store the program steps, a section to store the data list, and a section as the memory scoreboard to keep track of the variables (see Fig. 1.2).
- *Mass storage* is the "filing cabinet" used to store information that is not immediately required by the computer. The VAX uses one or more magnetic disks that look something like a thick phonograph record. This type of recording device allows rapid storage and retrieval of files.

The computer is capable of carrying out a wide variety of tasks. For example, a program can be stored in the disk memory, a file can be printed using the high-speed printer, or a program can be copied from the disk memory into main memory. These are all done under the control of the operating system using the appropriate commands.

The VAX computer has several different modes of operation and can communicate in different languages. The language used to carry out most system functions, like printing files on the high-speed printer, is called DEC Command Language (DCL). When you first sign on, the computer will be operating in DCL mode and will be expecting DCL system commands. Other modes of operation include BASIC mode for writing and running BASIC programs, EDIT mode for "word processing," MAIL mode for sending and reading messages, and PHONE mode for on-line communication with another person using the computer (see Fig. 1.5).

Each mode of operation has its own *command prompt* to indicate the type of command that the computer is ready for. The dollar sign ($) is the DCL command prompt. Other command prompts are indicated in Fig. 1.5.

FIGURE 1.3 The VAX 11/750 minicomputer. The left cabinet contains the central processor and main memory, the center cabinet houses a tape drive, and the right cabinet houses a disk drive.

1.4 THE VAX COMPUTER

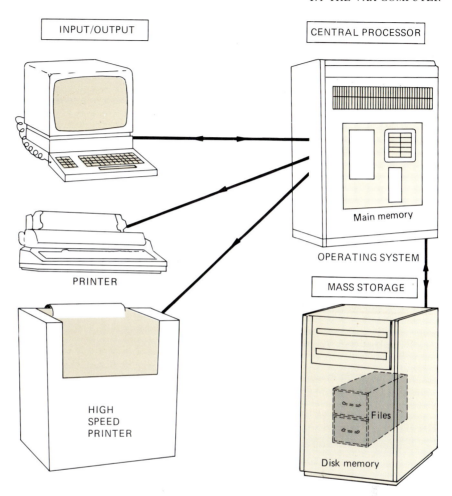

FIGURE 1.4 The main components of the VAX computer.

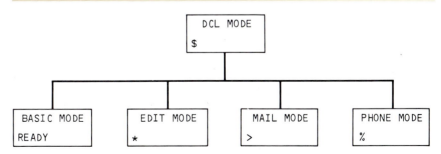

FIGURE 1.5 Some of the different modes of operation possible with the VAX computer. Each mode has its own command prompt shown in the lower left corner of the block.

TABLE 1.1 The most common DCL system commands.

DIRECTORY	Displays the names of files that are stored in your area of the disk memory.
TYPE	Displays the contents of a file on your terminal screen.
PRINT	Prints the contents of a file on the high-speed printer.
BASIC	Shifts from DCL mode to BASIC mode.
LOGOUT	Ends the session with the computer.

You will need to know a few DCL system commands in order to make effective use of the VAX computer. Some of these are shown in Table 1.1. A more complete list may be found in Appendix A. All DCL commands may be abbreviated to the first three letters and in some cases to the first two letters. For example the DIRECTORY command may be abbreviated to DIR and the PRINT command may be abbreviated to PRI or PR.

1.5 Using the Terminal

Two types of terminals are commonly used with the VAX-11 computer: the video terminal and the printing terminal. The video terminal uses a cathode ray tube (CRT) to display information. This type of terminal looks like a television with an attached typewriter keyboard (see Fig. 1.6). It is the fastest and easiest device to use for creating and changing programs. The printing terminal performs the same functions as the video terminal but prints the information on paper (hard copy).

Most of the keys on the terminal keyboard are similar to the usual keys on a typewriter (see Fig. 1.7). These include 26 letter keys and 10 number keys. The keys shown in Table 1.2 appear on a standard typewriter keyboard but may have a slightly different function on the computer. In addition to the keys described in Table 1.2, the terminal keyboard has a few keys that are not found on a standard typewriter. These are shown in Table 1.3.

Some Common Mistakes

It is easy to think of the terminal keyboard as simply a typewriter keyboard with a few extra keys. This can often lead to annoying errors. For example, typists often use the letter l (lowercase L) instead of the numeral 1. If this is done, say, in typing the number 12, the result will look like the number 12 but will be read as "L2" by the computer.

1.5 USING THE TERMINAL

FIGURE 1.6 The VT220 video display terminal.

FIGURE 1.7 A typical terminal keyboard.

TABLE 1.2 Terminal keys that may have a different function than the same keys on a typewriter.

CAPS LOCK	The CAPS LOCK key is used to shift the letter keys (and the letter keys only) to uppercase. You may wish to press the CAPS LOCK key at the beginning of a computer session because all BASIC commands are normally typed in uppercase letters.
SHIFT	Press the SHIFT key along with another key to get an uppercase letter or the second symbol on a dual-purpose key. The SHIFT key must be used to get the upper symbol on the nonletter keys even when the CAPS LOCK key is depressed.
RETURN ⟨ret⟩	The RETURN key (denoted by ⟨ret⟩ signals the computer that you have finished typing the current line. The computer will not respond to a command until the RETURN key is pressed. The RETURN key also begins a new line as it does on a typewriter.
BACKSPACE	The BACKSPACE key is similar to the backspace key on a typewriter. In general, the DELETE key should be used instead of the BACKSPACE key.

It is also easy to interchange the letter O and the numeral 0. For example, if you type "LOGOUT" using the numeral 0, the computer will read the command literally. It will not assume that you meant to type the command "LOGOUT" but will read what you have typed and then tell you that it does not understand your command. This leads to the confusing situation in which the computer will not respond to what appears to be a correct command.

TABLE 1.3 Terminal keys that are not found on a standard typewriter.

DELETE	The DELETE key backspaces and erases. (On some terminal keyboards, this key is called the RUBOUT key.) If you make a typing mistake, press the DELETE key one or more times until the mistake is erased and then retype.
CONTROL	The CONTROL key is similar to the SHIFT key in that it changes the function of the other keys. For example, the letter c is changed to a "cancel" button by the CONTROL key.
⟨ctrl/c⟩	Holding down the CONTROL key and pressing the letter c (denoted by ⟨ctrl/c⟩) cancels the last command entered to the computer. Use ⟨ctrl/c⟩ to stop a program before it is finished running.
NO SCROLL	The NO SCROLL key will stop the computer from printing output to the video terminal. This key is useful when the output is going too fast for you to read. Push the key once to freeze the screen, and push it again to resume output. It is not a good idea to push other keys while the output is frozen.

It is easy to make a similar mistake using the BACKSPACE key instead of the DELETE key. For example, typing the letter `D`, the letter `I`, the letter `S`, the BACKSPACE, and the letter `R` will end up looking like the three-letter command "`DIR`" on your terminal screen but will be read by the computer as the five-character sequence `DIS`⟨backspace⟩`R`. This problem can be avoided by using the DELETE key. The sequence `D`, `I`, `S`, ⟨delete⟩, `R` is read by the computer as the three-character sequence DIR.

Remember also that pressing the NO SCROLL key will freeze the output to the terminal screen. If nothing happens when you type something, the output may have been frozen by the use of the NO SCROLL key. Press the key again to resume the normal display.

1.6 Getting Started

Before you can use the computer, you must first obtain a *username* and a *password*. The username is your identification, and the password is your secret code word to verify that you are an authorized user. You also need to determine the location of the terminals that you will be using.

The rest of this section is a step-by-step description of a typical session with the computer. Here is an overview of what you will be doing:

- Log in to the system by giving your username and password
- Enter the BASIC mode using the DCL command `BASIC`
- Name a `BASIC` program
- Create a `BASIC` program
- `RUN` the program
- `SAVE` the program
- Leave `BASIC` mode using the BASIC command `EXIT`
- End the session using the DCL command `LOGOUT`

Some of these steps utilize DCL commands (also called system commands). The computer signals that it is ready to recognize a system command by printing a dollar sign "$" at the beginning of a new line on the terminal screen. Other steps require BASIC commands. The computer types the word "`Ready`" to indicate that it is ready for a BASIC command or program line.

The following examples show the words and symbols that will appear on the output screen when you are using the computer. As you type a command at the keyboard, it will be displayed on the terminal screen. When you press the RETURN key, the command will be sent to the computer for its action. The computer may then display something in response to your command.

Thus the terminal screen will contain the commands that you type as well as the responses from the computer. In the following examples, the words that you type are shown in color in order to set them off from the computer's response.

Ready? Find a terminal and make sure that it is turned on. You should check to see if there are any preliminary procedures that are peculiar to your installation. Some terminals must be connected to the computer through phone lines or electronic switches.

Signal your presence to the computer by pressing the RETURN key. The symbol `<ret>` will be used to denote this. The following examples will show this symbol as a reminder even though pressing this key actually causes nothing to be displayed on the screen.

The computer responds to ⟨ret⟩ with an identification message and then displays the word "`Username:`" and waits for your response. Now type your username. It will be displayed on the screen as you are typing it. The username will not be sent to the computer until you press the RETURN key. This gives you a chance to correct your typing mistakes. If you type the wrong letter, use the DELETE key to erase and then retype the correct username. When you press ⟨ret⟩, the computer reads your username and responds with the word "Password:" and waits for you to enter your password.

Next, enter your password. Notice that the computer will not display your password on the screen as you are typing it. This makes it more difficult to catch typing mistakes, but you still can make corrections by using the DELETE key. Send the password to the computer by pressing the RETURN key.

If you have logged in correctly, the computer will respond with a welcome message, followed by the dollar-sign prompt. If your login is not successful, repeat the above procedure.

Here's what it looks like so far:

1.6 GETTING STARTED

The $ is printed at the beginning of a new line to signal that the computer is in the DCL mode and is ready for a DCL command. You then type the word BASIC to shift to BASIC mode.

```
$ BASIC  <ret>

VAX-11 BASIC V2.x
Ready
```

The Ready prompt indicates that the computer is ready to accept a BASIC program or respond to BASIC commands. To indicate that this is a new program, you type the BASIC command NEW. The computer responds by asking for the file name of the new program. Type SUM, to give this program the name "SUM."

```
NEW  <ret>
  New file name-- SUM  <ret>
Ready
```

If you do not explicitly supply a name for the program, the computer uses "NONAME." This is called a *default* name.

You are now ready to enter the SUM program. Type the program exactly as shown below. The reason for the punctuation will be discussed later. Check each line before you press the RETURN key. Mistakes may be corrected by using the DELETE key as described earlier in this section. Section 1.7 will illustrate other methods for correcting errors.

```
100 LET A = 5  <ret>
110 LET B = 10  <ret>
120 LET C = A + B  <ret>
130 PRINT "A = "; A  <ret>
140 PRINT "B = "; B  <ret>
150 PRINT "A + B = "; C  <ret>
160 END  <ret>
```

The program consists of seven statements, numbered 100 to 160. Use the RUN command to have the computer carry out these program steps.

```
RUN <ret>
SUM  <date>  <time>

A = 5
B = 10
A + B = 15
Ready
```

If you have made a mistake in entering the program, one of the following may happen when you try to run it:

- The program may produce an output that is different from the one shown above.
- An error message may be printed.

Section 1.7 will show how these errors can be corrected.

In any case, you can save a copy of the program for future use by typing the SAVE command.

```
SAVE <ret>
Ready
```

When you save a program, a copy is put into a file in disk memory.

When you are finished with the BASIC language, return to DCL mode using the EXIT command. Omit this step if you wish to continue on to the example in the next section.

```
EXIT <ret>
$
```

The computer prints the DCL command prompt to indicate that it is ready to accept DCL commands.

Finally, use the LOGOUT command to end the session. Omit this step if you wish to continue at this time. The LOGOUT command may be abbreviated

1.7 CORRECTING ERRORS

to `LO` or `LOG`. It should be the last command that you type. If you neglect to logout before leaving, the next person to use the terminal will have access to your files.

```
$ LOGOUT <ret>
  <your username> logged out at <date> <time>
```

Note: In the following reviews, DCL system commands are shown with a dollar sign in front of them to remind you that these are DCL commands and not BASIC commands. Of course, there is no need to type the dollar sign when you use these commands in DCL mode.

Review: Getting Started

- The login procedure is used to begin a session with the computer.
- The `$BASIC` command is used to enter BASIC mode.
- The `NEW` command is used to erase main memory and name a program.
- The `RUN` command is used to start execution of the program steps.
- The `SAVE` command is used to store a copy of the program in a disk file.
- The `EXIT` command is used to leave BASIC mode and return to DCL mode.
- The `$LOGOUT` command is used to end the session.

1.7 Correcting Errors

As mentioned earlier, the DELETE key may be used to correct typing errors if they are detected before you press the RETURN key. In contrast, when you type a program line and press the RETURN key, the line is included in the program list in main memory, even if there are errors. These errors may not be detected until later when you try to RUN the program. If you have made an error in typing a BASIC command, the computer will probably be unable to interpret the command and will respond with an error message. Except for printing the error message, the computer will ignore the command, and it must be retyped.

If you notice an error in a line you have already typed, the error may be corrected by simply typing a correct version of the line using the same line number. That is, if you have typed line 110 of your program incorrectly, type a correct version of the line again, using line number 110. The computer will ignore all but the last version of lines with the same line number. To delete a line entirely, type the line number again, without typing anything else on that line. The lines of your program may be typed in any sequence, and the computer will arrange them in numerical order (according to line number).

The following example begins with the computer in BASIC mode. If you are continuing from the last section and have not used the `EXIT` command, then there is nothing more to do before starting the example. Otherwise, it is necessary to first login and enter BASIC mode as shown in Section 1.6.

Once in BASIC mode, use the `NEW` command to clear the previous program from main memory and name the new program. Remember, you will still have to press the RETURN key at the end of each line, but the reminder `<ret>` will no longer be shown.

```
NEW BOTTLES
Ready
```

Notice that the name of the program was typed right after the `NEW` command. The words NEW and BOTTLES may be typed on the same line with one or more spaces between them. This avoids the extra step of typing in the program name in response to the prompt "new file name--."

Each line of the BOTTLES program begins with a line number followed by a PRINT statement. Any number of spaces or tabs may be used between the line number and the `PRINT` statement. However, the line number must always be at the very beginning of the line.

When you type the program, use the TAB key to line up the `PRINT` statements. That is, type the line number, press the TAB key, and then type the rest of the statement. You should deliberately type the word PRIMT, not PRINT, in line 120 to insert a mistake into the program.

```
100 PRINT "100 BOTTLES OF BEER ON THE WALL"
110 PRINT "IF ONE OF THOSE BOTTLES"
120 PRIMT "SHOULD HAPPEN TO FALL"
130 PRINT X
140 PRINT "99 BOTTLES OF BEER ON THE WALL"
150 END
```

This program has a mistake in line 120 and a line that seems to perform no useful function (line 130).

1.7 CORRECTING ERRORS

Now type the `LIST` command to have the computer display the program that you just typed.

```
LIST

BOTTLES  <date> <time>

100 PRINT "100 BOTTLES OF BEER ON THE WALL"
110 PRINT "IF ONE OF THOSE BOTTLES"
120 PRIMT "SHOULD HAPPEN TO FALL"
130 PRINT X
140 PRINT "99 BOTTLES OF BEER ON THE WALL"
150 END
Ready
```

Notice that the computer displays what is stored as the program list in main memory (see Fig. 1.2). It does not try to do anything with the program until you give the `RUN` command. In terms of the game analogy of Fig. 1.1, the computer is simply displaying the game board and makes no attempt to play the game.

What happens when the `RUN` command is given? Now you are asking the computer to "play the game" and carry out the instructions given in the program list. It will not be able to do this because of the spelling error in line 120. The computer will not understand the instruction and generates an error message.

```
RUN
BOTTLES  <date> <time>
Error on line 120
        120     PRIMT "SHOULD HAPPEN TO FALL"
....................1
%BASIC-E-FOUND, 1: found string constant when expecting one of:
                            "("
                            ","
                            "="
                            "."
                            "::"

Ready
```

Unfortunately, the error message does not really tell you what you have done wrong, mostly because the computer does not know what you are

INTRODUCTION

trying to do. In this case, the approximate location of the error is enough information.

Correct the error by retyping line 120. At the same time, remove line 130 by typing the line number followed by a blank line.

```
120 PRINT "SHOULD HAPPEN TO FALL"
130
```

The `LIST` command may be used to verify that these changes have been made. First, see what happens when you incorrectly type the command.

```
    LIZT
Error in immediate mode
        LIZT
............1
%BASIC-E-FOUND, 1:  found end of line when expecting one of:
                                "("
                                ","
                                "="
                                ":"
                                "::"

Ready
```

Once again, the text of the error message is not important because it is pretty easy to see the problem.

Now type the command with no errors.

```
    LIST
BOTTLES   <date>   <time>

100 PRINT "100 BOTTLES OF BEER ON THE WALL"
110 PRINT "IF ONE OF THOSE BOTTLES"
120 PRINT "SHOULD HAPPEN TO FALL"
140 PRINT "99 BOTTLES OF BEER ON THE WALL"
150 END

Ready
```

1.7 CORRECTING ERRORS

This verifies that the error in line 120 has been corrected and line 130 has been deleted. You should enter the RUN command to verify that the computer is able to carry out all of the instructions (not shown).

If you run the BOTTLES program as it stands, you will notice that something is wrong with the song that it prints. The second line, "100 BOTTLES OF BEER," is missing. This is an example of a different kind of programming error, one that appears when you run the program and it produces the wrong output.

This error may be corrected by inserting a program line having a line number that is between 100 and 110 (say 105) with the missing second line of the song. Simply type the line, and the computer will insert that line in its proper position in the program.

```
105 PRINT "100 BOTTLES OF BEER"
```

The LIST command may be used to verify that the added line has been included in the program.

```
LIST
BOTTLES   <date>   <time>

100 PRINT "100 BOTTLES OF BEER ON THE WALL"
105 PRINT "100 BOTTLES OF BEER"
110 PRINT "IF ONE OF THOSE BOTTLES"
120 PRINT "SHOULD HAPPEN TO FALL"
140 PRINT "99 BOTTLES OF BEER ON THE WALL"
150 END

Ready
```

This program produces the desired result when the RUN command is given (not shown). Because changes have been made, the line numbers are not as neatly ordered as they were to begin with. Of course, the actual line numbers are not important as long as the program steps are in the proper sequence.

The RESEQUENCE command may be used to assign new line numbers to the program. This process will not change the output that is produced when the RUN command is given, but the line numbers will look neater when the program is listed. New line numbers are assigned, starting from 100 and going up in increments of 10 (100, 110, 120, etc.).

```
RESEQUENCE
Ready

LIST
BOTTLES   <date>   <time>

100 PRINT "100 BOTTLES OF BEER ON THE WALL"
110 PRINT "100 BOTTLES OF BEER"
120 PRINT "IF ONE OF THOSE BOTTLES"
130 PRINT "SHOULD HAPPEN TO FALL"
140 PRINT "99 BOTTLES OF BEER ON THE WALL"
150 END

Ready
```

Now, type the EXIT command.

```
EXIT
%BASIC-W-CHANGES, unsaved change has been made, ctrl-z or EXIT to exit
Ready
```

The bottles program is still in main memory, but you have not yet sent a copy to disk memory. The program list would be erased from main memory if you left BASIC mode, and so the computer prints a warning message to allow you one last chance to save your program.

Now save the program and exit from BASIC mode.

```
SAVE
Ready

EXIT
$
```

1.8 DISPLAYING AND RETRIEVING YOUR PROGRAMS

Review: Correcting Errors

- A program line may be corrected by retyping a correct version using the same line number.
- A program line may be deleted by typing the line number with nothing after it.
- Program lines may be typed in any order. The computer rearranges the lines into the proper order according to line number.
- The LIST command may be used at any time to display the current version of the program.
- The RESEQUENCE command may be used to assign new line numbers to a program.

1.8 Displaying and Retrieving Your Programs

When you are using BASIC and enter the SAVE command, the VAX computer will create a *file* that contains the program. The file will be stored in disk memory (see Fig. 1.8). Each file is identified by a *file specification* so that it can be found when you want to use it again (see Fig. 1.9). The VAX computer has to keep track of a large number of files, and so the complete file specification is quite complicated. Fortunately, most of the work is done

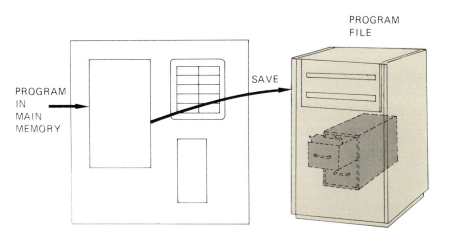

FIGURE 1.8 The file BOTTLES.BAS;1 is created and stored in disk memory when the SAVE command is given.

`DISKUS:[THIS.USER]BOTTLES.BAS;1`

FIGURE 1.9 The complete specification of a program file includes the name of the disk, the username, the file name, the file type, and the version number. The computer automatically provides the name of the disk and the username (dark shading). In BASIC mode, the computer also provides the file type and version number (color shading).

automatically by the computer; all you have to do is keep track of the *file name* (and sometimes the *file type* and *version number*). For a BASIC program, the file name is the name of the program, and the file type is BAS.

When you refer to a file without explicitly mentioning the disk or the username, the computer assumes that you mean your disk and username and automatically supplies this information. The operating system of the computer is designed to fill in missing information in this way, and the values that it uses are called *default* values.

All of the information contained in the file specification is shown in the output that appears when you type the DCL `DIRECTORY` command. The file name, file type, and version number are displayed for each file; and your disk and username are given in the heading (see Fig. 1.10). You can also determine the name of your disk and your username by typing the `SHOW DEFAULT` command in DCL mode. The username that appears in your file specification may differ slightly from the username that you use to login.

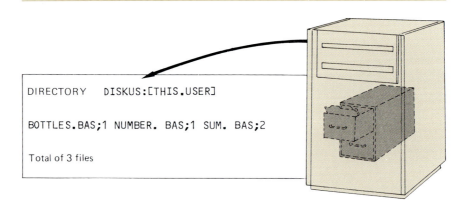

FIGURE 1.10 The `DIRECTORY` command displays a list of your files.

1.8 DISPLAYING AND RETRIEVING YOUR PROGRAMS

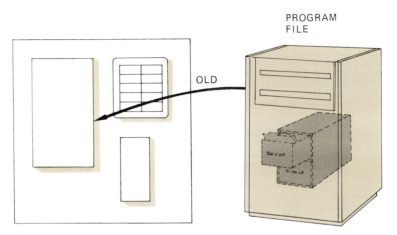

FIGURE 1.11 The OLD command is used to copy a program from disk memory into the program list section of main memory.

The DIRECTORY command shows a list of the names of your files. If you wish to see the contents of a file, use the (DCL) TYPE command. This command causes the computer to display the contents of a file on the terminal screen. Of course, you need to tell the computer which file to display. You can enter the TYPE command and the computer will ask you for the file specification, or you can enter the TYPE command followed by one or more spaces and then the file specification. When you enter the file specification, the file name and file type must be given explicitly. The remaining parts of the file specification are optional. If you do not type the optional parts, the computer will supply the disk and username using the values associated with your files and, if there is a choice, will display the file with the highest version number. Of course, you can explicitly specify the disk name, the username or the version number.

When you are working in BASIC mode, you may wish to use a program that you have saved as a disk file. This may be done using the OLD command (see Fig. 1.11). When you enter the OLD command followed by one or more spaces and then the name of the program, the computer will read a copy of the program from the disk file into the program list in main memory. Once again, the computer fills in the additional information necessary to determine the complete file specification so that it can find the file. In this case, the program name is the same as the file name portion of the file specification. Because you are in BASIC mode, the computer assumes a file type of BAS. As before, your disk and username are supplied by default and the highest version number is retrieved.

The following example illustrates the process of displaying and retrieving the program SUM, which was created in Section 1.6. First, the TYPE command is used in DCL mode to display the contents of the file SUM.BAS. Next, the OLD command is used in BASIC mode to put a copy of the program into the program list in main memory. The program is then displayed using the LIST command. The original file remains unchanged in disk memory.

```
TYPE SUM.BAS

100 LET A = 5
110 LET B = 10
120 LET C = A + B
130 PRINT "A = ";   A
140 PRINT "B = ";   B
150 PRINT "A + B = ";   C
160 END


$ BAS
VAX-11 Basic V2.x

Ready
OLD SUM
Ready

LIST
SUM   <DATE> <TIME>

100 LET A = 5
110 LET B = 10
120 LET C = A + B
130 PRINT "A = ";   A
140 PRINT "B = ";   B
150 PRINT "A + B = ";   C
160 END
Ready
```

At this point, there are two identical copies of the program: the disk file SUM.BAS and the program SUM in main memory.

Next, we will make a change in the program. Retype line 110, and LIST and RUN the revised program.

1.8 DISPLAYING AND RETRIEVING YOUR PROGRAMS

```
110 LET B = 46
LIST
SUM <DATE> <TIME>

100 LET A = 5
110 LET B = 46
120 LET C = A + B
130 PRINT "A = ";  A
140 PRINT "B = ";  B
150 PRINT "A + B = ";  C
160 END
Ready

RUN
SUM <date> <time>

A = 5
B = 46
A + B = 51
Ready
```

This new version of the program can be saved for future use using the `SAVE` command.

```
SAVE
Ready
```

Because there is already a file called `SUM.BAS;1`, the computer creates the file `SUM.BAS;2`. This can be verified by using the `DIRECTORY` command in DCL mode.

```
EXIT
$ DIR
Directory <disk name> : [ <username> ]
BOTTLES.BAS;   1 SUM.BAS;   2 SUM.BAS;1
Total of 3 files.
$
```

This sample directory listing shows that you now have three files stored in the disk memory: the BOTTLES program that had been saved earlier, along with two versions of the SUM program.

This example ends with the computer in DCL mode. At this point you can logout or continue on to the example in the next section.

> **Review:** Retrieving Programs from Disk Memory
>
> ■ When you save a program, a copy is written to disk memory. The file specification identifies the file so that it can be found later.
> ■ Use the `$DIRECTORY` command to see which files are stored in your section of disk memory.
> ■ Use the `$TYPE` command to display the contents of a file.
> ■ Use the `OLD` command to copy a program from disk memory into the program list in main memory.

1.9 Renaming and Deleting Programs

As you work on a program and make changes and additions, it is a good idea to save a copy of the program at various stages of its development. For instance, if you are about to try a major modification, `SAVE` the program just before you make the changes. If the changes do not work, you can recover the original version using the `OLD` command.

Each time you `SAVE` the program, another file is created with the same name but a higher version number. Presumably, as you work on a program, each time you `SAVE` a program it is closer to the desired result. If you do not wish to retain earlier versions of a program, your files can be cleaned out using the (DCL) `PURGE` command. In this process, the computer deletes files with the same name but different version numbers, keeping only the one with the highest version number. In particular, if you had typed the `PURGE` command at the end of the session described in Section 1.8, the file `SUM.BAS;1` would have been deleted from disk memory, whereas `SUM.BAS;2` and `BOTTLES.BAS;1` would have been retained.

If you make significant revisions to a program and wish to retain both the original and the revised version, it is a good idea to rename one of them. A carefully chosen name can help you remember how the revised program differs from the original one and can also prevent the inadvertent loss of a program if your files are purged. The `RENAME` command may be used in either BASIC or DCL modes. In BASIC mode, the `RENAME` command assigns a new name to the program in main memory. A subsequent `SAVE` command

1.9 RENAMING AND DELETING PROGRAMS

would then create a disk file with the new name. In DCL mode, the `RENAME` command assigns a new name to a disk file.

As your programming skills grow, you may look back on an earlier program and decide that you no longer need a copy of it. In this case, the `DELETE` command can be used in DCL mode to erase a specific program file from disk memory. In BASIC mode, the `UNSAVE` command may be used in a similar way to delete a program file from disk memory. Note that there is no need for a special command to erase the program in main memory, as this is done automatically when you enter the `OLD` or `NEW` commands to begin working on another program. (However, the `DELETE` command can be used in BASIC mode to erase part of the program from main memory by specifying a range of line numbers to be deleted [see Appendix B]. An example of the use of the `DELETE` command in this way will not be shown until Chapter 6.)

Most of these commands are illustrated in this section and Section 1.10. Additional information is contained in Appendixes A and B.

The following example illustrates the use of the `RENAME` and `UNSAVE` commands. The example begins with the computer in DCL mode. After entering BASIC mode, a copy of the SUM program is read into main memory using the command `OLD SUM`. The computer retrieves the latest version of the file (that is, `SUM.BAS;2`) and copies it into the program list in main memory.

```
BAS

VAX-11 Basic V 2.x
Ready

OLD SUM
Ready
```

At this point the program could be listed or run, and changes or additions could be made as shown in Section 1.8.

The program is now called SUM. Use the `RENAME` command to give it the new name ZUM.

```
RENAME ZUM
Ready
```

The command `RENAME ZUM` assigns the new name ZUM to the program that is now in main memory.

Next, the program is copied into the disk memory as the file ZUM.BAS;1, and the file SUM.BAS;2 is erased from disk memory.

```
SAVE
Ready

UNSAVE SUM
Ready
```

The command UNSAVE SUM instructs the computer to delete the highest version number of the file SUM.BAS from disk memory. Omit this step if you wish to retain this file.

Table 1.4 contains an outline of the steps used in this example.

As an alternative, the sequence of commands shown in Table 1.5 could have been used with the same end result.

TABLE 1.4 This series of commands may be used to change and rename a program.

Command	Action
OLD SUM	Copy SUM.BAS;2 into main memory.
(program changes)	
RENAME ZUM	Give the program in main memory the new name ZUM.
SAVE	Copy the program from main memory into the disk file ZUM.BAS;1.
UNSAVE SUM	Delete the highest version (2) of SUM.BAS from disk memory.

TABLE 1.5 An alternative method for changing and renaming a program.

Command	Action
OLD SUM	Copy SUM.BAS;2 into main memory.
(program changes)	
SAVE	Copy the program from main memory into the disk fie SUM.BAS;3.
EXIT	
$RENAME SUM.BAS ZUM.BAS	Rename SUM.BAS;3 (highest version) to ZUM.BAS;1.
$DELETE SUM.BAS;2	Delete SUM.BAS;2 from disk memory. (The version number must be specified for the DELETE command to work.)

1.10 USING DCL COMMANDS IN BASIC MODE

In both of these examples, we started out with the files `SUM.BAS;2` and `SUM.BAS;1` and ended up with the files `ZUM.BAS;1` and `SUM.BAS;1`.

Review: Renaming and Deleting Files

- Use the `RENAME` command to give the program in main memory a new name.
- Use the `$RENAME` command to assign a new name to a disk file.
- Use the `$PURGE` command to delete all but the latest version of your disk files.
- Use the `UNSAVE` command to erase the latest version of a program from disk memory.
- Use the `$DELETE` command to erase a specific file from disk memory.

1.10 Using DCL Commands in BASIC Mode

If you are in BASIC mode and wish to enter a DCL command, it is usual to `EXIT` into DCL mode before entering the command. However, DCL commands can be typed in BASIC mode by simply typing a dollar sign followed by the DCL command (see Fig. 1.12).

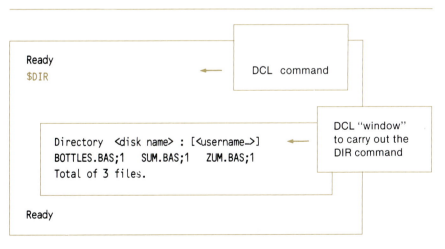

FIGURE 1.12 If you type a valid DCL command (including the dollar sign), the computer creates a window that looks out into DCL mode, where the command is carried out.

For example, assume you are working on a program in BASIC mode and have been saving and deleting files as shown in the previous section. At some point you may not be sure which files you have. Of course, you can `EXIT` and use the `DIRECTORY` command to see a list of the files, but this means that you will also have to `SAVE` the program you are working on and later use the `OLD` command to get it back again.

This can all be avoided by typing `$DIR` from BASIC mode. The computer will create a "window" to DCL mode and a list of your files will be displayed on the screen. Once the DCL command has been carried out, the Ready prompt is displayed to indicate that the computer is again ready for a BASIC command. The program that you had been working on is not altered.

The following example begins where we left off in Section 1.9. The computer is in BASIC mode, and we have been working on the program ZUM.

The `DIRECTORY` command is typed in BASIC mode to obtain a current list of disk files.

```
$DIR
Directory  <disk name> : [<username>]
BOTTLES.BAS;1    SUM.BAS;1    ZUM.BAS;1
Total of 3 files.
Ready
```

The `UNSAVE ZUM` command can be used to delete the file `ZUM.BAS;1` from disk memory. Alternatively, the DCL `DELETE` command may be used. The `DELETE` command is unique in that the file type and the version number must be explicitly specified. The `DIRECTORY` command is again used to verify that the file has been deleted.

```
$DELETE ZUM.BAS;1
Ready
$DIR
Directory  <disk name> : [<username>]
BOTTLES.BAS;1    SUM.BAS;1
Total of 2 files.
Ready
```

1.11 OBTAINING COPIES OF YOUR PROGRAMS

The program `ZUM.BAS` has been deleted from the disk file. However, the copy in the program list of main memory is unaffected.

```
LIST
ZUM    <DATE> <TIME>

100 LET A = 5
110 LET B = 46
120 LET C = A + B
130 PRINT "A = ";   A
140 PRINT "B = ";   B
150 PRINT "A + B = ";   C
160 END
Ready
```

This copy would have been erased if you had exited from BASIC mode to use the `DIRECTORY` command.

Review: Entering System Commands from BASIC Mode

- A system command may be entered from DCL mode or from BASIC mode.
- When a DCL system command is entered from BASIC mode, the dollar sign must be typed before the command.

1.11 Obtaining Copies of Your Programs

This section describes three methods of obtaining copies of your programs. The first method uses the DCL `PRINT` command to have a copy of a program file printed by the high-speed printer. This method is fast and easy but does not give you a copy of the output of the program.

The second method requires that you use a DECwriter or other printing terminal. The program may be printed using the `$TYPE` or the `LIST` command, and the output may be printed using the `RUN` command. This is an easy method to obtain a copy of both the program and the output.

The third method is the easiest method but can be used only after a special command procedure has been set up by your instructor.

Using the High-Speed Printer

The (DCL) `PRINT` command may be used to obtain a printed copy of a program disk file. This requires that you have previously used the `SAVE` command to create a disk file that contains the program.

The following example begins with the computer in BASIC mode. Assume that you wish to obtain a copy of the SUM program. Because you have already saved this program, you need only EXIT from BASIC mode and use the PRINT command to get a copy of the program file. Before using the PRINT command, you may wish to use the DIRECTORY and TYPE commands to inspect your files.

The DIRECTORY command displays a list of your program files, and the TYPE command causes the contents of the file to be displayed at your terminal. These are optional steps to ensure that you have the right file before it is printed.

```
EXIT
$ DIR
Directory  <disk name> : [<username>]
BOTTLES.BAS;1    SUM.BAS;1
Total of 2 files.
$ TYPE SUM.BAS
<program file is displayed at your terminal>
```

The `PRINT` command starts the printing process.

```
$ PRINT SUM.BAS
   Job 537 entered on queue LPA0
```

The `PRINT` command causes a copy of the file `SUM.BAS` to be sent to the high-speed printer. The job number message is your confirmation that the file will be printed. If you see a different message, it may indicate that an error has been made in typing the `PRINT` command. Check to see that you have correctly followed the above procedure, and retype the command if necessary.

Because there may be a number of different files waiting to be printed, a copy of your file is sent to a device called a spooler, which puts it into a

1.11 OBTAINING COPIES OF YOUR PROGRAMS

"queue," or waiting line. The original file is retained in disk memory. The printout can normally be picked up in a few minutes. Look for your username and the file name on the cover sheet that comes with the printout. The job number serves only to establish a place for your file in the print queue and does not appear on the output.

The `SHOW QUEUE` command may be used to obtain information about the number of files waiting to be printed. In this example, the queue is called `"LPA0."`

```
$ SHOW QUEUE LPA0
* Device queue "LPA0" Forms=0, Genprt Lower Burst Flag
CURR 529   <username> <jobname> <time entered> <size>
           [ 7 intervening Jobs Size = 35 ]
PEND 537  <yourname> <filename> <time entered> <size>
$
```

This gives you a status report indicating the position of your file in the print queue. CURR is the current job and PEND indicates that your job is pending. If your job is not listed and the PRINT command was entered correctly, then the file has already been printed.

Review: Obtaining Copies Using the High-Speed Printer

- Use the `DIRECTORY` and `TYPE` commands to review your files and display the contents of the file to be printed (optional).
- Use the `PRINT` command to obtain a copy of a program file.

Using a Printing Terminal

A printing terminal can be used to get both a copy of a program listing and the output of the program when the program is run. There are two situations when this method is useful:

- when the program runs correctly and you wish to get a copy of the program and the output to turn in for a homework assignment, and
- when the program does not run correctly and you wish to have a copy of the program together with the error messages.

Normally, you will be working on a video terminal. To use a printing terminal, you will need to `SAVE` the program, `EXIT` from BASIC mode, and

LOGOUT before moving to a DECwriter or other printing terminal. Once you have logged in on the printing terminal, enter BASIC mode and use the OLD command to retrieve the program. Use the LIST and RUN commands to get a copy of the program and the output.

Here is a step-by-step description of this procedure: Assume that you have just entered the BOTTLES program. When you are finished with the program, SAVE it, EXIT, and LOG off the system.

On a video terminal:

```
SAVE
Ready
EXIT
$  LO
<logout message>
```

Now go to a printing terminal, login, and enter BASIC mode (not shown). Once in BASIC mode, the OLD command is used to read a copy of the program from the disk file BOTTLES.BAS into main memory. A copy of the program is printed at the terminal by using the LIST command.

On a printing terminal:

```
Ready

OLD BOTTLES
Ready

LIST
<program will be listed>
```

Now a copy of the output of the program (or a copy of the error messages) is obtained by using the RUN command.

```
RUN
BOTTLES <date> <time>
<output of program or error messages>
Ready
```

1.12 OTHER BASIC COMMANDS

Once this has been done, the process may be repeated to obtain copies of other programs. (`OLD SUM`, `LIST`, `RUN`, etc.) Note that there is no need to use the `SAVE` command unless you make changes in a program and wish to keep a copy of the revised program. Afterward, `EXIT` and `LOG` off the system as usual.

Review: Using a Printing Terminal

- First write and `SAVE` the program using a video terminal.
- `EXIT` and `LOG` off the video terminal.
- Login and enter `BASIC` mode on a DECwriter terminal.
- Use the `OLD` command to retrieve the program.
- Use the `LIST` command to print the program.
- Use the `RUN` command to print the output.

Using the DOPRINT Command

DOPRINT is a special command that enables you to obtain a copy of your program and the output by simply typing the command followed by the name of the file:

```
$ DOPRINT ZUM.BAS
```

Your instructor will discuss the details of this procedure.*

1.12 Other BASIC Commands

Here are a few other BASIC commands that it is helpful to know about.

The SEQUENCE Command

Use the `SEQUENCE` command to have the computer type line numbers for you. Once this process has started, the computer types the line number and tabs over. You then type the rest of the line. Each time you press the return key, the computer generates a new line number and tabs over. New line numbers will continue to be generated until you press ⟨ctrl/c⟩.

---

*The command procedure is available on request from the publisher.

Here is how it looks on the terminal:

```
NEW EXAMPLE
Ready

SEQUENCE

100 LET A = 5
110 LET B = 10
120 LET C = A + B
130 <ctrl/c>
Ready
```

BASIC commands such as `LIST` or `RUN` cannot be entered until   has been used to stop the generation of line numbers. Note that the last line typed, line 130 in this case, will be wiped out when   is pressed even if you have typed something on that line. Thus you should sequence one line beyond the last line you wish to retain before you press

The EDIT Command

The `EDIT` command can be used to correct errors in a line without retyping the line. This is especially useful for correcting errors in long program statements. As an example, suppose you have typed the following program line:

```
400 PRINT "THIS LONG MESSAGE WILL BE TYPED BY THE COMPUTER
```

As we will see later, this program line has a mistake—it is missing a quotation mark at the end. The mistake can be corrected by typing

```
EDIT 400 /UTER/UTER"/
```

The 400 tells the computer what line to correct; the `UTER` tells the computer where to make the correction and what it looks like now; and the `UTER"` tells the computer what it should look like after the change. The "/" symbol marks the beginning and end of the old and new letters. There is nothing special about the choice of the letters UTER to tell the computer where to make the correction, as long as there is no ambiguity. In this case,

```
EDIT 400 /TER/TER"/
```

1.12 OTHER BASIC COMMANDS

would accomplish the same change. However, there are other situations that can be tricky. For example, suppose the line looked like:

```
600 PRINT "THIS IS ANOTHER LONG MESSAGE THAT GOES LIKE THIS
```

In this case, typing

```
EDIT 600 /HIS/HIS"/
```

or even:

```
EDIT 600 /THIS/THIS"/
```

would cause the quotation mark to be added after the first `THIS` and not at the end of the sentence as desired. In this case, either be more specific:

```
EDIT 600 /E THIS/E THIS"/
```

or type 2 at the end of the `EDIT` command to indicate that the correction should be made at the second occurrence of the letters HIS:

```
EDIT 600 /HIS/HIS"/ 2
```

The HELP Command

The `HELP` command can be used to get information about BASIC. This is generally not a good way to learn about new aspects of BASIC, but it is a good refresher when you have forgotten some detail, like where you need a comma or semicolon in a statement. To use the help facility in BASIC mode simply type the word HELP. A message will appear and you will then be asked to specify a topic. Type the word `COMMANDS` or the word `STATEMENTS` if you wish to have help with a BASIC command or statement. Each stage in the HELP process becomes more specific.

For example, the following sequence may be used to obtain information on the `SAVE` command.

```
HELP
...
Topic? COMMANDS
...
COMMANDS Subtopic? SAVE

<information about the SAVE command is displayed>

COMMANDS Subtopic?
```

At this point, you can enter a request for help on another command such as `LIST` or `EXIT`, or you can press the return key to go to the "Topic" level. At the Topic level, you can enter a request for help on another topic, like `STATEMENTS`, or you can press the return key again to end the help session. If you do not know what to do, type a question mark and the computer will display a list of the available topics or subtopics.

The `$HELP` command may also be used to obtain information on DCL commands. For example, type `HELP PRINT` in DCL mode to obtain information on the `$PRINT` command.

1.13 Exercises

1.1 Login to a video terminal, enter BASIC mode, and type the following program:

```
100 READ L1, L2, L3, L4, L5
200 DATA 39, 33, 29, 24, 25
300 READ H1, H2, H3, H4, H5
400 DATA 69, 69, 47, 50, 51
500 PRINT "LOW TEMPERATURES ARE: "
600 PRINT L1, L2, L3, L4, L5
700 PRINT "HIGH TEMPERATURES ARE: "
800 PRINT H1, H2, H3, H4, H5
900 END
```

After the program has been entered, LIST and RUN the program, and attempt to correct any typing errors. Note that the program will be called `NONAME` if you do not specify a name. After you have typed the program correctly, RENAME it TEMPS and SAVE it for later use.

1.2 Login to a DECwriter terminal, enter BASIC mode, and use the `OLD` command to retrieve the program TEMPS. LIST and RUN the program as described in the text in Section 1.11. Retain the hard copy for future reference.

1.3 The words `PRINT`, `DELETE`, and `RENAME` are used in both DCL mode and BASIC mode. Use the `HELP` command in DCL mode and in BASIC mode to obtain information about how these words are used in each mode.

1.4 While in DCL mode, type the `DIRECTORY` command to see if you have a file called `NUMBER.BAS` in your directory. If so, enter BASIC mode and type the command `RUN NUMBER` to run the program. Later, use the `PRINT` command to get a copy of this program for classroom reference.

1.5 After you understand how to play the NUMBER game of the previous problem, think about your strategy for guessing the number. Can you analyze the strategy? See if you can show that it is always possible to guess the number with at most 7 tries.

The BASIC language uses a vocabulary of words like `PRINT` and `INPUT`, called key words, together with identifiers like `X` and `Y`, called variables, in sentence-like structures, called *statements*.

This chapter deals with the rules of syntax for the `PRINT, LET, INPUT, READ, DATA, REMARK, GOTO,` and `END` statements. Most of the rules are quite natural and are designed to produce programs that are easy to understand. For example, the statement:

`100 LET A = 5`

means that `A` is to be given the value 5.

Note that this example begins with a line number (in this case, 100). Line numbers can be any whole number between 1 and 32767, inclusive. The computer uses the line number to determine the order in which program statements are displayed when a program is listed, and the order in which program steps are carried out when a program is run.

Although the rules of syntax are natural, they are quite strict. For example, the variations shown in Fig. 2.1 seem reasonable to the human reader but will not be understood by the computer and will result in error messages when you try to run the program.

ELEMENTARY GRAMMAR

```
100 SET A = 5
100 LET 5 = A
```

FIGURE 2.1 Examples of illegal grammar.

2.1 Variables

Variables are used in BASIC programs to provide a means of storing data and doing calculations. Note that the variable in the previous example has both a *name* or identifier (A) and a *value* (5). The name and value can be visualized as part of a single entity, which we will call a storage block (see Fig. 2.2).

FIGURE 2.2 A storage block for a program variable. The left side of the storage block gives the name of the variable, and the right side gives the value.

Naming Variables

Any letter or a letter followed by a number can be used as a variable name in minimal BASIC. For example, A, A2, X, and X6 are all valid variable names. In addition, VAX-BASIC allows variable names to be as many as 30 characters in length. The longer names must also start with a letter, but the rest of the variable name can contain letters, numbers, periods, or underscores. Note that spaces are not allowed, but a period or underscore can be used as a separator if more than one word is used for a given variable name. Some examples of valid variable names are shown in Table 2.1. When you are choosing names for the variables that appear in your programs, it is wise to use names that are descriptive but not excessively long.

TABLE 2.1 Examples of valid variable names.

X1	M.P.G.
TEMPERATURE	ELEVATION_IN_FT.
HIGHEST_SCORE	AVE.OF_25__SCORES

2.2 THE LET STATEMENT

Some key words (like `PRINT`, `LIST`, `NUM`) have special uses and are not allowed as variable names. Using one of these keywords as a variable name will cause an error message that is sometimes difficult to figure out. Appendix A of the *VAX-BASIC User's Guide* contains a complete list of key words that may not be used as variable names.

Here are some general rules to assure that you don't run into problems when naming the variables in your programs:

- A variable name must start with a letter and may contain up to 30 letters or numerals. Periods and underscore characters are also allowed.
- Any single letter or a single letter followed by one or more numerals is safe to use as a variable name. (For example, `X`, `A`, `B6`, `X24`, or `Z3794`.)
- Almost any variable name that contains one or more numerals is safe to use. (For example, `NUM23`, `TYPE4`, or `S2ET`.) The only exceptions are: `ATN2`, `LOG10`, `NUM1$`, and `NUM2`.
- Any variable name containing at least one period or underscore is safe to use. (For example, `NU.M`, `PR_INT`, `M.P.G.`, or `TYPE_A`.)
- Do not use variable names starting with the letters `FN` (these are reserved for user-defined functions).

2.2 The LET Statement

The LET statement is often called the assignment statement and is used to assign a value to a variable. Some examples of valid LET statements are shown in Fig. 2.3.

When a LET statement is executed, the expression to the right of the equals sign is evaluated. The resulting value is stored as the value of the variable named at the left of the equal sign. For example, the BASIC statement shown in Fig. 2.4 instructs the computer to take the number `23.45` and store it in main memory as the value of the variable `X`. When this statement is executed, a storage block for `X` is created, as shown in Fig. 2.4.

```
200 LET X = 23.45
500 LET Y = X + 5.8
900 LET Z = X + Z
```

FIGURE 2.3 Some valid LET statements. Each of these statements contains a variable name followed by an equal sign and an expression.

ELEMENTARY GRAMMAR

```
100 LET X = 23.45     →     [ X | 23.45 ]
```

FIGURE 2.4 When the computer executes a LET statement, it creates a storage block for the variable.

The LET statement shown in Fig. 2.5 instructs the computer to do a bit more work. It must first evaluate the expression X + 5.8, using the current value of X, and then store the result as the value of Y.

When a variable is mentioned for the first time, the computer sets up a storage block using the variable name that you have given. The variable starts out with a value of zero until an assignment is made. For example, in Fig. 2.5, a value of zero would be used for X if it had not been explicitly assigned a value in a previous step of the program.

Do not confuse the equals sign in the assignment (LET) statement with an equals sign in an algebraic formula. An equation such as X = X + 2 makes no sense as a formula in algebra, but it makes perfectly good sense to the computer (see Exercise 2.1). To understand why this is so, we have to take a closer look at what happens when the computer executes an assignment statement:

1. First the computer checks for syntax errors: Any grammatical error or illegal variable name will result in an error statement.
2. Then the variables are scanned. If any new variables are encountered, storage blocks will be created for each of them. New variables start out with a value of zero.
3. Next, the expression after the equals sign is evaluated. This expression might contain variables and numbers along with one or more algebraic operations. The computer obtains the current value of each variable and carries out the arithmetic calculations.

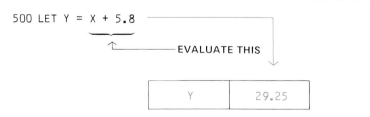

FIGURE 2.5 The expression at the right is evaluated and the value is assigned to Y. Assume that the current value of X is 23.45.

FIGURE 2.6 This shows the values in the storage blocks for Y and Z immediately before line 300 has been carried out.

4. Finally, the value obtained in the previous step is stored as the value of the variable named to the left of the equals sign. Of course, this wipes out the previous value of the variable.

As an illustration, consider the program fragment shown in Fig. 2.6. The statements on lines 100 and 200 set up storage blocks for Y and Z as shown. When the computer executes line 300, it first evaluates the expression Y + Z using the values 2 and 5, and the result (7) becomes the new value of Y (see Fig. 2.7).

The LET statement can be used to set a variable equal to a specific value (LET X = 23.45); it can be used to copy a value from one variable to another (LET W = X); or it can be used to instruct the computer to carry out a calculation and store the result as the value of a specified variable (LET Z = X + Y). Methods of doing more complicated calculations will be discussed in Chapter 3.

Review: The LET Statement

- The variable to be assigned a value must appear to the left of the equals sign.
- The expression to the right of the equals sign may contain variables or numbers. This expression is evaluated, and the resulting value is assigned to the variable on the left of the equals sign.

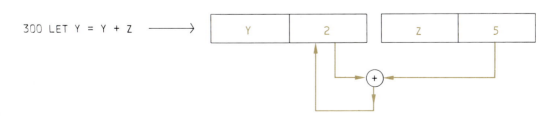

FIGURE 2.7 Line 300 calculates a new value for Y as shown.

ELEMENTARY GRAMMAR

2.3 The PRINT Statement

The PRINT statement provides a means of communication between the program and the outside world. It is a versatile statement that can be used to generate a variety of different outputs. In its simplest form, it can be used to display the value of a variable stored in the computer's memory (see Fig. 2.8).

The `PRINT` statement can also be used to display an expression with quotation marks around it such as "X = ". The characters inside the quotation marks are collectively called a *string*. A string may consist of letters, numbers, spaces, or any of the other printable characters on the terminal keyboard. When this kind of PRINT statement is executed, the string inside the quotation marks is displayed exactly as quoted.

The program of Fig. 2.9 shows the use of both of these types of PRINT statements. Notice that the number 10 is printed in columns 2 and 3 on the output screen. This is because the computer automatically prints a space before (and after) each positive number that it displays. This feature of the PRINT statement allows some separation between numbers that are printed one after the other.

The program of Fig. 2.9 may be modified so that, when run, both the quoted string and the value 10 are displayed on the same line of the output screen. This is done by placing a semicolon at the end of the first print statement. *When used as a separator or terminator in a print statement, a semicolon causes the next printed output to be displayed immediately after the previous output.*

In particular, if a semicolon is placed at the end of line 20 of the previous example, then the output of line 30 would be displayed immediately after the output of line 20 (see Fig. 2.10). Note that there are four spaces between the colon and the number 10 in the output. Three of these spaces are part of the quoted string of line 20, and the fourth space is printed before the number.

```
10 LET X = 10
20 PRINT X
30 END
```

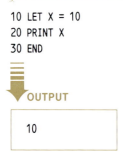

OUTPUT

```
 10
```

FIGURE 2.8 When this program is RUN and line 10 is carried out, the computer creates a storage block for X with the value 10. When line 20 is carried out, the value of X will be displayed on the output screen.

2.3 THE PRINT STATEMENT

```
10 LET X = 10
20 PRINT "THE VALUE OF X IS:    "
30 PRINT X
40 END
```

OUTPUT

```
THE VALUE OF X IS:
10
```

FIGURE 2.9 When the print statement in line 20 is executed, the string is displayed exactly as quoted. This includes the three blank spaces after the colon. When the print statement in line 30 is executed, the variable X is evaluated, and the value is printed on the next line of the output screen.

```
10 LET X = 10
20 PRINT "THE VALUE OF X IS:    " ;
30 PRINT X
40 END
```

OUTPUT

```
THE VALUE OF X IS:    10
```

FIGURE 2.10 Because of the semicolon, the output of line 30 is displayed immediately after the output of line 20.

The two types of print statements may be combined into a single line. For example, lines 20 and 30 of the previous example could be combined into the line:

```
20 PRINT "THE VALUE OF X IS: " ; X
```

The semicolon separates the quoted string from the variable and specifies that no extra spacing is to be inserted. As before, the output is printed one character after the other on a single line. Figure 2.11 shows an example similar to one used in the SUM program of Chapter 1.

```
10 LET Y = 32
20 PRINT "Y="; Y
30 END
```

OUTPUT

```
Y= 32
```

FIGURE 2.11 Another illustration of a two-part print statement. The first part of line 20 prints the string Y=, and the second part prints the value of Y with a leading and trailing space.

Tabbing Over

The placement of printed output can be controlled using preset tab settings. Tabs are set 14 spaces apart at spaces 14, 28, 42, 56, and 70. (Normally, a video terminal display is 80 spaces wide.) *A comma in a print statement causes the output to move to the next tab setting.*

The program of Fig. 2.12 illustrates the use of the preset tab settings. The first six `PRINT` statements will display a grid showing the location of the tab settings. Each of the first five quoted strings is exactly 14 characters wide, so that a vertical bar is printed at the beginning of a tab zone. The printed output of these five lines is $5 \times 14 = 70$ characters wide. Line 60 prints another 10 characters, so the output covers the entire 80 columns of the terminal display. There is no semicolon at the end of line 60, so the next print statement begins on a new line.

When line 70 is executed, the string `FIRST` is printed, and then the comma causes subsequent output to start in the next tab zone. This causes `SECOND` to be printed in the tab zone beginning at column 15. The comma after "SECOND" causes `THIRD` to be printed in the next available tab zone, and so on. Note that there is a comma at the end of line 70; this causes the output of line 80 to be printed on the same line as the output of line 70 in the next available tab zone.

```
10 PRINT "|............." ;
20 PRINT "|............." ;
30 PRINT "|............." ;
40 PRINT "|............." ;
50 PRINT "|............." ;
60 PRINT "|........."
70 PRINT "FIRST", "SECOND", "THIRD",
80 PRINT "FOURTH", "FIFTH", "SIXTH"
90 END
```

OUTPUT

```
|.............|.............|.............|.............|.............|.........
FIRST         SECOND        THIRD         FOURTH        FIFTH         SIXTH
```

FIGURE 2.12 This program illustrates the effect of semicolons and commas in PRINT statements. In particular, commas are used to display each of the six strings FIRST, SECOND, etc., in a different tab zone.

2.3 THE PRINT STATEMENT

Review: The PRINT Statement

- The PRINT statement begins with the key word PRINT.
- A PRINT statement may contain quoted strings or expressions.
- A quoted string consists of characters enclosed within quotation marks, which are printed exactly as quoted.
- An expression may contain variables and operations like addition or subtraction. The expression is evaluated and the resulting value is printed.
- Separate items in a PRINT statement must be separated by commas or semicolons. The output will be printed on a single line (if possible) with the commas and semicolons used to determine the spacing.
- A semicolon causes the next output to appear immediately after the previous output.
- A comma causes the next output to appear at the beginning of the next available tab zone.
- Tabs are set at columns 14, 28, 42, 56, and 70.
- If a PRINT statement ends with a comma or a semicolon, then the output of the next PRINT statement will appear on the same line.

The TAB Function

The TAB function is used in a PRINT statement to start printing output in any one of the 80 columns on the page. The TAB function is used only in PRINT statements and can have the form:

```
PRINT <item>; TAB(N); <item>
```

where ⟨item⟩ may be an expression or a quoted string as described earlier. The TAB(N) function will move the output to column N so that the next output will begin in column N + 1.

Some examples of the use of the TAB function are shown in Fig. 2.13. Line 200 will print the string LEFT beginning at the left edge of the screen and then tab to column 75 so that the word RIGHT will be printed at the right edge of the screen, in columns 76 through 80. In line 500, the expression N+4

```
200 PRINT "LEFT"; TAB(75); "RIGHT"
300 PRINT   X; TAB(10); Y; TAB(20); Z
400 PRINT   TAB(37); "CENTER"
500 PRINT   TAB(N+4); "*"
```

FIGURE 2.13 Some examples of the use of the TAB function.

is evaluated, and the resulting number is used to determine the position of the asterisk. That is, if `N` has the value `10`, then the computer will tab to column `14`, and the asterisk will be printed in column `15`.

The `TAB` function will move the output to the right only. If the output has gone beyond column `N`, `TAB(N)` has no effect. For example, the `TAB` function has no effect in:

```
600 PRINT "FIRST"; TAB(2); "SECOND"
```

In this case, `TAB(2)` will be ignored and the strings will be printed one after the other.

Review: The TAB Function

- The `TAB` function can be used in a `PRINT` statement only.
- Semicolons should always be used to separate the `TAB` function from the rest of the `PRINT` statement.
- If the output has not yet reached column `N`, `TAB(N)` tabs right to column `N`. The following output will begin printing in column `N+1`. `TAB(N)` does not tab over `N` spaces.
- The `TAB` function can tab to the right only. `TAB(N)` is ignored if the output has already passed column `N`.

2.4 The READ and DATA Statements

The `READ` statement provides another way to assign a value to one or more variables. The `READ` statement must be accompanied by a `DATA` statement somewhere in the program. The `READ` and `DATA` statement pair is like a `LET` statement in that a predetermined value is assigned to a variable as the program is running. However, the `READ` and `DATA` statements can be more efficient than `LET` statements in dealing with a large number of variables. Figure 2.14 shows a program in which six variables are assigned values and added together. This program will read the values of the variables `X1` through `X6`—the values are the numbers in the data statement—and print them along with the value of the sum. Note that commas are used to separate variables and data elements in `READ` and `DATA` statements.*

When more than one pair of `READ` and `DATA` statements is present in a program, the *first* value in the *first* `DATA` statement is assigned to the *first* variable in the *first* `READ` statement, and so on. For example, the program in

---

*Caution: Commas are used as separators and therefore should never be used when you write a number in a BASIC program; that is, you should write 1579, not 1,579.

2.4 THE READ AND DATA STATEMENTS

```
100 READ X1, X2, X3, X4, X5, X6
150 DATA 83, 76, 1579, 452, 92, 15
200 PRINT "THE NUMBERS ARE: ";
250 PRINT X1; X2; X3; X4; X5; X6
300 LET S = X1 + X2 + X3 + X4 + X5 + X6
400 PRINT 'THE SUM IS '; S
500 END
```

FIGURE 2.14 This program reads the numbers in the DATA statement and prints the numbers and their sum.

Fig. 2.14 is logically equivalent to the following one:

```
100 READ X1
110 READ X2, X3
120 READ X4, X5, X6
200 PRINT "THE NUMBERS ARE: ";
250 PRINT X1; X2; X3; X4; X5; X6
300 LET S = X1 + X2 + X3 + X4 + X5 + X6
400 PRINT 'THE SUM IS '; S
500 DATA 83, 76, 1579, 452
510 DATA 92, 15
600 END
```

Here is an outline of what happens when the computer executes a program containing one or more **READ** and **DATA** statements:

First the computer looks for all of the **DATA** statements and creates a data list. The computer arranges the list so that the first data item in the first **DATA** statement is on top and the last data item in the last **DATA** statement is on the bottom (see Fig. 2.15).

Next, the program steps are carried out. Each time the computer executes a **READ** statement:

- the computer reads one or more numbers from the data stack, starting at the position of the pointer (see Fig. 2.16);
- each time a number is read, the pointer is moved down to the next number in the data list; and
- each value read from the data stack is assigned to the corresponding variable in the READ statement.

Each time a READ statement is carried out, one or more numbers are transferred into a storage block. All of the variables are then available for calculations later in the program.

If the program has too many READ statements (fewer values in the DATA statement than variables in the READ statement), an error message

52
ELEMENTARY GRAMMAR

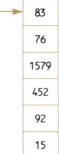

FIGURE 2.15 The data list created for the program of Fig. 2.14. When the program is RUN, the data list is created as shown and the pointer is positioned in front of the first data item.

will be printed when the computer attempts to read beyond the end of the data list. However, the RESTORE statement may be used to reset the pointer to the top of the data list (see Fig. 2.17).

Because of the confusion that can result when READ and DATA statements are scattered throughout a program, it is a good idea either to group all of the DATA statements together at the end of the program or to put each DATA statement immediately after the corresponding READ statement.

Review: The READ/DATA Statement Pair

- A READ statement must always be used with a DATA statement.
- Unless the RESTORE statement is used, the number of variables assigned using READ statements must be no more than the number of data items contained in DATA statements.
- The DATA statement may not be used in combination with any other statement on the same line.

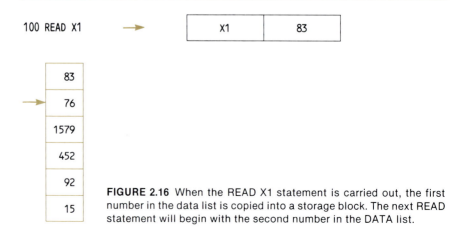

FIGURE 2.16 When the READ X1 statement is carried out, the first number in the data list is copied into a storage block. The next READ statement will begin with the second number in the DATA list.

```
100 READ U, V, W
200 RESTORE
300 READ X, Y, Z
400 PRINT U + V + W , X + Y + Z
500 DATA 3, 6, 9
600 END
```

FIGURE 2.17 This illustrates the use of the RESTORE statement. After the first three variables have been read, the pointer is reset to the beginning of the data list using the RESTORE statement. This allows the same data to be reused for the next three variables.

2.5 The INPUT Statement

The INPUT statement may be used to get the value of a variable from the user at the time that the program is run. For example, when the computer executes the statement:

```
100 INPUT X
```

it will stop and ask you to type in a number to be used as the value of X.

The following example shows what happens when the program SUM of Chapter 1 is modified so that the LET statements are replaced by INPUT statements.

Login as usual, enter BASIC mode, retrieve the SUM program, and list it.

```
OLD SUM
Ready

LIST
SUM  <date> <time>

100 LET A = 5
110 LET B = 10
120 LET C = A + B
130 PRINT "A= ";  A
140 PRINT "B= ";  B
150 PRINT "A + B = ";  C
160 END
Ready
```

ELEMENTARY GRAMMAR

We will replace the LET statements with INPUT statements, rename the program, and list it.

```
100 INPUT A
110 INPUT B
RENAME SUM2
Ready

LIST
SUM2   <date>  <time>

100 INPUT A
110 INPUT B
120 LET C = A + B
130 PRINT "A= "; A
140 PRINT "B= "; B
150 PRINT "A + B = "; C
160 END
Ready
```

Now RUN the program. At each INPUT statement, the computer will stop and print a question mark to indicate that it is waiting for you to type in a number.

```
RUN
SUM2   <date>  <time>

?  23.45
```

When line 100 is executed, the computer prints the first question mark and waits for a number to be entered. If the user types the number 23.45, as shown, then the variable A is given the value 23.45. If a different number had been typed, then that number would have been assigned as the value of A.

Similarly, when line 110 is executed, a question mark is printed and the computer waits for input. In this case, the variable B is given the value 17.23. After these numbers are entered, the program proceeds as usual.

2.5 THE INPUT STATEMENT

```
?  17.23
A = 23.45
B = 17.23
A + B = 40.68
Ready
```

The major difference between this program and the earlier version is that this program can be RUN with different numbers. By changing the LET statements to INPUT statements, we have changed the nature of the program from one that adds two given numbers (5 and 10) to one that can add any numbers that we choose to type in.

The INPUT statement can be modified so that a string is printed before the question mark. This is a very useful feature that can be used to prompt the user to enter a number. The following example shows the use of the EDIT command to modify lines 100 and 110 of the SUM2 program to include a prompt string.

```
EDIT 100 /A/"FIRST NUMBER"; A/
100 INPUT "FIRST NUMBER"; A

Ready
EDIT 110 /B/"SECOND NUMBER"; B/
110 INPUT "SECOND NUMBER";   B

Ready
```

Now when the program is run, the prompt string and a question mark are printed and the computer waits for input.

```
RUN
SUM2   <date> <time>

FIRST NUMBER?  23.45
SECOND NUMBER?
```

It is almost always a good idea to use some type of printed message with each INPUT statement. This makes the program a lot easier to use. You can

ELEMENTARY GRAMMAR

```
100 INPUT "FIRST NUMBER"; A
101 PRINT "SECOND NUMBER";
102 INPUT B
```

FIGURE 2.18 The `INPUT` statement that contains a quoted string (line 100) is equivalent to a `PRINT` statement followed by the plain version of an `INPUT` statement (lines 101 and 102).

```
100 PRINT "CURRENT VALUE IS:"; A ;"ENTER THE NEW VALUE" ;
102 INPUT A
```

FIGURE 2.19 A situation in which a separate `PRINT` statement must be used to prompt for input.

use an `INPUT` statement with a prompt string or a `PRINT` statement followed by the simple form of the `INPUT` statement (see Fig. 2.18).

Note: There are a few situations in which it is necessary to use separate `PRINT` and `INPUT` statements. This results from the restriction that only a single quoted string may be used in an `INPUT` statement. For example, if the value of a variable is to appear as part of the prompting message, then a separate `PRINT` statement must be used (see Fig. 2.19).

> **Review:** The INPUT Statement
>
> ■ The `INPUT` statement is used to obtain the value of a variable from the user when the program is run.
> ■ The `INPUT` statement may include a quoted string. The quoted string must be placed immediately after the word `INPUT` and must be followed by a comma or a semicolon.
> ■ The last part of the `INPUT` statement consists of one or more variable names. If more than one variable name is given, they must be separated by commas.

2.6 The REMARK Statement

The `REMARK` statement may be used to insert comments that make your programs easier to read and understand. The standard REMARK statement has

```
<line #> REM <text of the remark>
```

FIGURE 2.20 The standard REMARK statement begins with the key word REM. The text serves to explain the contents of the program but has no effect when the program is run.

2.6 THE REMARK STATEMENT

```
<line #> <any statement except DATA or END> ! <comment text>
<line #> ! <more comment text>
```

FIGURE 2.21 The exclamation point begins a comment field. All text to the right of the exclamation point is ignored by the computer. The second line shows how the comment separator may be used instead of a `REM` statement.

---

the form shown in Fig. 2.20. REMARK statements are listed along with the rest of your program but are otherwise ignored by the computer.

VAX-BASIC also provides for a comment field to allow insertion of remarks on a program line (see Fig. 2.21). The comment field begins with an exclamation point and continues to the end of the line. This type of comment may not be used in a DATA statement, but may be placed at the end of any other type of program statement. The exclamation point may also be used instead of REM in a remark statement.

An example showing the use of comments is shown in Fig. 2.22. The two programs differ only in the use of remark statements and hence will produce identical output when run.

Review: REMARK and !

- REM is a program statement, whereas ! is a separator that may be used after other program statements or by itself.
- Comment text is listed along with the rest of the program but is ignored when the program is run.

```
100 INPUT "FIRST NUMBER";  A       10  !****************************************
110 INPUT "SECOND NUMBER"; B       20  ! PROGRAM: S U M T W O
120 LET C = A + B                  30  !****************************************
130 PRINT "THE SUM IS";  C         40      ! THIS IS A PROGRAM TO FIND THE
140 END                            50      ! SUM OF TWO NUMBERS
                                   60      !
                                   70      ! --- get the two numbers ---
                                   100 INPUT "FIRST NUMBER";  A
                                   110 INPUT "SECOND NUMBER"; B
                                   115     ! --- determine the sum ----
                                   120 LET C = A + B
                                   125     ! --- print the results ---
                                   130 PRINT "THE SUM IS";  C
                                   140 END
```

FIGURE 2.22 Two equivalent programs. The remark lines in the second program add explanatory comments but do not affect the output of the program.

ELEMENTARY GRAMMAR

2.7 The GOTO Statement

The `GOTO` statement may be used to alter the usual sequence of statement execution:

600 GOTO 300

Program steps are carried out in the usual order until line 600 is reached. At that point the program jumps back to line 300 (see Fig. 2.23). In this case, the GOTO has created a loop in which steps 300, 400, and 500 are repeated over and over. Unless some other provision has been made to stop this process, the program will go on repeating these steps until ⟨ctrl/c⟩ is used to interrupt it.

The possibility of creating a never-ending loop is only one reason why the unconditional `GOTO` should be used very sparingly and carefully. Frequent use of the `GOTO` statement can also result in programs that are difficult to understand because the program logic jumps around too much.

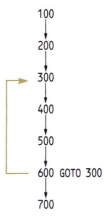

FIGURE 2.23 The `GOTO` statement has altered the usual sequence of program flow. This results in the formation of an "infinite loop" in which steps 300, 400 and 500 are repeated over and over.

2.8 The END Statement

The `END` statement marks the last line of a program. A program should contain only one `END` statement, and it must have the highest line number. Any other statement after the `END` statement, even a blank comment line, will cause an error message to be printed.

2.9 Using These Statements

We now have enough tools to begin writing some simple programs to illustrate how the `LET`, `INPUT`, `READ`, `DATA`, and `PRINT` statements may be used to accomplish specific tasks.

An Age Graph

The process of writing a program always begins with defining what the program is supposed to do, the *objective* of the program. Here is the objective of the program we are going to write next:

- The program should produce a graphical display of the user's age. (The "user" is any person who runs the program.) The display should show an asterisk (*) correctly positioned along a scale that represents ages from 0 to 60.

Once the objective has been defined, we can begin to think about a step-by-step procedure to accomplish it. Here is a first outline:

- Get the user's age.
- Display the age on an "age line."

The next step is to determine the variables that are required and give them names. In this case, the one variable required for this program will be called `AGE`.

Next, go back to the outline and determine how each step can be programmed. This may require another look at the programming tools at our disposal. For example, the first step is to get the user's age and store it in the variable `AGE`. There are three types of statements that may be used to do this: `LET`, `READ`, or `INPUT`. We assume that the user's age is not known in advance, so the `INPUT` statement must be used.

The next step is to display the age on a scale from 0 to 60. If you do not know how to do this, try breaking the step down into smaller pieces. For example:

- Print an asterisk in the correct column.
- Print a line with vertical marks every ten spaces.
- Print numbers to indicate the scale.

Each of these steps is a more manageable task.

It may also be necessary to experiment with a test program. For example, we might need to try some variations with the `TAB` function in a `PRINT` statement in order to get the output to look right.

Figure 2.24 shows a solution of the problem along with outputs for two typical runs.

ELEMENTARY GRAMMAR

```
100 INPUT "HOW OLD ARE YOU" ; AGE
110 PRINT "HERE IS A 'GRAPH' OF YOUR AGE:"
120 PRINT \PRINT
130 PRINT TAB(AGE); "*"
140 PRINT "|.........|.........|.........";
150 PRINT "|.........|.........|.........|"
160 PRINT "0"; TAB(9); "10"; TAB(19); "20"; TAB(29); '30';
170 PRINT TAB(39); '40' ;TAB(49); '50' ;TAB(59); '60'
180 END
```

OUTPUT

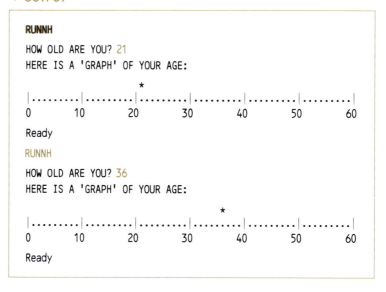

FIGURE 2.24 A program that displays an age graph.

A Retirement Table

Assume that we have been given the following information: If you save 10 dollars a month in an account that pays 10 percent interest, then after 10 years you will have 2,048 dollars, after 20 years you will have 7,593 dollars, after 30 years 22,604 dollars, and after 40 years 63,240 dollars.

- The objective of the program is to display a table containing the above information.

A simple outline of the program might include the steps:

- READ the dollar amounts from a DATA table.
- PRINT a header.

2.9 USING THESE STATEMENTS

- PRINT in appropriate columns the number of years and the total amount saved.

Assume that you have gone through the process of working out the solution and are ready to enter the program. The following example illustrates the procedure for entering the program with the aid of the SEQUENCE command. The process begins by entering the command SEQ, which tells the computer to begin generating line numbers starting with 100. Lines 120–160 produce output that identifies the program and gives headings for each column. The other `PRINT` statements contain two commas in order to tab the output over to column 28.

```
Ready
SEQ
100 READ S1, S2, S3, S4
110 DATA 2048, 7593, 22604, 63240
120 PRINT "IF YOU SAVE 10 DOLLARS A MONTH AT "
130 PRINT "TEN PERCENT INTEREST, YOU WILL HAVE:"
140 PRINT
150 PRINT "NUMBER OF YEARS" , "TOTAL AMOUNT SAVED"
160 PRINT "---------------" , "------------------"
170 PRINT 10 ,,S1
180 PRINT 20 ,,S2
190 PRINT 30 ,,S3
200 PRINT 40 ,,S4
210 END
220     <ctrl/c>
Ready
```

OUTPUT

```
RUN
NONAME  <date>  <time>

IF YOU SAVE 10 DOLLARS A MONTH AT
TEN PERCENT INTEREST, YOU WILL HAVE:

NUMBER OF YEARS               TOTAL AMOUNT SAVED
---------------               ------------------
10                            2048
20                            7593
30                            22604
40                            63240
```

2.10 Exercises

2.1 The program
```
100 LET X = X + 2
200 PRINT "X = ";X
300 END
```
will produce the output
```
X =  2
```
Use the discussion in Section 2.2 to explain why this is true.

2.2 Consider the following program:
```
100 INPUT "WHAT NUMBER" X
200 LET "Y= "; X+2
300 PRINT "TWO PLUS"; X ; " IS " ; Y
400 END
```
If you try to run this program you will get error messages for lines 100, 200, and 300 indicating that there are grammatical mistakes. Fix the mistakes and run the corrected program.

2.3 Determine the output of the following program:
```
100 READ X,Y,Z
200 LET W = X + Y + Z
300 PRINT W
400 DATA 2,4,6
500 END
```

2.4 Determine the output of the following program:
```
100 PRINT "FOURSCORE AND " ;
110 PRINT "SEVEN YEARS"
120 PRINT "AGO", "OUR FATHERS"
130 END
```

2.5 Determine the output of the following program:
```
100 LET Z = 2
200 LET W = 9
300 PRINT "Z=";Z , "W="; W
400 END
```
What happens if the comma in line 300 is replaced by a semicolon? Convince yourself that the values of Z and W are printed with a leading and trailing space by running the revised program. What happens to the spacing if Z and/or W are assigned negative values?

2.10 EXERCISES

2.6 Determine the output of the following program:
```
100 DATA 37
200 PRINT 'THIS IS A PROGRAM TO PRINT ';
250 PRINT 'THE VALUE OF '
300 PRINT 'THE VARIABLES A, B, AND C.'
400 READ A, B, C
500 DATA 10, 20, 30
550 PRINT "A= ";  A, "B= ";  B, "C= ";  C
600 END
```
Note that the placement of READ and DATA statements may lead to unexpected results.

2.7 Write a program to print the numbers 1 through 3 and the names of three Greek letters. The output should look like this:

```
1           ALPHA
2           BETA
3           GAMMA
```

Your program should show that three different methods can be used to align the printed output. For example, use commas to print the first line, quoted spaces to print the second line, and the TAB function to print the last line.

2.8 Modify the program TEMPS of Problem 1.1 so that the high and low temperatures for the first day are displayed graphically using the TAB function. Your output should have a temperature scale printed along the top with an L and an H on the next line to denote the low and the high temperature for the day. Your program should work correctly with different numbers in the data statement.

2.9 Modify the age graph program in Section 2.9 by adding a comment header that contains the program name "AGESCALE." Insert the following comment lines at the appropriate spots in the program:

```
---get the user's age---
---display the age on an age scale---
```

Run the program to ensure that the output is not affected by the comment lines.

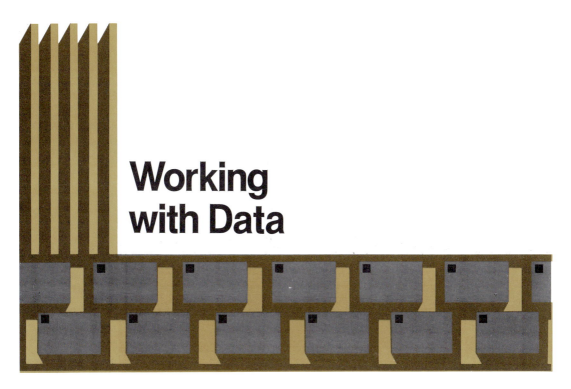

Working with Data

Chapter 2 showed how the assignment (LET) statement, the INPUT statement, and the READ statement can be used to name variables and give them values. This chapter will cover some of the calculations that can be carried out using these variables. For example, the computer can be instructed to calculate the square root of a number or to determine the average of several numbers.

3.1 More about the LET and the PRINT Statements

The standard form of an assignment statement is shown in Fig. 3.1. Oddly enough, the word LET is actually an optional part of the LET statement. This is indicated symbolically by the square brackets around the word LET in Fig. 3.1. The three essential parts of the assignment statement are

1. a variable name,
2. an equals sign, and
3. an algebraic or arithmetic expression.

WORKING WITH DATA

```
<line #> [ LET ] <variable name> = <expression>
```

FIGURE 3.1 The assignment statement contains the name of a variable and an expression to be evaluated. The square brackets are not part of the statement, but indicate that the word LET may be omitted. Pointed brackets indicate that enclosed words are descriptive rather than literal. That is, the words "variable name" are not part of the LET statement but should be replaced by an actual variable name like X or AVE.

$$\text{<line \#> PRINT} \left\{ \begin{array}{c} \text{<quoted string>} \\ \text{or} \\ \text{<expression>} \end{array} \right\} \left\{ \begin{array}{c} , \\ \text{or} \\ ; \end{array} \right\} \left\{ \begin{array}{c} \text{<quoted string>} \\ \text{or} \\ \text{<expression>} \end{array} \right\} \ldots$$

FIGURE 3.2 A PRINT statement may contain one or more algebraic expressions. Each such expression will be evaluated and the resulting value will be displayed.

The third part of the assignment statement, the algebraic expression, is the important one for this discussion. This is where calculations like addition, subtraction, multiplication, division, exponentiation (raising to a power), and finding square roots can be carried out. Most of the calculations in the program examples of the following chapters are carried out in the "expression" part of an assignment statement.

All of the algebraic and arithmetic expressions that can be used in a LET statement can also be used in a PRINT statement (see Fig. 3.2). The computer will carry out the calculations given in the expression and print the result.

Section 3.2 gives more specific rules for writing algebraic and arithmetic expressions.

3.2 Algebraic Operations

It is occasionally necessary to have the computer evaluate complicated algebraic expressions, such as

$$\frac{x^2 + axy - 2z}{78ax^4}.$$

If you wanted to write this expression as part of a BASIC program, several problems would soon become obvious. Program execution proceeds line by line, but the written symbols for division and exponentiation require two lines. Furthermore, the quantity axy could be interpreted as A times X times Y or as a variable called AXY.

3.2 ALGEBRAIC OPERATIONS

TABLE 3.1 The symbols used for algebraic operations.

Symbol	Meaning
+	Add
−	Subtract (when it appears between two variables)
−	Negative sign (when it appears alone in front of a variable)
*	Multiply
/	Divide
** (or ^)	Raise to a power

To avoid these problems, BASIC has its own set of rules to allow the user to give unambiguous directions for evaluating algebraic expressions (see Table 3.1). For example, the asterisk * is used as the multiplication sign and the "slash" / is used as the division sign, and so a times x times y would be denoted A*X*Y, and

$$\frac{(x)(y)}{a}$$ is written as X * Y / A.

Similarly, ** means "raise to a power," and so x^2 is written as X ** 2.

Even with all this notation, there are times when the computer might not know what to do. For example, does 3 * 4 ** 2 mean 12 squared or 3 times 16? Of course, these answers are different and depend on which operation (* or **) is carried out first. Additional rules to avoid this type of ambiguity are outlined in Table 3.2. In particular, 3 * 4 ** 2 always means 3 * 16 because ** is carried out before *.

Because of these rules, it is often necessary to add a set of parentheses to assure that the correct quantity is calculated. For example,

$$\frac{(x)(y)}{a+b}$$ must be written as X * Y / (A + B).

TABLE 3.2 Order of precedence (priority) for evaluating an algebraic expression in BASIC.

FIRST	Evaluates expressions contained within parentheses, starting from the innermost set.
THEN	Within a set of parentheses, carries out algebraic operations in the following order: 1. exponentiation (raising to a power), 2. minus signs, 3. multiplication or division, and 4. addition or subtraction.

WORKING WITH DATA

```
X + ( Y / Z * W )
    ↑         ↑
  first     next
```

FIGURE 3.3 Within a given set of parentheses, operations of the same priority are carried out from left to right.

If the parentheses are left off, the computer will evaluate an expression that is very different:

X * Y / A + B is evaluated as $\frac{(x)(y)}{a} + b$.

There are still times when ambiguities may arise. For example, does

12 / 3 / 2

mean 4 / 2 or 12 / 1.5? A similar problem arises with an expression like

12 / 3 * 2.

In each case, the answer depends on which operation is carried out first. The applicable rule is shown in Fig. 3.3. Table 3.3 shows a number of examples of how an algebraic equation can be written in computer notation. In some cases alternative representations are given. All of the parentheses used in the expressions on the right side of Table 3.3 are necessary to assure that the correct quantity is computed. In some cases, one or more extra sets of parentheses will make an expression easier to read and understand. For example,

$\frac{xy}{ab}$ is better written as (X * Y) / (A * B).

TABLE 3.3

Algebraic Expression	Computer Notation
$\frac{(x)(z)}{y}$	X * Z / Y
$\frac{x}{(y)(z)}$	X / Y / Z or X / (Y * Z)
$\frac{xy}{ab}$	X * Y / (A * B) or X * Y / A / B or X / A * Y / B

3.2 ALGEBRAIC OPERATIONS

Note: Parentheses do not indicate multiplication in BASIC. The asterisk must always be used. Therefore $(x + y)(a + b)$ should be written as (X + Y) * (A + B).

In some cases it is necessary to use parentheses inside parentheses. Such *nested* sets of parentheses are evaluated from the innermost set first. For example,

$\frac{r + st}{x(y + z)}$ is written as (R + S * T) / (X * (Y + Z)).

Once again, this expression might be clearer if extra parentheses were used:

(R + (S * T)) / (X * (Y + Z)).

Some algebraic expressions can look quite lengthy and complicated. For example, the expression at the beginning of this section,

$$\frac{x^2 + axy - 2z}{78ax^4},$$

can be written as

(X ** 2 + A * X * Y - 2 * Z) / (78 * A * X ** 4).

Nevertheless, algebraic expressions written in computer notation can easily be interpreted by applying the rules outlined above. These rules are summarized in Table 3.2. Operations of equal priority are carried out from left to right.

An algebraic expression can be used in a LET statement to calculate a new value for a variable (see Fig. 3.4) or in a PRINT statement to perform a calculation and display the result (see Fig. 3.5).

An algebraic expression can also be calculated in "immediate mode." That is, if you type a PRINT statement without a line number, the computer will not include the statement as part of your program but will evaluate and display the expression immediately. This allows you to use the computer as a calculator. For example, if you type the second statement of Fig. 3.5 without

---

110 LET Z = (X * Y) / (A + B)

FIGURE 3.4 A typical use of an algebraic expression in an assignment statement. The computer will calculate the value of the expression (X * Y) / (A + B) and store the result as the value of Z.

120 PRINT X * Y / A
130 PRINT "15 SQUARED IS "; 15 ** 2

FIGURE 3.5 Two examples of the use of an algebraic expression in a PRINT statement. In line 120, the expression X * Y / A is evaluated and the resulting value is printed. Line 130 illustrates the use of a quoted string and an algebraic expression in the same PRINT statement.

WORKING WITH DATA

a line number, the computer will immediately carry out the instruction and print

```
15 SQUARED IS 225
```

Example: Present-Worth Factor. The present-worth factor is given by the formula

$$\text{P.W.F.} = \frac{r}{1 - (1 + r)^{-n}}.$$

Assuming that the values of n and r have been established, the value of P.W.F. may be calculated using the program statement

```
LET P.W.F. = R / (1 - (1 + R) ** (-N) )
```

In evaluating this expression, the computer first evaluates (1 + R) and (-N), carries out the exponentiation (1 + R) ** (-N), performs the subtraction (1 - (1 + R) ** (-N)), and then the division.

The present-worth factor can be used to calculate the monthly payment on a mortgage or loan. In this case, N is the number of months that the loan is to be paid, and R is the monthly interest rate expressed as a decimal. The monthly payment is given by the formula

```
PAYMENT = LOAN-AMOUNT * P.W.F.
```

3.3 Exponential Notation

In order to make accurate computations, the VAX computer keeps track of numbers with more precision than we normally need. For example, the number 0.2 may be represented in the computer as 0.2000000000. Here, 2 is a *significant* digit, whereas the zeros are not. When the computer displays such a number, it normally shows only the significant digits, because the extra zeros do not provide any useful information.

TABLE 3.4 Very large or small numbers may be represented in a standard way as a power of 10.

```
    1,000 = 1 * 10 **  3 = 0.1 * 10 **  4
   10,000 = 1 * 10 **  4 = 0.1 * 10 **  5
  100,000 = 1 * 10 **  5 = 0.1 * 10 **  6
1,000,000 = 1 * 10 **  6 = 0.1 * 10 **  7
   0.0001 = 1 * 10 ** -4 = 0.1 * 10 ** -3
  0.00001 = 1 * 10 ** -5 = 0.1 * 10 ** -4
 0.000001 = 1 * 10 ** -6 = 0.1 * 10 ** -5
```

```
.2923E+05    →    29230
.843E-02     →    0.00843
```

FIGURE 3.6 Conversion from E format to standard notation. The decimal point must be moved the number of places given by the exponent.

If a number has more than six significant digits, it may be converted and displayed using *exponential notation*. This is a method of displaying a very large or very small number as a number between 0 and 10 multiplied by a power of 10 (see Table 3.4). For example, the very large number 1,269,238,000 can be represented as 1.269238000 * 10 ** 9, or as 0.1269238000 * 10 ** 10; and the very small number 0.0000045920 can be represented as 4.5920 * 10 ** −6, or as 0.45920 * 10 ** −5.

Expressing a value as a number multiplied by a power of 10 is called scientific, or exponential, notation. A closely related method, called E format, is used by the computer.

To represent a number using E format, first convert it to scientific notation with the decimal point positioned in front of the first nonzero digit. This number is rounded to six significant digits, if necessary, and is printed followed by an E and the power of 10 in the scientific representation of the number. For example, the numbers 1,269,238,000 and 0.0000045920, mentioned above, would be printed as **.126924E+10** and **.4592E−05**, respectively. In the first example, the number 0.1269238000 is rounded to six significant digits; in the second, the final zero in 0.45920 is not printed because it is not a significant digit.

To convert a number from E format to standard form, move the decimal point to the right if the exponent is positive and to the left if the exponent is negative. The two-digit exponent gives the number of places that the decimal point must be moved (see Fig. 3.6).

3.4 Built-in Functions

A function is a means of giving a name to a specific type of calculation. For example, ABS(X) means, "Calculate the absolute value of X," and SQR(Y) means, "Calculate the square root of Y." The quantity inside parentheses is called the *argument* of the function. Information about numeric functions is contained in Table 3.5; a more complete list appears in Appendix D.

A function may be used as part of an arithmetic expression in a LET or PRINT statement. Some typical examples are shown in Fig. 3.7 and in the program of Fig. 3.8. The absolute value function (**ABS**) is used in line 60 of the program of Fig. 3.8 to assure that Y is always a positive number. Then the

WORKING WITH DATA

TABLE 3.5 The most common numeric functions.

Function	Action
ABS( )	Calculates the absolute value of the argument. That is, if the argument is a negative number it is changed to a positive one with the same value. ABS(-5.2) returns a value of 5.2.
INT( )	Finds the largest integer that is less than or equal to the argument. If the argument is positive, the result is the same as dropping the decimal part. INT(3.65) returns a value of 3, whereas, INT(-4.6) returns a value of -5.
RND	Generates an unpredictable or random number between 0 and 1. The RND function has no argument.
SQR( )	Calculates the square root of the argument. SQR(16) returns a value of 4.

square root of Y is calculated in line 70. In fact, lines 60, 70, and 80 may be combined in various ways (see Fig. 3.9). Each variation requires that the ABS and the SQR functions be nested. In line 65 of Fig. 3.9, the absolute value of X is determined, then its square root is calculated and the resulting number is assigned to the variable Z. Line 85 of Fig. 3.8 differs from line 80 because Y is no longer used. Line 75 shows how all three lines may be combined into a single PRINT statement.

```
300 LET W = (X + Y) * SQR(Z)
310 LET U = SQR(ABS(X) )
320 PRINT INT(X + 3 * Y)
```

FIGURE 3.7 Typical uses of the SQR, ABS, and INT functions in LET and PRINT statements. Line 310 illustrates "nested" functions. In this case, one function serves as the argument of another one. Nested functions are evaluated by working out from the inner set of parentheses.

```
10 PRINT "SQUARE ROOT CALCULATOR"
20 PRINT
30 PRINT "THIS PROGRAM CALCULATES THE SQUARE ROOT"
40 PRINT "OF THE ABSOLUTE VALUE OF A NUMBER"
50 INPUT "WHAT IS THE NUMBER"; X
60 LET Y = ABS(X)
70 LET Z = SQR(Y)
80 PRINT "THE SQUARE ROOT OF"; Y; "IS"; Z
```

FIGURE 3.8 The square root calculator first changes negative numbers to positive ones using the ABS function.

3.4 BUILT-IN FUNCTIONS

```
65 LET Z = SQR(ABS(X))
85 PRINT "THE SQUARE ROOT OF"; ABS(X); "IS";   Z
```
or

```
75 PRINT "THE SQUARE ROOT OF";   ABS(X); "IS";   SQR(ABS(X))
```

FIGURE 3.9 Two ways of combining lines 60, 70, and 80 of Fig. 3.8.

The RND (random) function is remarkable for two reasons. First, it is the only function that does not require an argument. Second, it will produce a different number each time you use it.

The value of the RND function will always lie between 0 and 1,

$$0 \leq \text{RND} < 1,$$

but the actual value obtained will be different each time RND is used in a program. The computer actually generates a value for the RND function using a carefully selected algorithm. The algorithm provides a method of obtaining millions of different numbers that do not seem to have any systematic pattern.

In order to visualize this process, imagine using a book that contains millions of numbers that were selected at random (see Fig. 3.10). Each time the RND function is used, the next number is obtained from the table. The first time you use the RND function, the first number in the table is used; the next time, the second number is used, and so on. The program of Fig. 3.11 will obtain and display the first three numbers generated by RND (that is, the first

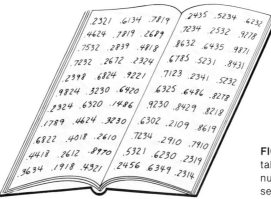

FIGURE 3.10 A random-number table may contain millions of numbers that have been carefully selected to have no pattern.

```
100 LET X = RND
110 LET Y = RND
120 LET Z = RND
130 PRINT X, Y, Z
```

FIGURE 3.11 These statements will display the first three random numbers generated by RND.

```
 90 RANDOMIZE
100 LET X = RND
110 LET Y = RND
120 LET Z = RND
130 PRINT X, Y, Z
```

FIGURE 3.12 Inserting the RANDOMIZE statement will create a totally unpredictable output. The three numbers will always be between 0 and 1 but will be different each time the program is run.

three numbers in the random number table). Each time you run the program of Fig. 3.11 the same output will be produced because the computer will always be starting at the beginning of the random number table.

The RANDOMIZE statement can be used to scramble things up. RANDOMIZE instructs the computer to go to some undetermined spot in the table and start there rather than at the beginning of the table (see Fig. 3.12). The results are totally unpredictable.

Example: Root of a Quadratic Equation. A root of a quadratic equation is a value of x that satisfies the relation

$$ax^2 + bx + c = 0$$

for specific values of a, b, and c. The solution is given by the quadratic formula

$$\frac{-b \pm \sqrt{b^2 - 4ac}}{2a}.$$

Assuming that the values of a, b, and c have been established, we may calculate the roots using the following statements:

```
200 LET R1 = (-B + SQR(B ** 2 - 4 * A * C)) / (2 * A)
210 LET R2 = (-B - SQR(B ** 2 - 4 * A * C)) / (2 * A)
```

Example: Game Simulations Using RND. The values of RND are uniformly distributed over the numbers between 0 and 1. This means that there are just as many numbers less than 0.5 as numbers greater than 0.5 in the random-number table.

```
100 LET T = INT(2 * RND)
```

FIGURE 3.13 This produces a value of 0 or 1 with equal likelihood. This can be used to simulate the tossing of a coin.

```
|••••|o•••|o•••|o•••|o•••|o•••|o•••|••••|
  0   1   2   3   4   5   6   7   8
```

FIGURE 3.14 Possible values of 6 * RND + 1 range between 1 and 7 so that INT(6 * RND + 1) will have a value of 1, 2, 3, 4, 5, or 6.

```
100 RANDOMIZE
110 LET D1 = INT(6 * RND + 1)
120 LET D2 = INT(6 * RND + 1)
130 PRINT  'YOU ROLLED A'; D1; 'AND A'; D2
140 END
```

FIGURE 3.15 A program to simulate the roll of a pair of dice.

Using this fact, we can accurately simulate the tossing of a coin by defining "Heads" to be a number less than 0.5 and "Tails" to be a number greater than 0.5. Figure 3.13 shows another method. In this case, the values of 2 * RND are numbers between 0 and 2. Therefore INT(2 * RND) is either 0 or 1. (The value of 2 * RND is never actually 2 because RND is always less than 1.)

The same technique can be used to generate other numbers. For example, 6 * RND has values between 0 and 6. All of these values are equally likely. By using INT(6 * RND + 1), one of the six numbers 1, 2, 3, 4, 5, or 6 may be randomly generated (see Fig. 3.14).

Figure 3.15 shows a program that uses the RND function to simulate the roll of a pair of dice.

Review: Using Functions

- All functions except RND require an argument. The argument is placed inside parentheses immediately after the function name.
- The argument of a function may consist of another function or an algebraic expression. The computer evaluates the argument first and then determines the value of the function.

3.5 Exercises

3.1 Translate the following algebraic expressions into computer notation:
   a) $(32.4)(x)(y)$
   b) $(x + 3)y/z$
   c) $\dfrac{(x + y)a}{b(c + d)}$
   d) $\dfrac{(37)\sqrt{4.5}}{3(x + y)}$

WORKING WITH DATA

3.2 Write the following numbers using scientific notation and E format:
   a) 1284.5   b) 0.00238
   c) 0.0000362910 d) 3492300.00

   Indicate how each of these numbers would be printed in a BASIC program.

3.3 Use the PRINT statement in immediate mode to calculate the following algebraic expression:

   $$\frac{56.8}{24.3} + 24.3 + (29.5)(17.6).$$

   Put the same calculation into a program.

3.4 Write a program to compute the values of **ABS**, **SQR**, **INT** for three numbers. Your program should use READ and DATA statements to assign the values 34.76, −2.45, and 0.0235 to the variables X1, X2, and X3. The answers should be displayed in four columns with a header that looks like this:

   ```
   NUMBER    ABS    SQR    INT
   -------------------------------
   ```

3.5 Write a program to convert an English length (yards, feet, and inches) into the equivalent number of meters. Your program should use INPUT statements to get the number of yards, feet, and inches and express this length as an equivalent number of inches. The number of meters is obtained by multiplying the number of inches by 0.0254. When run, your program should look like this:

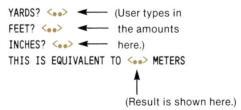

3.6 Write a program to convert a temperature from degrees centigrade to degrees Fahrenheit. Your program should use an INPUT statement to get the number of degrees centigrade and print out the equivalent temperature in degrees Fahrenheit. To convert from centigrade to Fahrenheit, first multiply by 9/5 and then add 32. When run your program should look like this:

3.7 Write a program HEART that computes the value of the maximum heart rate, in heartbeats per minute, that a person should encounter while exercising. An approximate formula for the maximum heart rate is

$$200 - \frac{AGE - 20}{2},$$

where AGE is the person's age in years.

Your program should ask for the user's age and then compute and display the maximum heart rate. Your program should also display a line that mentions that this is only an approximate value.

3.8 Write a program that uses the formula

```
PAYMENT = LOAN_AMOUNT * P.W.F.
```

to calculate the payment on a loan. The present-worth factor (P.W.F.) is described in Section 3.2. Your program should ask the user for the loan amount, the number of years that the loan is to be paid, and the annual interest rate on the loan. Note that the last two quantities must be converted before they are used in the P.W.F. formula.

3.9 Write a program that uses the compound-amount factor C.A.F. to calculate the amount of accumulated savings using the formula

```
NET_SAVINGS = AMOUNT_SAVED_EACH_MONTH * C.A.F.
```

The compound amount factor is given by the formula

$$\text{C.A.F.} = \frac{(1 + r)^n - 1}{r},$$

where r is the monthly interest rate expressed as a decimal, and n is the number of months.

Your program should ask for the amount saved each month, the annual interest rate, and the number of years of savings. The annual interest rate must be translated to a monthly interest rate and converted from a percent to a decimal value, and the number of years must be converted to the equivalent number of months.

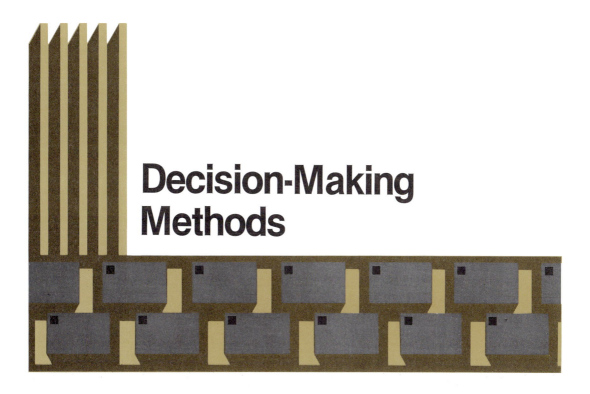

Decision-Making Methods

All of the program statements discussed so far are unconditional statements in the sense that they are always carried out when their turn comes during program execution. In this chapter we discuss conditional program statements.

A *conditional program statement* is one that may or may not be executed, depending on some specified condition. In the game analogy of Chapter 1, these correspond to instructions of the form

```
IF THERE IS ENOUGH MONEY, THEN PAY THE RENT
```

In particular, a statement such as

```
110 LET Z = SQR(X)
```

is an unconditional statement that computes the square root of X and assigns the value to the variable Z. On the other hand, a statement like

```
120 IF X > 0 THEN   LET Z = SQR(X)
```

is a conditional statement that will compute the square root only when X is a positive number.

We will use the phrase *decision making construct* to denote a collection of one or more program steps

DECISION-MAKING METHODS

that, taken together, accomplish a specific task. The `IF-THEN` and `IF-THEN-ELSE` statements described below are used for decision-making constructs in BASIC programs.

4.1 Conditional Execution (IF-THEN)

The conditional execution, or `IF-THEN`, statement is the simplest form of decision-making construct (see Fig. 4.1). The ⟨condition⟩ is a relational or logical condition, such as `X > 0`, and the ⟨statement⟩ is a standard program statement, such as a `PRINT` statement. The computer decides if a statement is to be carried out based on the value of some variables in the program. For example, the print statement in

```
200 IF X > 0 THEN PRINT X
```

will be carried out only if X is a positive number; otherwise nothing happens, and the computer goes on to the next step in the program. In the statement

```
320 IF A + B <> 0 THEN LET Y = A * B / (A + B)
```

"⟨⟩" is the symbol for "not equal to," and so the value of `Y` is computed only if `A + B` is nonzero. This avoids the possibility of dividing by zero. In the statement

```
340 IF A == B THEN PRINT "A AND B ARE NEARLY EQUAL"
```

the symbol "==" means "approximately equal to," and the variables are tested to see if they are nearly equal. Normally, this occurs when the two numbers agree to within the first six significant figures. That is, the statements `PRINT A` and `PRINT B` would produce the same output even though the values of `A` and `B` might be different.

    IF ⟨condition⟩   THEN ⟨statement⟩

FIGURE 4.1 The format for an `IF-THEN` statement.

4.2 Logical Conditions

Logical conditions are used in decision-making constructs to determine if one or more statements are to be carried out. The computer must evaluate the logical condition and determine if it is true or false. For example, the logical

4.2 LOGICAL CONDITIONS

TABLE 4.1 The relational operators and their meanings when used with numeric variables.

Operator	Meaning
=	Exact equality
<	Less than
<= or =<	Less than or equal to
>	Greater than
>= or =>	Greater than or equal to
<> or >< or #	Not equal to
==	Approximate equality

condition X < Y is true if the value of x is less than the value of y. This condition contains the variables X and Y together with the relational operator <.

There are a number of different *relational operators* that can be within the logical condition in an IF statement. Table 4.1 contains a summary of the operators and their meanings when used with numeric variables.

The difference between exact equality "=" and approximate equality "==" has to do with the fact that numbers are stored with more precision than when they are displayed. Two numbers are exactly equal if their internal representation is the same. Two numbers are approximately equal if they produce the same output when displayed. Normally, this happens when the first six significant digits are the same.

In addition, relational operators and variables may be combined into compound conditions by means of *logical operators*. The most useful logical operators are AND, OR, and XOR (exclusive OR). Specifically, suppose the two conditions cond1 and cond2 are combined using these logical operators. Table 4.2 indicates when the resulting compound condition is true. When this kind of compound condition is used as the ⟨condition⟩ part of an IF-THEN statement, the compound condition is evaluated according to the rules of Table 4.2 and the statement is carried out only when the compound condition is found to be true.

Here are two examples of the use of compound logical conditions in IF-THEN statements. Remember that the ⟨condition⟩ part of an IF-THEN

TABLE 4.2 How logical operators combine two conditions into one compound condition.

⟨cond1⟩ AND ⟨cond2⟩	is true if both condition 1 and condition 2 are true.
⟨cond1⟩ OR ⟨cond2⟩	is true if at least one of the two conditions is true.
⟨cond1⟩ XOR ⟨cond2⟩	is true if exactly one of the two conditions is true.

statement consists of everything between the words IF and THEN and the ⟨statement⟩ part consists of everything after the word THEN.

In the first statement

```
100 IF X < 100 AND X > 0 THEN  PRINT "X IS BETWEEN 0 AND 100"
```

the message is printed only if the value of X actually lies between 0 and 100. In the second statement

```
500 IF R1 = 0 XOR R2 = 0 THEN PRINT "THERE IS EXACTLY ONE ZERO"
```

the exclusive or, XOR, assures that exactly one of the two variables is zero when the message is printed.

4.3 The Multiline IF-THEN Statement

A single condition can be used to control the execution of more than one program statement (see Fig. 4.2). A few short statements can be executed conditionally if they are placed in an IF-THEN statement separated by the backslash symbol (\). For example, the decision construct

```
300 IF X > 0 THEN  LET SUM = SUM + X \ PRINT X
```

tests to determine if X is positive and if so, carries out the LET and the PRINT statements. Neither of the statements is carried out if X is negative or zero.

The IF-THEN statement can be split into different lines before and after the key word THEN and between each statement. For example,

```
300 IF  X > 0
      THEN
         LET SUM = SUM + X
         PRINT X
      END IF
```

```
IF <this condition is true>
   THEN <do all of the following statements:>
       <statement T1>
       <statement T2>
         etc.
```

FIGURE 4.2 A single condition may be used to control the execution of a group of program statements.

4.3 THE MULTILINE IF-THEN STATEMENT

```
<line #>  IF <condition>
             THEN
                <statement T1>
                <statement T2>
                <statement T3>
                  etc.
             END IF
```

FIGURE 4.3 The `IF-THEN` statement may be arranged as shown for maximum clarity. The `END IF` clause is optional under normal conditions.

Notice that only one line number has been used even though the construct occupies several lines of text. Each continuation line should begin with at least one space or tab character. It is recommended that you use this form of the `IF-THEN` statement because it makes complicated decision-making constructs a lot easier to read and understand (see Fig. 4.3).

Line Continuations Using the Sequencer

If you are using the sequencer to generate the line numbers of your program, you will not be able to type the `IF-THEN` statement in the form given above. There are two alternatives. One is to stop the sequencing process before entering the multiline IF statement, enter the statement as usual, and then resume sequencing, as shown in Fig. 4.4. The alternative is to use the ampersand character (&) at the end of each line as shown in Fig. 4.5. The

```
SEQ
100 LET SUM = 10
110 INPUT  X
120 <ctrl/c>
Ready

120 IF X > 0          <R>
       THEN           <R>
          LET SUM = SUM + X  <R>
          PRINT X     <R>

SEQ 130
130 ...
```

FIGURE 4.4 Entering a multiline statement by stopping the sequencer.

DECISION-MAKING METHODS

```
SEQ
100 LET SUM = 10
110 INPUT  X
120 IF   X > 0 &
      THEN &
         LET SUM = SUM + X &
         PRINT X
130 ...
```

FIGURE 4.5 Entering a multiline statement using the ampersand character.

ampersand character may be used at any time to continue a line of your program onto a new line of text. If the ampersand is used while sequencing, the computer will not generate a new line number and you can then type the next line of the multiline statement.

Whenever a line ends with the ampersand character it is regarded as a line that is to be continued, and no new line number is generated. When the final line in the multiline statement, in this case PRINT X, is typed without an ampersand, the computer resumes generation of line numbers. Whenever lines are continued in this way, the ampersand must be the *last* character on the line. Even a blank space after the last ampersand character will cause problems.

4.4 The IF-THEN-ELSE Statement

The condition in an IF statement may be used to determine which of two statements or groups of statements is to be executed (see Fig. 4.6). If the condition is true, the first statement (indicated by ⟨stmt T⟩) is executed; if the condition is false, the second statement (⟨stmt F⟩) is carried out.

For example, the following decision construct will choose one of the two PRINT statements PRINT X,Y or PRINT Y,X depending on the relative values of X and Y:

```
300 IF X < Y THEN PRINT X,Y ELSE PRINT Y,X
```

IF ⟨condition⟩ THEN ⟨stmt T⟩ ELSE ⟨stmt F⟩

FIGURE 4.6 The form of the IF-THEN-ELSE statement.

If the value of X is less than the value of Y then `PRINT X,Y` is executed; otherwise `PRINT Y,X` is executed. The result is that the smaller number is always printed at the left edge of the screen and the larger number in the next tab zone.

The `IF-THEN-ELSE` statement can also be split at the words `THEN` and `ELSE`:

```
340 IF X < Y
      THEN PRINT X,Y
      ELSE PRINT Y,X
```

This format is used in the NUMBER program (see Chapter 7):

```
3900 IF GUESS > NMBR
        THEN  PRINT "THAT NUMBER IS TOO BIG"
        ELSE  PRINT "THAT NUMBER IS TOO SMALL"
```

If the condition is true, the guess is bigger than the number to be guessed and the first message is printed. If the condition is false, then the second message is printed.

The condition in the `IF-THEN-ELSE` statement can be used to determine which of two groups of program statements is to be carried out (see Fig. 4.7). If the condition is true, all of the statements between `THEN` and `ELSE` are carried out; if the condition is false, all of the statements following `ELSE` are carried out. (The text in brackets, { }, is explanatory and should not be included in the program.) Figure 4.8 shows the `IF-THEN-ELSE` construct as it

```
{test the condition}
IF {the} <condition> {is true}
        THEN {do all of these statements}
                <stmt T1>
                <stmt T2>
                <stmt T3>
                   etc.
        ELSE {if the condition is false, do these:}
                <stmt F1>
                <stmt F2>
                   etc.
```

FIGURE 4.7 The condition in an `IF-THEN-ELSE` construct may be used to control which of two groups of program statements is executed.

```
<line #> IF <condition>
         THEN
                <statement T1>
                <statement T2>
                <statement T3>
         ELSE
                <statement F1>
                <statement F2>
                ...
         END IF
```

FIGURE 4.8 This shows how the multiline `IF-THEN-ELSE` construct may be arranged for maximum clarity.

```
320 IF D >= 0
      THEN
        LET R1 = (-B + SQR(D)) / (2 * A)
        LET R2 = (-B - SQR(D)) / (2 * A)
        PRINT "THE ROOTS ARE "; R1 ; " AND "; R2
      ELSE
        PRINT "SORRY BUT THIS EQUATION DOES NOT HAVE"
        PRINT "A REAL VALUED SOLUTION "
    END IF
```

FIGURE 4.9 An IF-THEN-ELSE statement.

appears in a program. A line number is used only on the first line. Each subsequent line must begin with one or more blank spaces or tabs. The END IF is optional unless the next line numbers are omitted as described in Chapter 12.

Figure 4.9 presents an IF-THEN-ELSE statement taken from the program discussed in the example that follows. The three statements between the keywords THEN and ELSE are carried out if the value of D is greater than or equal to zero. The two statements after the keyword ELSE are carried out if D is a negative number.

Example: Roots of a Quadratic Equation. The roots of a quadratic equation are values of x that satisfy the equation

$$ax^2 + bx + c = 0$$

for specific values of the constants a, b, and c. In most cases, the roots may be determined from the formulas

$$\frac{-b + \sqrt{b^2 - 4ac}}{2a} \quad \text{and} \quad \frac{-b - \sqrt{b^2 - 4ac}}{2a}. \tag{4.1}$$

The quantity under the square root is called the discriminant. If the discriminant is negative, then the square roots cannot be calculated as real numbers. There is no way of knowing in advance if the discriminant is positive or negative, and so this must be tested before attempting to compute the square root.

This example includes a step-by-step procedure for writing a program to compute the roots of a quadratic equation.

The first step is to make sure that you understand the problem: Write a program to calculate the roots of a quadratic equation using the above formulas. The next step is to develop a rough outline of the program.

4.4 THE IF-THEN-ELSE STATEMENT

> Get the values of a b and c.
>
> Determine the discriminant $D = b^2 - 4ac$.
>
> Is the discriminant nonnegative?
>
> > If *yes*, calculate the roots R1 and R2 using the formulas in Eq. 4.1.
> >
> > If *no*, print a message telling the user that the roots cannot be computed.

The above outline includes names for all of the variables used in the program. Otherwise, naming the variables would have to be a separate step. The program uses three "input" variables, A, B, and C, and three "program" variables, D, R1, and R2.

The values of A, B, and C must be obtained from the user before anything else can happen. The program then calculates the values of the discriminant D and uses this to determine if the roots R1 and R2 can be calculated.

Here is a more detailed outline of the program:

> INPUT the values of A, B, and C.
>
> LET D = B ** 2 - 4 * A * C.
>
> IF D >= 0 {is true},
>
> > THEN {do these steps:}
> >
> > > calculate the values
> > > of R1 and R2 using the
> > > above formulas;
> >
> > ELSE {if D >= 0 is not true, do this:}
> >
> > > display a message.

```
100 INPUT  A
120 INPUT  B
130 INPUT  C
140 LET D = B ** 2 - 4 * A * C
150 IF D >= 0
       THEN
          LET R1 = (-B + SQR(D)) / (2 * A)
          LET R2 = (-B - SQR(D)) / (2 * A)
          PRINT "THE ROOTS ARE "; R1 ; " AND " ; R2
       ELSE
          PRINT "SORRY, NO SOLUTION "
       END IF
160    END
```

FIGURE 4.10 Test version of a program to compute the roots of a quadratic equation.

DECISION-MAKING METHODS

At this point, a short "test" version of the program can be written (see Fig. 4.10). The test version runs correctly in most cases. However, there is a "bug" in the program that shows up if 0 is used as the value of **A**. In this case the program will attempt to divide by 0 and an error condition will result.

The final version of the program is shown in Fig. 4.11. It uses an **IF-THEN** statement to ensure that **A** is nonzero before going on to the calculations. Comments were added to the test version, and the **INPUT** and **PRINT** statements were expanded. Finally, lines were renumbered using the **RESEQUENCE** command.

Example: Calculating the Exercise Value of a Run. Here's a program that is based on actual experiments to determine the amount of "aerobic" exercise value there is in running a given distance in a given amount of time. The formulas are realistic and are based on a scale that uses 100 exercise units per week as the norm for fitness.

In order to compute the exercise value, we need to know the distance in miles of the run or walk and the time in hours that it took. Obviously, if you run faster, you get more exercise, and so the speed or rate plays a role in the calculation.

Here are some preliminary formulas and variable definitions:

- **DIST** = the distance in miles of the run or walk;
- **TOT.TIME** = the total time in hours that it took;
- **RATE** = $\dfrac{\text{DIST}}{\text{TOT.TIME}}$ = the speed in miles per hour.

There are two different formulas for the exercise value **EXVAL** of the run or walk, depending on the speed.

1. IF the value of **RATE** is less than 6,

   $$\text{EXVAL} = \frac{10*(\ \text{DIST}*(\text{RATE}-1)\ -1\ )}{3}.$$

2. IF the value of **RATE** is 6 or more,

   $$\text{EXVAL} = \frac{10*(\ \text{DIST}*(5+\ 2*(\text{RATE}-6)/3)\ -1\ )}{3}.$$

The program must calculate the value of the **RATE** and use this to determine the correct formula for calculating the exercise value (**EXVAL**). This may be accomplished using an **IF-THEN-ELSE** construct.

4.4 THE IF-THEN-ELSE STATEMENT

```
100 ! *******************************************
110 ! PROGRAM: Q U A D R A
120 ! -------------------------------------------
130         ! PROGRAM TO SOLVE FOR THE REAL ROOTS
140         ! OF A QUADRATIC EQUATION
150         ! LIST OF VARIABLES:
160         !  A,B,C - coefficients of the quadratic
170         !  D     - the discriminant
180         !  R1, R2 - the real roots
190         !
200 PRINT "THIS SOLVES FOR THE ROOTS OF A QUADRATIC"
210 PRINT "EQUATION OF THE FORM:"
220 PRINT
230 PRINT "       2"
240 PRINT " A X   +  B X  + C  =  0"
250 PRINT
260 PRINT "YOU NEED TO TYPE IN THE VALUES OF A, B and C"
270 INPUT  "WHAT IS THE VALUE OF A"; A
280 INPUT  "WHAT IS THE VALUE OF B"; B
290 INPUT  "WHAT IS THE VALUE OF C"; C
300 IF A = 0
     THEN
        PRINT "THIS IS NOT A QUADRATIC EQUATION"
        PRINT "THE VALUE OF A MUST BE NONZERO"
        GOTO 200
     END IF
310 LET D = B ** 2 - 4 * A * C
320 IF D >= 0
     THEN
        LET R1 = (-B + SQR(D)) / (2 * A)
        LET R2 = (-B - SQR(D)) / (2 * A)
        PRINT "THE ROOTS ARE "; R1 ; " AND " ; R2
     ELSE
        PRINT "SORRY BUT THIS EQUATION DOES NOT HAVE"
        PRINT "A REAL VALUED SOLUTION "
     END IF
330 END
```

FIGURE 4.11

Here is an outline of the program:

Get the distance in miles (DIST).

Get the time it took in hours and minutes (TIME.HR, TIME.MIN) and calculate the total time in hours (TOT.TIME).

Compute the RATE using the formula given above.

Test the value of RATE and calculate the EXVAL using the appropriate formula.

Convert negative values of EXVAL to zero and check for suspicious answers.

Print the results.

The program is shown in Fig. 4.12. Line 240 is a check for suspicious answers. A `RATE` greater than 15 MPH represents running a mile in less than four minutes. An `EXVAL` greater than 800 is the equivalent of running a marathon in near record time.

Review: The `IF-THEN-ELSE` Construct

The standard form of the IF-THEN-ELSE construct is

```
<line #> IF
            THEN
                    <statement T1>
                    <statement T2>
                    <statement T3>
            ELSE
                    <statement F1>
                    <statement F2>
                    ...
         END IF
<line #> ...
```

- The ⟨condition⟩ is used to determine which group of statements is to be carried out.
- Any number of statements may appear between the key words `THEN` and `ELSE` and between the key word `ELSE` and the end of the construct.
- If the condition is true, all of the statements between `THEN` and `ELSE` are carried out.
- If the condition is false, all of the statements after the `ELSE` are carried out.
- The END IF clause may be used to mark the end of the IF-THEN-ELSE construct, otherwise, the IF-THEN-ELSE construct terminates whenever a line number is used to begin a new program line.

```
100 ! ************************************************
110 ! PROGRAM: R U N V A L
120 ! ----------------------------------------------
130       ! PROGRAM TO DETERMINE THE EXERCISE
140       ! VALUE OF A RUN.
150       !
160 INPUT 'HOW FAR DID YOU RUN (MILES)'; DIST
170 PRINT 'HOW LONG DID IT TAKE (HOURS AND MINUTES)'
180 INPUT 'HOW MANY HOURS'; TIME.HR
190 INPUT 'HOW MANY MINUTES'; TIME.MIN
200 LET TOT.TIME = TIME.HR + TIME.MIN/60
210 LET RATE = DIST/TOT.TIME
220 IF RATE < 6
       THEN
          LET EXVAL = 10/3*(DIST*(RATE-1) -1)
       ELSE
          LET EXVAL = 10/3*(DIST*(5+2/3*(RATE-6)) -1)
    END IF
230 IF EXVAL < 0 THEN EXVAL = 0
240 IF RATE > 15 OR EXVAL > 800
       THEN
          PRINT 'WHO DO YOU THINK YOU ARE, BILL ROGERS?'
          GOTO 290
    END IF
250 PRINT 'YOUR RUN HAD AN EXERCISE VALUE OF';
260 PRINT EXVAL; 'UNITS. '
270 PRINT '100 UNITS OF EXERCISE PER WEEK'
280 PRINT 'IS ADEQUATE TO MAINTAIN YOUR FITNESS '
290 END
```

FIGURE 4.12 Final program to compute the exercise value of a run.

4.5 Multiple Alternatives Using the SELECT Statement

The IF-THEN-ELSE statement provides a means of telling the computer to "do one thing or another." There are two alternatives; do one statement or group of statements (the THEN statements), or do the other (the ELSE statements).

DECISION-MAKING METHODS

Grade-point average	Evaluation
3.8 to 4.0	High honors
3.5 to 3.8	Dean's list
2.5 to 3.5	Satisfactory
1.5 to 2.5	Poor
0.0 to 1.5	Unsatisfactory

FIGURE 4.13 The grade-point average is to be evaluated using the above rules.

There are times when there may be more than two alternatives. For example, we may wish to look at a student's grade-point average and print an evaluation on a grade-report summary using the criteria presented in Fig. 4.13.

In situations like this, the SELECT statement provides a convenient method of giving the computer instructions for choosing from among a number of different alternatives. In particular, if G.P.A. represents the value of the grade-point average, the evaluation can be accomplished using the SELECT statement as shown in Fig. 4.14.

Note the structure of the SELECT statement. The first line contains the key word SELECT followed by the name of the variable to be tested. The

INPUT "WHAT IS YOUR G.P.A."; G.P.A.

```
1000 SELECT G.P.A.
        CASE 3.8 TO 4.0
            PRINT "HIGH HONORS"
        CASE 3.5 TO 3.8
            PRINT "DEAN'S LIST"
        CASE 2.5 TO 3.5
            PRINT "SATISFACTORY"
        CASE 1.5 TO 2.5
            PRINT "POOR"
        CASE 0.0 TO 1.5
            PRINT "UNSATISFACTORY"
        CASE ELSE
            PRINT "G.P.A. IS OUT OF RANGE"
     END SELECT
     END
```

FIGURE 4.14 Evaluating a grade-point average using the SELECT statement.

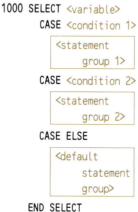

FIGURE 4.15 The structure of the SELECT construct for two statement groups and one default statement group.

CASE statement is followed by a condition that is to be tested. In this example, the condition is a range of values, but conditions like

    CASE = 4.0

or

    CASE > 3.8

are also allowed. If the condition in the CASE clause is found to be true, then the statement or group of statements immediately after the CASE clause is carried out (see Fig. 4.15). If the condition in the first CASE clause is not true, then the computer checks the condition in the next CASE clause. Additional CASE clauses may be added before the CASE ELSE clause. The statement group immediately following the first true CASE clause will be carried out. If there is no true condition, the default statement group following the CASE ELSE clause will be carried out.

*4.6 Nested IF-THEN-ELSE Statements

An IF-THEN-ELSE construct normally contains two groups of statements, as illustrated in Fig. 4.8. A nested IF-THEN-ELSE construct is created by inserting a second IF-THEN-ELSE construct into the statement group following the ELSE key word (see Fig. 4.16).

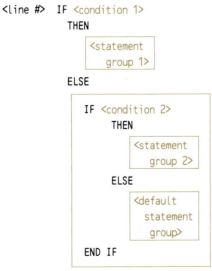

FIGURE 4.16 The nested IF-THEN-ELSE construct provides a method of dealing with multiple alternatives.

DECISION-MAKING METHODS

```
<line #>   IF <condition 1> THEN
               <statement
                  group 1>
           ELSE IF <condition 2> THEN
               <statement
                  group 2>
           ELSE
               <default
                statement
                  group>
           END IF
           END IF
```

FIGURE 4.17 A nested IF-THEN-ELSE construct.

When `IF-THEN-ELSE` constructs are nested, it is usual to arrange the statements as shown in Fig. 4.17. This particular example shows two conditions, but any number of conditions may be included by adding additional `ELSE IF` clauses. There should be one `END IF` for each `IF`, but the `END IF` clauses are optional if the next statement begins with a line number. The arrangement shown in Fig. 4.17 makes it a lot easier to see the nature of the construct and also emphasizes the fact that the logic is similar to a `SELECT` construct (see Exercise 4.4).

4.7 Exercises

4.1 Write a program that asks the user to type in an age. The program should then determine if the user is old enough to vote and display the result.

4.2 Modify your solution of Exercise 3.7. This time, your program should use the following formula to compute the maximum heart rate if the user's age is less than 20:

   $220 - AGE$.

4.3 Write a program that asks the user to type in a grade-point average. Your program should use the SELECT construct of Fig. 4.15 to evaluate the G.P.A. and print a message. Test your program using a number of different inputs.

*4.4 Revise the program of Exercise 4.3. This time your program should use a nested IF-THEN-ELSE construct instead of the SELECT construct. Which method do you think is easier?

4.5 a) Write a program to guess the minimum value of the quadratic equation
$$y = Ax^2 + Bx + C$$
on the interval between -10 and 10.

Your program should do the following:

1. Obtain values for A, B, and C from the user.
2. Set starting values for the variables
   XMIN and YMIN (use XMIN $= 0$, YMIN $= C$).
3. Repeatedly generate a random guess for X and compute the corresponding value for Y. Test the value of Y against YMIN. If Y is smaller than YMIN, then replace XMIN and YMIN with the current values of X and Y.

Use the statement

```
LET X = 20*RND - 10
```

to generate random guesses between -10 and 10.

Repeat step (3) 100 times or more to obtain a reasonably good estimate for XMIN. (Of course, step (2) should not be repeated.)

b) If your program makes 200 guesses, how close would you expect to come to the actual value of XMIN?

4.6 Modify the program of Exercise 4.5 so that the maximum value is also determined.

***4.7** From calculus, the maximum or minimum value of a quadratic equation must occur at a "critical" point. In particular, the maximum and minimum value of the quadratic equation of Exercises 4.5 and 4.6 must occur at one of the end points
$$X = -10 \text{ or } X = 10,$$
or at the point $X = -B/2A$ provided this lies within the interval between -10 and 10.

Write a program to determine the actual maximum and minimum value of the quadratic equation of Exercise 4.5. Your program should do the following:

1. Evaluate the quadratic equation for each of the end points -10 and 10.
2. If appropriate, evaluate the quadratic for $X = -B/2A$.
3. Determine the largest and smallest value obtained for Y.
4. Display the result.

How does the result compare with the values obtained in Exercise 4.6?

Loops

The term *loop* is used to describe a situation in which the program departs from the usual procedure of carrying out one program step after another in order to repeat a step or group of steps more than once. A typical situation is illustrated in Fig. 2.23. In that case, steps 300 to 600 are carried out and then the program "loops back" to repeat these steps over and over. A more useful loop would contain some provision to stop the program from repeating these steps indefinitely.

5.1 Situations in Which Loops Are Useful

Loops are useful when one or more program steps must be repeated. For example, the TABS program of Section 2.3 contains five identical PRINT statements of the form

```
<line #>  PRINT "|............";
```

Rather than type out the same print statement five times, it is possible to put a single print statement into a loop that repeats five times.

LOOPS

The advantage of a loop is more apparent when statements must be repeated tens or hundreds of times. For example, suppose we wish to display a table containing all of the numbers from 1 to 100 along with their square roots. Rather than write out 100 statements of the form

```
100 PRINT 1, SQR(1)
200 PRINT 2, SQR(2)
300 PRINT 3, SQR(3)
         .
         .
         .
```

It would save a lot of typing if the same table could be produced by putting one or two identical program statements into a loop that is repeated 100 times. Of course, the statements to be repeated are not all identical, but they do have the same form:

```
<line #> PRINT N, SQR(N)
```

where N takes on the values 1, 2, 3, 4, and so on.

The table can be produced by beginning with the statement

```
200 LET N = 1
```

and repeating the following steps 100 times:

```
300 PRINT N, SQR(N)
400 LET N = N + 1
```

5.2 The FOR Loop

The FOR and NEXT statements in BASIC make it easy to set up loops to repeat program steps. The first line of a FOR loop is always a FOR statement, and the last line is always a NEXT statement.

```
FOR N = 1 TO 100
    <steps to
    be repeated>
NEXT N
```

FIGURE 5.1 An example of a FOR loop to repeat a group of program steps 100 times. The statements are repeated with N taking values ranging from 1 through 100.

```
100 FOR N = 1 TO 100
200    PRINT N, SQR(N)
300 NEXT N
```

FIGURE 5.2 A FOR loop to display a table showing the numbers from 1 to 100 together with their square roots.

5.2 THE FOR LOOP

```
10 FOR N = 1 TO 5
20   PRINT "|............." ;
30 NEXT N
60 PRINT "|........."
70 PRINT "FIRST", "SECOND", "THIRD",
80 PRINT "FOURTH", "FIFTH", "SIXTH"
90 END
```

FIGURE 5.3

The FOR statement has the form

`100 FOR N = 1 TO 100`

and specifies a control variable (N), a starting value (1) and a stopping value (100).

The NEXT statement has the form

`300 NEXT N`

The FOR/NEXT statement pair set up a loop in which all of the statements that appear between FOR and NEXT are repeated (see Fig. 5.1). In particular, the square-root table of Section 5.1 could be created using the FOR loop of Fig. 5.2.

FOR loops are often used simply to repeat one or more program statements a specified number of times. Figure 5.3 shows how the TABBING program of Fig. 2.12 can be rewritten using a FOR loop to repeat the first PRINT statement five times.

In general, the FOR loop has the form shown in Fig. 5.4. This shows that the FOR loop can contain an optional STEP clause that specifies how much the loop variable is increased or decreased each time the loop is repeated. The loop-control variable, ⟨loop variable⟩, begins with a value of ⟨start value⟩, and ⟨step size⟩ is added to ⟨loop variable⟩ each time the loop is repeated. If no STEP is specified, ⟨loop variable⟩ is increased by one each time the loop is repeated. The loop continues until ⟨loop variable⟩ reaches ⟨end value⟩ or is less than ⟨end value⟩, but the addition of ⟨step size⟩ would cause it to exceed ⟨end value⟩.

```
FOR <loop variable> = <start value> TO <end value> [ STEP <step size>]
        ┌─────────────────┐
        │ <program        │
        │  statements>    │
        └─────────────────┘
NEXT <loop variable>
```

FIGURE 5.4 The format of a FOR loop showing the optional STEP clause.

```
100 FOR N = 10 TO 70 STEP 10
110    PRINT TAB(N-2); N ;
120 NEXT N
130 PRINT

200 FOR N = 10 TO 1 STEP -1
210    PRINT N
220 NEXT N
230 PRINT 'BLASTOFF'
```

FIGURE 5.5 The use of the STEP clause in a FOR loop.

Figure 5.5 shows an example of the use of the STEP clause to count up or down by a specified amount: The PRINT statement in line 110 is repeated with N = 10, 20, 30, 40, 50, 60, and 70. Lines 100 to 130 print a "scale" across the output screen showing a 10 in column 10, a 20 in column 20, and so on. Lines 200 to 230 print a "countdown": 10, 9, 8, and so on down to 1, followed by the word BLASTOFF.

Example: Sums and Averages. This example shows how to write a program that adds a list of 15 numbers. If you had to figure out a procedure for doing this, you might start out with a long list of numbers and think about how you would add the numbers using a calculator:

> Press the clear button.
> Enter the first number.
> Press the "+" key.
> Enter the next number.
> Press the "+" key.
> Continue this process until all 15 numbers have been entered, and write down the result.

The repetitive nature of the process is apparent. Each time you enter a number, it is shown on the calculator screen. Each time you press the "+" key, the "accumulated sum" of the numbers you have entered is shown on the screen. The calculator is keeping track of two numbers: the last number you have entered and the sum of the numbers you have entered so far.

We can use the same procedure in a program. We can put the numbers into a DATA list and use a FOR loop to read through the numbers. As each number is read, its value is added to the accumulated sum. We will use the variable X for the number being added and the variable SUM for the accumulated sum. Here is an outline of the procedure.

5.2 THE FOR LOOP

Start with SUM = 0

FOR N = 1 TO 15

    READ the next number from the DATA list into X

    add the value of X to SUM and store the result in SUM

NEXT N

Print the SUM

After the loop has been repeated 15 times, all numbers in the DATA list will have been added to SUM, and the result can be printed. Notice that the variable used for loop control (N) is different from the variables used inside the loop (X and SUM). N simply counts how many times the steps inside the loop are repeated. The program is shown in Fig. 5.6. Note that it would not be wise to place the PRINT statement before line 500 of this program because it would be inside the loop and therefore would be repeated 15 times. Similarly, the program would not work correctly with the first LET statement inside the loop. In this case, the accumulated sum would be lost each time the program repeated the statement "LET SUM = 0".

The program of Fig. 5.6 can be modified to compute and print the average of the numbers by adding one or two statements after line 500 (see Fig. 5.7).

```
100   LET SUM = 0
200   FOR N = 1 TO 15
300     READ X
400     LET SUM = SUM + X
500   NEXT N
600   PRINT "THE SUM OF THE NUMBERS IS "; SUM
1000  !
1100  DATA 23, 45, 18, 67, 45, 23, 56, 98, 34
1200  DATA 86, 93, 100, 45, 76, 87
1300  END
```

FIGURE 5.6 A program to add the 15 numbers in the DATA list.

```
700   LET AVE = SUM/15
800   PRINT "THE AVERAGE IS "; AVE

700   PRINT "THE AVERAGE IS "; SUM/15
```

FIGURE 5.7 The program of Fig. 5.6 may be modified to print the average of the 15 numbers in either of these two ways.

LOOPS

Example: Retirement Fund Table. This example shows a method of printing a table that shows the value of a retirement fund. Here we incorporate the calculation of the Compound Amount Factor first seen in Exercise 3.9. Recall that the calculation requires two numbers: the interest rate I and the number of years Y.

The amount in the retirement fund is computed using the formula

```
retirement_fund = monthly_saving * C.A.F.
```

A FOR loop is used to calculate and print the value of the retirement fund after 10, 20, 30, and 40 years.

Here is an outline of the program:

    Set the value of the variables I and M.SAV
        I = annual interest rate
        M.SAV = amount saved each month

    PRINT a header

    FOR N = 10 TO 40 STEP 10

        compute the compound amount factor (C.A.F.)

        PRINT: The number of years (N)

            the value of the retirement fund

    NEXT N

In the program of Fig. 5.8 an interest rate of 10 percent and a monthly savings of $10 is used to calculate the values shown in Fig. 2.25. When correctly finished, this program produces a table that is similar to the one displayed in Fig. 2.25. However, there is one important difference between the two programs. The earlier program simply prints a list of numbers, whereas this program computes them. This type of program is more useful because it can be modified to show a retirement table for other values of I, Y, and M.SAV (see Exercise 5.6).

Review: FOR Loops

The FOR loop has the form

    <line #>   FOR N = 1 TO 20 [STEP 1]
    <line #>

```
<line #>
<line #>       <statements to
                be repeated>
<line #>
<line #>  NEXT N
```

- Any number of program statements may be repeated under the control of the loop variable.
- The optional STEP clause can specify a positive or negative value of the change.
- The control variable (N) begins with the starting value specified.
- The statements in the loop are repeated and then the loop variable is tested to see if the STEP change can be added without exceeding the ending value; if so, the STEP change is added and the loop is repeated.
- The statements in the loop may use the control variable (N) but should not alter its value.

```
110 ! *******************************************
120 ! PROGRAM: I R A
130 ! *******************************************
140         ! this program prints a retirement table
150         !
160 LET M.SAV = 10
170 LET I = 10
180 PRINT 'IF YOU SAVE'; M.SAV ; 'DOLLARS A MONTH AT '
190 PRINT I; 'PERCENT INTEREST, YOU WILL HAVE:'
200 PRINT
210 PRINT 'NUMBER OF YEARS' , 'TOTAL AMOUNT SAVED'
220 PRINT '---------------' , '------------------'
230 FOR N = 10 TO 40 STEP 10
240   ! --- calculate the compound amount factor ---
250   LET C.A.F. = 0 ! <-- replace the 0 with the
260         !            correct formula ---
270   PRINT N,, 10*C.A.F.
280 NEXT N
290         !
300 END
```

FIGURE 5.8

5.3 Nested FOR Loops

The structure of a FOR loop is depicted diagrammatically in Fig. 5.9. If the statement group contained within a FOR loop includes another complete FOR loop, then these loops are said to be *nested* (see Fig. 5.10).

An example of a nested loop is shown in Fig. 5.11. The outside loop variable N controls execution of statements 110 through 140. This group of statements includes another FOR loop in lines 110 through 130. (The statements in each loop have been indented to help clarify the structure of the overall program construct.) The output of the program is shown at the bottom of Fig. 5.11. Each time the PRINT statement in line 120 is carried out, the value of N * M is calculated and printed, and because of the comma, the computer tabs over to the next tab zone. After three numbers have been printed by the inside loop, the PRINT statement in line 140 finishes the line and moves to the next one. The inside loop must go through a complete cycle (M = 2, 3, and 4) for each value of the outside loop variable N.

A nested loop like the one shown in Fig. 5.11 may be analyzed in detail using the diagram shown in Table 5.1. Each program step is represented by a number across the top of the table. Program steps go from left to right, and the program begins in the upper left corner. When step 100 is carried out, N is given a value of 1. Next, M is given a value of 2 in step 110. In step 120, the value of N * M is computed and printed. When step 130 (NEXT M) is carried

FIGURE 5.9 The structure of a FOR loop. The heavy line indicates the group of statements that are repeated under the control of the loop variable N.

FIGURE 5.10 A typical nested FOR loop structure. The inside loop, which has the control variable M, is contained within the outside loop, which has the control variable N.

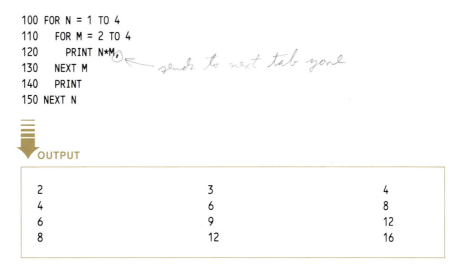

FIGURE 5.11 An example of a nested FOR loop construct.

out, the program loops back to line 110, where M is given a value of 3. Each NEXT statement causes either a loop back to the corresponding FOR statement or a continuation to the next program statement. The process continues as shown in the diagram.

Other types of nested loop structures are possible. Each inside loop must lie entirely within the body of the outside loop. Up to twelve layers of nesting are permitted on the VAX computer, but it is very difficult and confusing to use more than two layers. A few possibilities are depicted in Fig. 5.12.

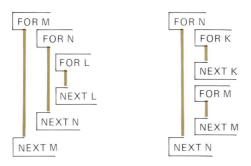

FIGURE 5.12 Other ways in which loops may be nested.

TABLE 5.1. Systematic analysis of a nested loop structure.

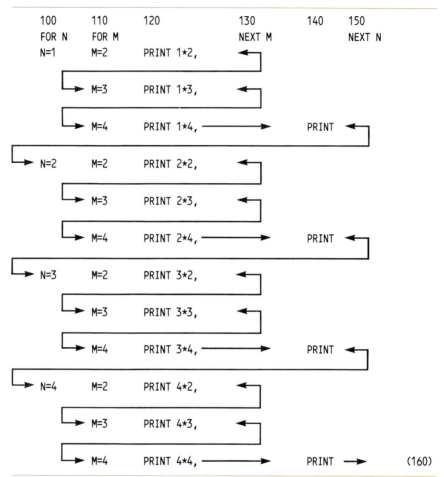

5.4 The Use of the FOR Loop

Here are a number of examples that illustrate the use of the FOR loop.

Bar Graphs. A graph is a way to show a picture of data. In the example of Section 2.9, we used the TAB function to depict the age of the user by printing an asterisk at the proper position along a scale from 0 to 60. An alternate

5.4 THE USE OF THE FOR LOOP

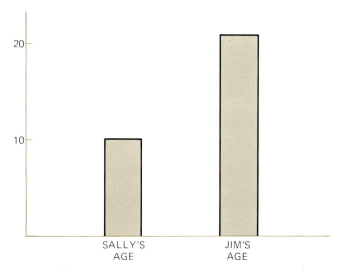

FIGURE 5.13 A bar graph showing ages of 10 and 21.

method of displaying an age is to print a line of asterisks, using one asterisk for each year of age. Using this method, an age of 10 would be depicted as

****

and an age of 21 would be shown as

****

This type of graphical representation is analogous to a bar graph, which is shown in Fig. 5.13. A horizontal "bar" of asterisks representing an age can be printed using the program statements of Fig. 5.14. This program uses a

```
100 INPUT 'WHAT IS YOUR AGE'; AGE
110 FOR N = 1 TO AGE
120    PRINT "*" ;
130 NEXT N
140 PRINT
150 END
```

FIGURE 5.14 This program prints a "bar" of asterisks representing an age.

loop that repeats the first `PRINT` statement `AGE` times. The semicolon at the end of line 120 is important because it causes all of the asterisks to be displayed one after the other on the same line. Statement 140 is also important because it completes the display line.

The program of Fig. 5.15 uses a bar graph representation of the retirement amounts computed in the program of Section 5.2. Because the retirement amounts are large, each symbol printed in the bar graph represents a thousand dollars of savings.

The program uses nested loops to produce the graph. The inside loop is the program segment that goes from line 310 to line 340. These lines are much like the example of Fig. 5.14, which prints a row of asterisks, except that a row of `THOU` dollar signs is printed. Because of the semicolon at the end of line 300, the row of dollar signs is printed starting from column 5.

Lines 260 through 340 print a single line of output consisting of a number (5, 10, 15, and so on) followed by a row of dollar signs. These program lines are repeated eight times to produce the graph.

When this program has been completed to include the proper calculation of the compound amount factor `C.A.F.`, it produces the output shown at the bottom of Fig. 5.15.

FIGURE 5.15

```
110 ! ******************************************
120 ! PROGRAM: I R A G R A P H
130 ! ******************************************
140         ! this program prints a retirement graph
150         !
160 LET M.SAV = 10
170 LET I = 10
180 PRINT "THIS SHOWS HOW A MONTHLY SAVINGS OF "; M.SAV
190 PRINT "DOLLARS AT"; I ; "PERCENT INTEREST"
200 PRINT "WILL GROW WITH THE YEARS. EACH DOLLAR SIGN"
210 PRINT "REPRESENTS A THOUSAND DOLLARS OF SAVINGS"
220 PRINT
230 PRINT "YEAR              AMOUNT SAVED"
240 PRINT "-------           --------------"
```

5.4 THE USE OF THE FOR LOOP

```
250 FOR N = 5 TO 40 STEP 5
260    ! --- calculate the compound amount factor ---
270    LET C.A.F. = 0 ! <-- replace the 0 with the
280           !          correct formula ---
290    LET THOU = INT( 10*C.A.F./1000 )
300    PRINT N; TAB(4);
310    FOR K = 1 TO THOU
320      PRINT "$";
330    NEXT K
340    PRINT
350 NEXT N
360           !
400 END
```

OUTPUT

```
THIS SHOWS HOW A MONTHLY SAVINGS OF 10
DOLLARS AT 10 PERCENT INTEREST
WILL GROW WITH THE YEARS. EACH DOLLAR SIGN
REPRESENTS A THOUSAND DOLLARS OF SAVINGS

YEAR       AMOUNT SAVED
------     ------------
5
10  $$
15  $$$$
20  $$$$$$$
25  $$$$$$$$$$$$$
30  $$$$$$$$$$$$$$$$$$$$$$
35  $$$$$$$$$$$$$$$$$$$$$$$$$$$$$$$$$$$$$
40  $$$$$$$$$$$$$$$$$$$$$$$$$$$$$$$$$$$$$$$$$$$$$$$$$$$$$$$$$$$
```

Geometric Patterns. Most interesting geometric patterns require the use of nested FOR loops. The example of Fig. 5.16 shows a program that displays a triangular pattern of asterisks.

The FOR/NEXT loop contained in lines 100 to 150 is used to repeat lines 110 to 140 ten times. These lines are similar to the ones in Fig. 5.15, used to print the bar graph for the previous example. Each time lines 110 to 140 are repeated, a line of N asterisks is printed. The output of this program is shown at the bottom of Fig. 5.16.

```
100 FOR N = 1 TO 10
110     FOR M = 1 TO N
120         PRINT "*";  continues printing on same line
130     NEXT M
140     PRINT
150 NEXT N
```

OUTPUT

```
*
**
***
****
*****
******
*******
********
*********
**********
```

FIGURE 5.16

Time Delays and SLEEP. One sometimes encounters a loop that seems to do nothing, such as

```
100 FOR N = 1 TO 1000
110 NEXT N
```

or

```
100 FOR N = 1 TO 1000 \ NEXT N
```

Loops such as these simply have the computer count from 1 to 1000 in order to introduce a time delay into a program. This does not work well on the VAX computer because it counts much faster than the average microcomputer. Furthermore, this type of loop would produce a time delay that is of unpredictable duration. Instead of an empty loop, use the SLEEP statement to introduce a delay of a specified number of seconds. The SLEEP statement has the form

```
<line #>  SLEEP <secs>
```

5.5 WHILE AND UNTIL LOOPS

```
200 FOR N = 10 TO 1 STEP -1
210    PRINT N
215    SLEEP 1
220 NEXT N
230 PRINT 'BLASTOFF'
```

FIGURE 5.17 A modification of the countdown example.

Figure 5.17 shows a modification of the countdown example of Fig. 5.5. The use of SLEEP 1 produces a pause of one second between each count.

5.5 WHILE and UNTIL loops

Other types of program loops may be constructed using the `WHILE` and `UNTIL` statements. The WHILE loop begins with the `WHILE` statement and ends with the `NEXT` statement (see Fig. 5.18). When the computer executes a `WHILE` loop, it first checks the condition in the `WHILE` statement to see if it is true. If the condition is true, the entire statement group is executed. After all of the statements have been carried out, the condition is again checked. If the condition is again found to be true, the entire statement group is executed once more. The process is repeated until the condition is no longer true when checked (see Fig. 5.19). Naturally, there must be something going on inside the loop that will eventually change the condition so that it becomes false, or else the `WHILE` loop will never terminate.

The UNTIL loop construct is shown in Fig. 5.20. The UNTIL loop is similar to the WHILE loop, but in this case the condition is checked and the entire statement group is executed each time the condition is found to be false (see Fig. 5.21).

The `WHILE` and `UNTIL` loops are more or less interchangeable. For example, `WHILE X > 0` is the same as `UNTIL X <= 0`. In some cases one may be easier to use or clearer than the other.

```
WHILE  <condition>
           <statement
            group>
NEXT
```

FIGURE 5.18 The general format for the WHILE loop.

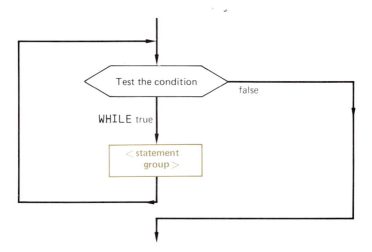

FIGURE 5.19

UNTIL <condition>
    <statement
    group>
NEXT

FIGURE 5.20 The general format for the UNTIL loop.

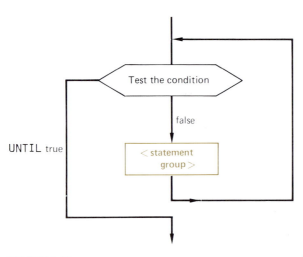

FIGURE 5.21

5.5 WHILE AND UNTIL LOOPS

```
100  LET C = 0 \ LET SUM = 0
200  READ X
300  WHILE X <> -1
400    LET SUM = SUM + X
500    LET C = C + 1
600    READ X
700  NEXT
800  PRINT "THE SUM OF THE NUMBERS IS "; SUM;
900  PRINT " AND THE AVERAGE IS "; SUM/C
1000
1100 DATA 23, 45, 18, 67, 45, 23, 56, 98, 34
1200 DATA 86, 93, 100, 45, 76, 87, -1
1300 END
```

FIGURE 5.22

Figure 5.22 shows an example of a program that uses a WHILE loop to read a data list and find the sum and average of the numbers. A value of −1 indicates the end of the data list. This number is not meant to be part of the data, but simply serves to terminate the WHILE loop. This method allows us to write a program that will work correctly with a longer or shorter data list.

The order of the statements is important to ensure that −1 is not counted in the average (see Fig. 5.23).

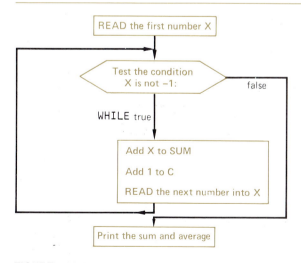

FIGURE 5.23 The order of the statements in the example program assures that −1 is not counted in the sum.

Line 300 of Fig. 5.22 could be replaced by the equivalent UNTIL statement:

    300 UNTIL X = -1

and this would not change the nature of the program.

5.6 Exercises

5.1 Find at least three mistakes in the following program, which tries to add the five numbers in the DATA list.

```
100 FOR N = 1 TO 5
110    LET SUM = 0
120    READ N
130    LET SUM = SUM + N
140 NEXT
150 PRINT SUM
160 DATA 2, 4, 7, 10, 3
```

Revise the program and test it to ensure that it runs correctly.

5.2 a) Write a program to find the sum of the numbers from 1 to 1000 (that is, 1 + 2 + 3 + 4 + 5, and so on, up to 1000).

b) Write a program to find the sum of the odd numbers from 1 to 1000 (that is, 1 + 3 + 5 + 7, and so on, up to 999).

5.3 Write a program to graph the values of the SIN function. Use a FOR loop starting with

    FOR N = 0 TO 7 STEP 0.2

to plot values of the function for every 0.2 radian from 0 to 7 (SIN(0), SIN(0.2), SIN(0.4), and so on, up to SIN(7)).

(*HINT:* The value of SIN(N) lies between −1 and 1, and so 25*SIN lies between −25 and 25. Therefore, the change of scale (25*SIN+45) can be used with the TAB function to plot asterisks in columns 20 through 70 representing the values of the SIN function.)

5.4 Use Table 5.1 to analyze the following program:

```
100 FOR N = 1 TO 4
110    FOR M = 2 TO 4
120       PRINT N*M,
130    NEXT M
140    PRINT
150 NEXT N
```

Also analyze the output with line 120 changed to

```
120 PRINT N + M;
```

What happens if line 140 is removed? Test your analysis by running the programs.

5.5 The following program violates the rule that the control variable of a FOR loop should not be altered by statements within the loop.

```
100 FOR K = 1 TO 15
110   READ K
120   LET SUM=SUM+K
130 NEXT K
140 PRINT SUM
150 DATA 5, 7, 3, 9, 1, 2, 8, 4, 2, 3, 4, 2, 7, 16, 5
160 END
```

Does the program run? If so, how many numbers does it sum? (You may wish to insert statements 105 PRINT K; and 115 PRINT K.) What happens if the 16 in the DATA list is changed to 6? What happens if the second number in the data list is changed from 7 to 17?

Rewrite the program so that it correctly sums all 15 numbers.

5.6 Enter and run the IRA program of Fig. 5.8 using your solution of Exercise 3.9. The output of the program should agree with the retirement table printed by the program of Section 2.9.

Next, modify the program so that the user is asked to supply the interest rate I and the amount of monthly savings M.SAV. Note that line 240 will require modification.

5.7 Run the IRAGRAPH program of Fig. 5.15. The output should be consistent with the output shown in the figure.

Modify the program so that the user is asked to supply the interest rate I and the monthly savings M.SAV. What special problems arise with this version of the program?

5.8 Write a program that uses nested loops to produce a triangular pattern:

5.9 Explain why the PRINT statement should be inside the FOR loop of Fig. 5.8 but not inside the FOR loop of Fig. 5.6.

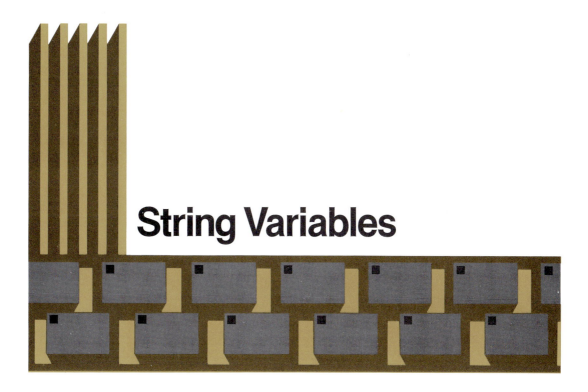

String Variables

So far, we have been dealing with variables like X or AGE, which represent numbers. This chapter introduces a different kind of variable, called a string variable, that can be used to store and manipulate symbols or characters. A string variable is given a name that ends with a dollar sign ($) to emphasize that it stores a different type of information. Figure 6.1 shows some typical storage blocks for the string variables A$ and DATA$.

Like a numeric variable, each string variable has a name and a value. Values can be assigned using LET, INPUT, or READ/DATA statements and displayed using a PRINT statement.

Roughly speaking, string variables are like the variables we have been using all along, except that they store characters instead of numbers. Of course, there are many differences between the ways that the two types of variables can be manipulated. For example, it would be pretty hard to imagine multiplication of strings.

The figures and diagrams used in this chapter are meant to emphasize the unique characteristics

STRING VARIABLES

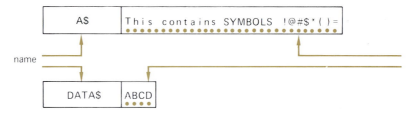

FIGURE 6.1 Typical storage blocks for string variables. The length of the storage block depends on the number of characters stored.

of string variables. For example, Fig. 6.2 emphasizes the fact that string variables are made up of a collection of individual characters.

Because the electronic circuits of the computer can store only numbers, each character of a string is converted to a number using the special code shown in Appendix F. This code is called the ASCII code (American Standard Code for Information Interchange). Each character of the string corresponds to a number that occupies one *byte* of storage in the computer's memory (see Fig. 6.3). (A byte is a unit of storage that uses eight binary integers or bits.) Of course, this is all happening behind the scenes when the computer creates the storage block for a string variable. For example, when the computer stores the character "**A**" it automatically uses the ASCII code 65. When the computer displays the character, it converts the number into the character "**A**" before displaying it.

FIGURE 6.2 Each of the four storage spots for this string is indicated by a colored dot to emphasize that strings store information as individual characters.

FIGURE 6.3 The storage block for the four-character string **MM$** is represented as a collection of four "cells." Each cell occupies one byte of storage in main memory and is represented here as a cube with the character on the front face and the ASCII equivalent on the top face.

6.1 Assigning a Value to a String Variable

When you first use a string variable in a program, the computer sets up a storage block using the variable name that you have selected. Until the string variable is assigned a value, the storage block will contain no characters (Fig. 6.4). A string variable with no value is often called a *null* string or an *empty* string. The empty string's value is like a zero value for a numeric variable. A string variable may be given a value using either a `LET` statement, a `READ` statement together with a `DATA` statement, or an `INPUT` statement. The value of a string variable may be displayed using the `PRINT` statement. The use of the `LET`, `READ`, `DATA`, `INPUT`, and `PRINT` statements or string variables is similar to the use of these statements for numeric variables. In addition, the `LINPUT` statement may be used to obtain the value of a string variable.

The LET and PRINT Statements

Just as the statement

    100 LET X = 23.7

assigns the value `23.7` to the numeric variable `X`, so the statement

    200 LET D$ = "18-Aug-85"

assigns the value `18-Aug-85` to the string variable `D$` (see Fig. 6.5). The quotation marks are necessary in this type of LET statement to mark the beginning and the end of the character string. When the value of `D$` is actually assigned, the quotation marks themselves do not become part of the string.

A string enclosed within quotation marks is called a *quoted string*. Quotation marks used in this way to mark the beginning and the end of a string are called *delimiters*. Single quotes (') or double quotes (") may be used to delimit strings provided that the same type of quote is used at each end of the string.

Generally speaking, the right side of a string assignment statement may consist of a quoted string as shown above or it may contain an expression that involves string variables.

FIGURE 6.4 The storage block for a null or empty string.

FIGURE 6.5 The nine-character storage block produced by statement 200.

STRING VARIABLES

TABLE 6.1 A comparison of the LET and PRINT statements used for string variables and numeric variables.

String Variables	Numeric Variables
100 LET AA$ = "ABCD"	1100 LET X = 23.7
200 LET BB$ = AA$	1200 LET Y = X
300 LET CC$ = AA$ + 'EF'	1300 LET Z = X + 34
400 PRINT AA$, BB$; CC$	1400 PRINT X, Y; Z
500 PRINT AA$ + "36"	1500 PRINT X + 78.9

If a string expression appears in a PRINT statement, the computer evaluates the expression and displays the result. For example, the statement PRINT D$ would display the value of the string variable D$. In the specific case of the string D$ shown in Fig. 6.5, the string 18-Aug-85 would be displayed.

Table 6.1 shows the similarities between string variables and numeric variables in LET and PRINT statements. In line 100, the variable AA$ is given the value ABCD. In line 200, the string variable AA$ is evaluated and the resulting value is assigned to the variable BB$. The right side of line 300 contains a valid string variable expression. The "+" denotes a special type of "addition" that will be described below. The expression AA$+'EF' is evaluated and the resulting value of ABCDEF is assigned to CC$.

The PRINT statement in line 400 will display the values of the variables AA$, BB$, and CC$. As usual, the comma will cause the computer to tab over to the next tab zone before printing the value of BB$, and the semicolon will cause the value of CC$ to be printed immediately after BB$. Line 500 shows the use of a string expression in a PRINT statement. The expression is evaluated, and the resulting string expression, ABCD36, is displayed.

The READ, DATA, and INPUT Statements

The READ statement may be used to assign the value of a string variable from a DATA statement. In this case, it is not necessary to use quotation marks to delimit the strings in the DATA statement unless the data item contains commas, quotation marks, leading spaces or trailing spaces. Similarly, there is no need to use quotation marks when typing a string in response to an INPUT statement.

The program of Fig. 6.6 illustrates the use of the READ, DATA, and INPUT statements for strings. Notice that the DATA statement contains three strings separated by commas. The first string, HELLO, is quoted and includes a space at the end. The second string HOW ARE YOU is not quoted. In this case, the spaces before HOW and after YOU are ignored. Single quotes have been used to delimit the third string because it already contains double

6.1 ASSIGNING A VALUE TO A STRING VARIABLE

```
100 READ  B$, C$, D$
200 DATA  "HELLO " ,  HOW ARE  YOU  , '  "FINE", I HOPE '
300 INPUT  "WHAT IS YOUR NAME"; E$
400 PRINT  B$; E$; C$; D$
500 END
```

OUTPUT

```
WHAT IS YOUR NAME? DAVID JONES
HELLO DAVID JONESHOW ARE   YOU  "FINE", I HOPE
```

FIGURE 6.6

quotes. The computer interprets the double quotes around FINE and the comma as part of the string.

When this program is run, the computer first sets up a list that contains the three strings given in the **DATA** statement (see Fig. 6.7).

The quoted strings are reproduced exactly as quoted. Leading and trailing spaces are ignored in the unquoted string. Next, the **READ** statement in line 100 sets the values of **B$**, **C$**, and **D$**, the prompted message is displayed, and the computer waits for input.

If we assume that the name DAVID JONES is typed at the terminal, then this string is used as the value of the variable **E$**. The resulting storage blocks for the variables **B$**, **C$**, **D$**, and **E$** are represented in Fig. 6.8. Notice that the computer prints the *value* of each of the string variables **B$**, **C$**, **D$**, and **E$**, just as it would have printed the value of a numeric variable. Because of the semicolons in statement 400 of Fig. 6.6, the strings are printed one after the other with no spaces between them.

Extra spaces or punctuation can be added by using quoted strings. For example, we can replace statement 400 of Fig. 6.6 with

```
400 PRINT B$;   E$;   ". ";   C$;   "? ";  D$
```

FIGURE 6.7 The data list formed by the program of Fig 6.6.

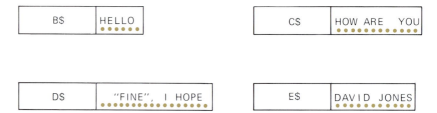

FIGURE 6.8 The storage blocks created by the program of Fig. 6.6.

This PRINT statement contains two quoted strings: The first adds a period and a space after E$, and the second adds a question mark and two spaces after C$. This version of line 400 would produce the following output:

```
HELLO DAVID JONES. HOW ARE YOU?   "FINE", I HOPE
```

The LINPUT Statement

We have seen that the INPUT statement may be used to obtain the value of either a numeric variable or a string variable. In addition, one INPUT statement may be used to obtain the values of several variables. Here are some examples:

```
700 INPUT "TYPE THREE NUMBERS SEPARATED BY COMMAS"; X, Y, Z
800 INPUT "TYPE A NUMBER, A COMMA, AND A NAME"; N, A$
900 INPUT "ENTER YOUR NAME (last,first)"; L.NAM$, F.NAM$
```

When one of these statements is executed, the input you type into the computer must be separated by commas or typed on different lines. Thus commas are interpreted as data separators when typed in response to an INPUT statement. If you wish to include a comma in the value of a string variable, the string must be enclosed within quotes or the LINPUT statement must be used.

The LINPUT statement is an input statement used for string variables. It is used in much the same way as an INPUT statement and has a similar format:

```
260 LINPUT "WHAT IS YOUR NAME"; M$
```

When this statement is executed, the computer prints WHAT IS YOUR NAME? and waits for input from the terminal. The user then types a line of text and presses the return key. Unlike the INPUT statement, the LINPUT statement accepts all of the text as the value of the string variable M$. This includes quotation marks, commas, leading spaces, and trailing spaces. Table 6.2 illustrates the difference between the INPUT and LINPUT statements when assigning the value of a string variable.

6.1 ASSIGNING A VALUE TO A STRING VARIABLE

In contrast, if you use an `INPUT` statement to get the value of the string variable `N$`:

`270 INPUT "WHAT IS YOUR NAME"; N$`

then the computer will ignore leading spaces and trailing spaces and will stop reading input when a comma is encountered unless the comma is inside a quoted string. If quotes are used in your response, they will be interpreted as delimiters, and the enclosed string will be assigned as the value of `N$` (see Table 6.2).

Because of the special nature of the `LINPUT` statement, only a single string variable may be assigned in each statement. That is, LINPUT N$, M$ is not a valid use of the `LINPUT` statement.

Review: Assigning the Value of a String Variable

- In most cases, use a quoted string in a string assignment just as you would use a number in a numeric assignment.
- Quotation marks are optional to delimit strings in a `DATA` statement and strings typed in response to an `INPUT` statement.
- Quotation marks should be used around a string in a `DATA` statement if the string is to include quotes, commas, or leading or trailing spaces. Use single quotes around a string containing double quotes and double quotes around a string containing single quotes.
- The right side of a `LET` statement for a string variable may contain a quoted string, string variables, string functions, or a string expression that uses the " + " operation. The expression is evaluated, and the resulting string value is assigned to the string variable at the left of the equals sign (more about this in Chapter 10).
- Use the `LINPUT` statement if the input string may contain quotation marks or commas.

TABLE 6.2 Difference between the INPUT and LINPUT statements.

String Typed at Terminal	Value Assigned to N$ (INPUT)	Value Assigned To M$ (LINPUT)
JOHN DOE	JOHN DOE	JOHN DOE
"JOHN DOE"	JOHN DOE	"JOHN DOE"
BOSTON, MASS.	BOSTON	BOSTON, MASS.
"BOSTON, MASS."	BOSTON, MASS.	"BOSTON, MASS."
"FIRST","SECOND"	FIRST	"FIRST","SECOND"

STRING VARIABLES

6.2 String Comparisons

The relational operators <, >, and = may be used with string variables. For example, the statement

```
470 IF A$ < B$ THEN PRINT A$, B$
```

uses a string comparison as the condition in an IF statement. In this case "<" means "comes before" with respect to the values assigned in the ASCII code (see Appendix F). The ASCII ordering is the same as alphabetical ordering if the strings are all uppercase letters or all lowercase letters. Therefore the strings A$ and B$ will be printed only if A$ comes before B$ in ASCII "alphabetical" order.

The following string comparison is used in a conditional GOTO statement:

```
600 IF ANS$="YES" THEN GOTO 200
```

Here, the condition is true only if the value of the string variable ANS$ is identical to the three character string YES. Because uppercase letters are different from lowercase letters for this comparison, the condition is false if the value of ANS$ is Yes or yes.

All of the relational operators discussed in Chapter 4 may be applied to string variables. Table 6.3 summarizes the most useful relational operators and their interpretation when used with strings.

Example: Obtaining a Word at Random from a List. Assume that we would like to be able to pick out a word at random from a DATA list that contains 50 words. Remember that the DATA list is read through one word at a time, from beginning to end. Therefore, each time a READ GW$ statement is carried out, the next word in the DATA list is read into the storage block GW$. In Fig. 6.9, the READ statement appears in a loop that is repeated M times. Therefore,

TABLE 6.3 Some relational operators and their meaning when used with string variables.

String Operator	Meaning
A$ = B$	Character for character, the strings are the same (except possibly for spaces at the end).
A$ < B$	Starting from the left, the strings are compared, character for character, until a mismatch is found. Then A$ < B$ is true if the first mismatched character in A$ is one that "comes before" the corresponding character in B$ (in ASCII alphabetical order).
A$ > B$	Starting from the left, the strings are compared, character for character, until a mismatch is found. In this case A$ > B$ means that the first mismatched character in A$ is one that "comes after" the first mismatched character in B$ (in ASCII order).

```
100 LET M = INT(50*RND+1)
200 FOR I = 1 TO M
210    READ GW$
220 NEXT I
      .
      .
      .
820 DATA ... (LIST OF 50 WORDS)
```
FIGURE 6.9

at the completion of M read operations, word number M is stored as the value of GW$. This results in the selection of an unpredictable word, because, as we see from statement 100, M has been randomly generated. This can be the basis of a "guess-the-word" game (Exercise 6.2).

6.3 Exercises

6.1 Write a program that asks the user to enter two words. Your program should compare the strings and print a message that gives the strings in (ASCII) alphabetical order. Check your program by typing a few names. What happens when you type AAZ and AAa? What happens with AA1 and AAa? 356 and 2597? Explain the results in terms of the ASCII code of Appendix F.

6.2 Write a "guess-the-word" game. Your program should pick a word at random using the method described in Fig. 6.9. The user should be asked to guess the word. With each guess the program should indicate whether the guess is before or after the correct word (in ASCII order). The program should keep track of the total number of guesses required to get the correct word. For simplicity, you might wish to use only uppercase letters.

6.3 Write a program that asks the user to type in a word and then displays the word diagonally across the screen:

```
xxxx
 xxxx
  xxxx
   xxxx
    xxxx
```

6.4 Write a program that "talks" to the user. Your program should ask at least one Yes/No question and should make an appropriate response.

Building Programs

We have seen several examples of the process of planning and writing a program. This chapter reviews this process and outlines a step-by-step procedure designed to help you produce programs that are well organized and easy to understand and modify.

7.1 Planning the Program: The First Outline

The procedure for planning a program may be summarized in the following steps:

I. *Define the problem.* Make sure that you understand the problem completely before you do anything else. What should the program do? What data is required and how is it stored? How is the output to be presented?

II. *Think about the problem.* What calculations must be done? What formulas are needed? What variables are needed to carry out the calculations?

It is often helpful to think about similar problems that might be easier to solve. This will frequently provide insights that will help solve the problem at hand.

Generally speaking, the more you think about the problem, the less time you'll need to spend revising your program: It is much easier to rethink your approach than it is to rewrite your program.

III. *Write a preliminary outline.* Next, outline a step-by-step procedure for solving the problem. This step-by-step procedure is called an *algorithm*. Your outline might be rather sketchy, but it should include all of the important steps that you must go through in order to solve the problem.

You may wish to draw a block diagram showing the steps of the algorithm. In any case, the outline should include a description of each step in plain language.

7.2 Refine the Algorithm

The first outline should be expanded and refined. You may wish to do this in two or more stages. Each stage should bring you closer to the point where you can write a successful program. As the algorithm is refined, it should be rechecked to ensure that the logic is correct and that it actually does solve the problem. Here are some specific steps:

IV. *List the variables.* Go through the first outline and decide what variables are required. Some variables might get the initial data (input variables); others might store the results of computations carried out in the program (program variables). Give each variable a name, and write out a list that indicates what each variable represents.

V. *Refine the outline of the program.* Write a more detailed outline of the program. Once again, each step should be described in plain language, but this time the outline should be more specific. Where appropriate, refer to the variables by name and write out the formulas using computer notation. If possible, use BASIC key words like INPUT or PRINT in your outline.

When you finish your outline, you should have a clear understanding of how to translate most of the steps of your algorithm into programming language.

Of course, there may be steps that you are not so sure about and that will require more thought before you are able to see how to program them. Each of these difficult steps becomes a separate problem that can be attacked in a way similar to the way you tackled the problem as a whole.

V(a). *Refine hazy program blocks.* You have identified the parts of the algorithm that are presenting problems. Now perform steps I, II, and III for these sections of the algorithm.

- *Redefine.* Make sure you understand what this program block is supposed to do.
- *Rethink.* Think about what is going on in the program block and how it relates to the program as a whole.
- *Refine your algorithm.* See if you can break the program block into several logical units that are easier to translate into programming language.
- *Refine your tools.* What types of program statements relate to the problem at hand? Are there ways that these statements can be used to achieve the desired result? There may be program statements that you think will work but you are not sure of. Try them out. That is, write a small program and run it to see if the desired end is achieved.

The refinement process is one of looking back at the previous outline of the algorithm to try to break it down into more manageable pieces, while looking ahead at the available programming tools to try to find a match between the task and the tool. This may involve changing the algorithm so that it better utilizes the available programming tools or finding a new programming tool that is better suited to the problem at hand.

Finally, if all else fails, it may be necessary to go back and revise the entire algorithm. It is important to remember that this is part of the programming process and that it is much easier to revise your approach at this point than it would be after you have spent fruitless hours at the terminal.

VI. *Review.* Now that you have a reasonably detailed outline of your program, go over it to ensure that it does what it should. Consider some typical values for the variables and inputs and trace through each step to ensure that the logic is correct.

Here are some general suggestions for planning your program:

- *Review the variable list.* Make sure that the variable list is complete and that it gives an accurate description of the purpose of each variable.
- *Arrange topics logically.* Arrange the steps of your outline so that they show the logical flow of your algorithm.
- *Avoid GOTO.* Avoid the use of the unconditional GOTO statement if possible.

7.3 Writing the Program

You may wish to write the program in two or more stages. If so, begin by writing a test program. This version of the program will enable you to try out all of the essential features of the algorithm. Build the program gradually, starting with the parts you are not sure about. Write a section and test it before adding more. This procedure helps to isolate problems and makes them easier to find and correct.

You may also wish to write out a preliminary version of the program on a piece of paper. This can help you organize your thoughts and makes more effective use of the time at the terminal.

In any case, you should not start to enter the program at the computer until you have a fairly good outline that contains all of the important steps of the solution.

VII. *Write a test version of your program.* Here are some suggestions:

- *Use the variable list.* Have the list of variables handy as you enter the program into the computer. If you need to use an additional variable, add that variable to the list. Keep in mind that the inconsistent use of variables is one of the most frequent errors in BASIC. In particular, make sure the variable is spelled the same way each time you use it, and make sure that you do not use the same variable for two different purposes at once.

- *Align program statements.* Use the ⟨tab⟩ key to line up the left side of the statement text. That is, type the line number and then press the tab key before typing the rest of the statement. Use the SEQUENCE command if you wish to have the computer do this for you.

- *Indent loops.* Indent the statement group in a FOR, WHILE, or UNTIL loop by two spaces. That is, type the line number, then press the tab key, and then add two spaces before typing the rest of the statement. Indent nested loops an additional two spaces for each layer of nesting.

- *Use the multiline form of the IF-THEN-ELSE statement.* The IF-THEN and IF-THEN-ELSE statements should normally be written on several lines of text as shown in Chapter 4.

- *Separate major program sections.* Insert a blank comment line between the major logical sections of the program. Later, descriptive comments may be inserted at these locations.

- *Check as you go.* Make sure that each program statement has the proper format. Check the program one section at a time by running it and correcting errors before adding the next section.

- *Initialize variables.* Even though a variable is automatically given an initial value, this happens only once. If you forget and use the same variable again, it may not have the value you think it has. Thus it is good programming practice to assign starting values to variables.

7.4 Getting the Bugs Out

According to Murphy's law, it is almost certain that your program will have something wrong with it. You should always allow some time for correcting errors in the program. Indeed, there may be times when the process of debugging a computer program can take more time than planning and writing it. This is especially true if the preliminary steps have been rushed.

VIII. *Test run your program.*

There are three general types of common errors: grammatical, run-time, and logical. In general, grammatical errors and run-time errors will generate error messages, whereas logical errors cause weird results.

Grammatical errors show up when the computer tries to translate the program from BASIC into the machine language of the computer. This translation process is called *compilation*, and this type of grammatical error is often called a "compile-time" error.

Grammatical or compile-time errors, which include spelling and punctuation errors, generally are the easiest to correct. If you have followed the previous "check as you go" suggestion, most grammatical errors will have been corrected as the program is typed in. Nevertheless, first check each program line mentioned in an error message for grammatical errors. This is especially true if you cannot understand the error message. It is often the case that a simple spelling or punctuation mistake can produce a long-winded error message that is misleading or cryptic.

Run-time errors also produce error messages, but these happen when the computer tries to carry out the machine language version of the program and discovers that something is wrong. Some common examples of run-time errors are:

- *Out of data.* This happens when the program attempts to read data that is not there. This can be caused when there are too many **READ** statements or when a **READ** statement is repeated too many times inside a loop.

- *Subscript out of range.* This can happen when the program attempts to use a subscript bigger than 10 in an array that has not been dimensioned (see Chapter 9).

- *Data format error.* This can happen when you type in a letter or character in response to an INPUT statement for a numeric variable. This error will not stop the program. The error message is printed and the computer repeats the INPUT request.

In general, the text of the error message for a run-time error provides information that is helpful in tracking down the mistake. It contains a description of the problem and the line number where it occurs in the program.

Finding Logical Errors

The last type of error, the logical error, is the hardest to find and correct. *Logical errors* do not produce error messages but cause the program to produce erroneous results. This kind of error can result from mistakes such as the incorrect use of a formula, the improper spelling of a variable name, or the use of faulty logic in your algorithm.

Think of finding logical errors as a detective game. The computer gives you clues, and you try to interpret these clues to locate the problem. Sometimes the clues are insufficient, and you have to ask the computer to provide more hints. This means that you may have to make some temporary changes in your program to have the computer display additional information.

Go back to your program and insert `PRINT` statements that display the value of suspected variables. These `PRINT` statements will provide you with more information that may be used to determine where the problem arises. You can interrupt the program at any point by inserting a `STOP` statement. When the program is stopped, the current value of any of the variables can be determined by using the `PRINT` statement in immediate mode. The `CONTINUE` command may be used to resume program execution from the point where it stopped.

Once you have isolated the problem, examine the program for mistakes. Also review your algorithm for faulty reasoning. The extra information gained from your detective work should enable you to focus your efforts in an effective manner. Remember that this is a normal step in the process of developing a program. Avoid frustration by thinking of this as a puzzle to solve and by allowing yourself enough time to work out the solution.

7.5 The Final Draft

Now that you have a program that runs correctly, add some finishing touches. This is an important step in ensuring that your program will be easy to read, that the logic will be easy to understand, and that the final program will be easy to use and modify.

IX. *Write a final draft of your program.* Here are some suggestions:

- *Add a title and description.* Insert comment lines that provide a header displaying the name and a brief description of the program. It may also be helpful to provide a list of variables within the comment text.

- *Print an introduction.* Add `PRINT` statements to print a brief description of the program for the user.

- *Improve the input.* Insert quoted strings in the `INPUT` statements or additional `PRINT` statements to provide detailed instructions for input. In addition, it is often a good idea to have the computer check for numbers that are too big or too small to make sense.

- *Improve the output.* Insert additional `PRINT` statements that describe the program output in greater detail.

- *Introduce each section.* Insert a comment line that describes the task being carried out in each section of the program. The comments should provide a rough outline of your program.

- *Set comments off.* Comments should be set off so that they are apart from the main program text. This makes it easy to tell the difference between statements and comment text. One method is to indent comments by using the tab key twice before typing the exclamation point (or REM) to begin the comment. That is, type the line number, press the tab key twice, then type an exclamation point and begin the comment. The text of the comment can be further set off by using hyphens (---) before and after the text and by writing the text in lower-case letters.

- *Comment wisely.* Make sure that comments help improve the readability of the program. Too many comments will clutter things up.

Example—The Number Game

Here is a step-by-step outline of how the above procedure can be applied to the number game.

PLANNING THE PROGRAM

I. *Statement of the problem.* Write a program to guess a number between 1 and 100. The number to be guessed is generated by the computer in an unpredictable way. The computer will ask for a guess and check to see if the guess is correct. If not, the computer will indicate whether the number is too big or too small. The program should keep track of the total number of guesses made and the number of games played, and compute the average number of guesses per game.

II. *Some thoughts about the problem.* A number between 1 and 100 must be generated in an unpredictable way. The program must keep track of the total number of guesses and the total number of games played, and must compute the ratio of the two to determine the average number of guesses per game.

III. *First outline of the algorithm.* A block outline of the algorithm is shown in Fig. 7.1. This is a simple outline, but it provides a good starting point.

BUILDING PROGRAMS

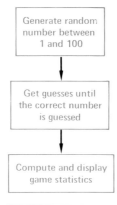

FIGURE 7.1

IV. *List of variables.* A list of variables is shown in Fig. 7.2.

V. *Refine the algorithm.* We will refine the algorithm in two steps. Figure 7.3 shows the second outline. At this point, the algorithm is sufficiently detailed to attempt a preliminary outline of the actual program (see Fig. 7.4).

V(a). *Refine hazy program blocks.* Steps A and G of Fig. 7.4 have not been fully translated into informal programming language. Translating step A might require you to get more information about the functions RND, and INT, and the RANDOMIZE statement. Step G might be programmed using a string comparison. One solution is shown in Fig. 7.5. The final version of the NUMBER program uses a slightly different method to accomplish the same thing.

VI. *Review.* After thinking about steps A and G, we have a pretty good idea of what the program should look like. A careful review of the logic would uncover a need for an additional variable to keep track of the number of guesses in the current game, but we assume that we have not caught this error before going on to the next step.

VII. *Write a test version.* Figure 7.6 shows a typical test version of the program.

NMBR	a random number between 1 and 100
GUESS	the number guessed by the user
GAMES	the number of games played by the user
TRYS	the number of guesses taken

FIGURE 7.2

7.5 THE FINAL DRAFT

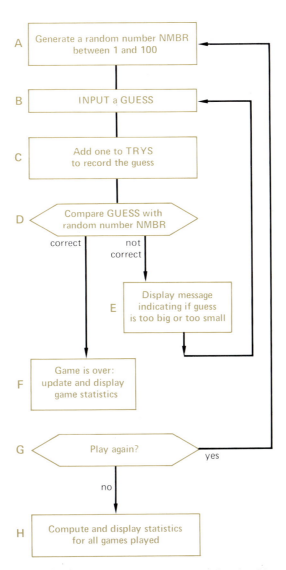

FIGURE 7.3 A more detailed outline of the algorithm.

VIII. *Test run the program.* The program runs as expected for the first game. However, an unexpected thing happens at the end of the second game: The computer displays a value that is much too large for the number of guesses in the second game. This is because the variable `TRYS` is used in the `PRINT` statement on line 2100 to give the number of guesses for the

BUILDING PROGRAMS

```
A    generate a random number NMBR

B    INPUT "WHAT GUESS"; GUESS

C    LET TRYS = TRYS + 1

D    IF GUESS = NMBR THEN GOTO F

E    IF GUESS > NMBR
        THEN PRINT "THAT NUMBER IS TOO BIG"
        ELSE PRINT "THAT NUMBER IS TOO SMALL"
     GOTO B

F    PRINT "THAT'S RIGHT!";GUESS;"IS THE CORRECT NUMBER"
     PRINT "IT TOOK "; TRYS ; "GUESSES TO GET IT"
     GAMES = GAMES + 1

G    PLAY AGAIN?
        IF YES THEN A
        IF NO THEN H

H    PRINT "YOU PLAYED "; GAMES ; " GAMES "
     PRINT "YOU TOOK AN AVERAGE OF "; TRYS/GAMES ;" GUESSES PER GAME"
```

FIGURE 7.4 A preliminary outline of the program.

---

current game, but TRYS is not reset to zero when a new game begins because it is also used to keep track of the total number of guesses made in all of the games played thus far. This can be corrected by using separate variables for the number of guesses made in the current game (TRYS) and the total number of guesses made in all of the previous games (TOTRY). The revised program is shown in Fig. 7.7.

IX. *Write a final draft.* There are many ways to write up a final version of the program. The NUMBERS program of Fig. 7.8 is but one example and does not necessarily represent the best solution.

```
INPUT "DO YOU WISH TO PLAY AGAIN (Y/N) ";  A$
IF A$ = "Y" THEN GOTO A ELSE GOTO H
```

FIGURE 7.5 An alternative method of programming step G of Fig. 7.4.

7.5 THE FINAL DRAFT

```
1000 RANDOMIZE
1100 LET NMBR = INT(100*RND)+1
1200 INPUT "WHAT IS YOUR GUESS"; GUESS
1300 LET TRYS = TRYS + 1
1400 IF GUESS = NMBR THEN GOTO 2000
1500 IF GUESS > NMBR
        THEN PRINT "THAT NUMBER IS TOO BIG"
        ELSE PRINT "THAT NUMBER IS TOO SMALL"
1600 GOTO 1200
2000 PRINT "THAT'S RIGHT ! "; GUESS ; "IS THE CORRECT NUMBER"
2100 PRINT "IT TOOK "; TRYS ; "GUESSES TO GET IT"
2200 LET GAMES = GAMES + 1
2300 PRINT "TYPE 1 IF YOU WANT TO PLAY AGAIN "
2400 PRINT "TYPE 0 IF YOU WANT TO STOP "
2500 INPUT X
2600 IF X = 1 THEN 1100
2700 PRINT "YOU PLAYED "; GAMES ; " GAMES "
2800 PRINT "YOU TOOK AN AVERAGE OF "; &
        TRYS/GAMES ;" GUESSES PER GAME"
```

FIGURE 7.6 The first version of the test program.

```
1000 RANDOMIZE
1100 LET NMBR = INT(100*RND)+1
1150 LET TRYS = 0
1200 INPUT "WHAT IS YOUR GUESS"; GUESS
1300 LET TRYS = TRYS + 1
1400 IF GUESS = NMBR THEN GOTO 2000
1500 IF GUESS > NMBR
        THEN PRINT "THAT NUMBER IS TOO BIG"
        ELSE PRINT "THAT NUMBER IS TOO SMALL"
1600 GOTO 1200
2000 PRINT "THAT'S RIGHT ! "; GUESS ; "IS THE CORRECT NUMBER"
2100 PRINT "IT TOOK "; TRYS ; "GUESSES TO GET IT"
2200 LET GAMES = GAMES + 1
2250 LET TOTRY = TOTRY + TRYS
2300 PRINT "TYPE 1 IF YOU WANT TO PLAY AGAIN "
2400 PRINT "TYPE 0 IF YOU WANT TO STOP "
2500 INPUT X
2600 IF X = 1 THEN 1100
2700 PRINT "YOU PLAYED "; GAMES ; " GAMES "
2800 PRINT "YOU TOOK AN AVERAGE OF "; &
        TOTRY/GAMES ;" GUESSES PER GAME"
```

FIGURE 7.7 This version of the test program has been revised to remove a logical error.

BUILDING PROGRAMS

FIGURE 7.8 The final draft of the program includes comments and expanded instructions to the user.

```
1000  ! *******************************************************
1100  !    PROGRAM:    N U M B E R
1200  ! *******************************************************
1300          !
1400          !    LIST OF VARIABLES:
1500          !        NMBR  - A number between 1 and 100
1600          !        GUESS - The current guess
1700          !        TRYS  - The number guesses this game
1800          !        GAMES - The number of games played
1900          !        TOTRY - The total number of guesses
2000
2100          !------------- header message --------------
2200  PRINT   "GUESS THE NUMBER GAME - "
2300  PRINT
2400  PRINT   "I WILL THINK OF A NUMBER BETWEEN 1 AND 100"
2500  PRINT   "YOUR GOAL IS TO GUESS THE NUMBER "
2600  PRINT   "I WILL TELL YOU IF YOUR GUESSES ";
2700  PRINT   "ARE TOO HIGH OR TOO LOW."
2800  PRINT
2900          !
3000          !-- generate random number and initialize ----
3100  RANDOMIZE
3200  LET   NMBR = INT(100*RND)+1
3300  LET   TRYS = 0
3400          !
3500          ! -----------------begin input loop --
3600  INPUT   "WHAT IS YOUR GUESS"; GUESS
3700  LET   TRYS = TRYS + 1
3800  IF   GUESS = NMBR THEN 4400
3900  IF   GUESS > NMBR
         THEN   PRINT "THAT NUMBER IS TOO BIG "
         ELSE   PRINT  "THAT NUMBER IS TOO SMALL"
4000  GOTO  3600
4100          ! ---------------- bottom of input loop --
4200          !
4300          !-- when correct number has been guessed -----
4400  PRINT   "THAT'S RIGHT !"; GUESS; "IS THE CORRECT NUMBER"
4500  PRINT   "IT TOOK "; TRYS; " GUESSES TO GET IT"
4600          !
4700          !-------- keep track of statistics ----------
```

```
4800  LET   GAMES = GAMES + 1
4900  LET   TOTRY = TOTRY + TRYS
5000        !
5100        !---------- play again or stop? ----------
5200  PRINT "TYPE  1  IF YOU WANT TO PLAY AGAIN "
5300  PRINT "TYPE  0  IF YOU WANT TO STOP "
5400  INPUT X
5500  IF  X = 1  THEN 3200    ! ------ play again -------
5600  IF  X <> 0  THEN  PRINT "INVALID INPUT " \ GOTO 5200
5700        !
5800        !---------- display statistics ------------
5900  PRINT "O.K. HERE'S HOW YOU DID: "
6000  PRINT
6100  PRINT "YOU PLAYED ";GAMES ;" GAMES"
6200  PRINT "YOU TOOK AN AVERAGE OF "; TOTRY/GAMES ;
6300  PRINT " GUESSES PER GAME."
6400  PRINT "THANKS FOR PLAYING THE NUMBER GAME "
6500  END
```

7.6 Exercises

7.1 The NUMBER program uses `GOTO` statements in lines 3800 and 4000. This is often considered bad programming practice. Alter the program so that

    a) the statement `UNTIL NMBR = GUESS` is used to set up a loop for steps 3600 through 4000, thus eliminating the GOTO at line 4000, and

    b) lines 4400 and 4500 are included in step 3800, thus eliminating the GOTO there.

Have you introduced any logical errors in making these changes? In particular, what happens if you play the game once and then the computer happens to generate the same random number for the next game?

7.2 Apply the methods outlined in this chapter to some of the programs that you have already written. Can you see ways in which these programs can be improved?

7.3 Get together with a classmate and critique each other's programs. Can you understand his or her programs? Is the logic clear? Do comments help? Try running one of the programs. Does the program do a good job of explaining what is going on?

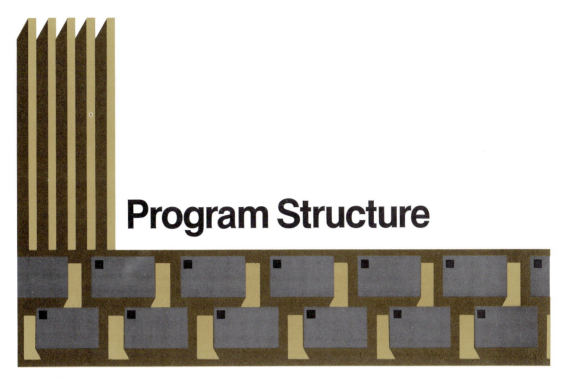

Program Structure

Every program can be broken down into segments that perform a specific task, such as printing a header for the output or finding the largest number in a data list. We have seen some examples of programs that have been developed by writing a block outline. Each block represents a step or group of steps in the program. In large programs, each program block may carry out a complex task that requires a page or more of program steps. Such programs tend to become cluttered with details that make it difficult to see the main flow of ideas.

It is possible to write blocks of program steps in a separate section of the program, out of the way of the main flow of ideas, while, at the same time, preserving the order in which the program steps are executed. This can be done by putting these steps into a separate *subroutine* or *function*.

8.1 Subroutines

A SUBROUTINE is a collection of program steps that usually accomplishes a specific task. Each subroutine

PROGRAM STRUCTURE

```
10000   ! --- subroutine to do a task --
10100
10200       < program steps to
10300       carry out the task>
11000
11300
11400   RETURN
```

FIGURE 8.1 The general arrangement of a subroutine.

has a distinct beginning and end. A subroutine usually begins with a comment line that describes its purpose and ends with a RETURN statement. See Fig. 8.1 for the general form of a subroutine.

A GOSUB 10000 statement anywhere in the program begins execution of the subroutine that begins at line 10000. The RETURN statement at the end of the subroutine ends execution of the steps in the subroutine and causes the program to continue, starting with the next step after the GOSUB statement.

A model of a program containing a subroutine is shown in Fig. 8.2. In this case, the subroutine consists of lines 10000 through 11400 (in color). Program steps 100 through 500 are executed in the usual order, and then line 600 of the main program causes the statements in the subroutine to be executed. When the subroutine is finished, the RETURN statement at the end of the subroutine causes the program to continue at line 700.

The GOTO statement at line 3300 is necessary to ensure that the subroutine is not inadvertently carried out after the main program has finished at line 3200. Omission of this GOTO statement will cause an error message when the program is RUN.

As an example, suppose a program is to contain a long section with instructions for the user. These instructions are important and make the program easier to use, but they take up a lot of room and would tend to distract one from seeing the main program steps. It makes sense to put these instructions into a subroutine.

The use of a subroutine in this way also allows the same instructions to be repeated at several different points in the program. Simply insert a GOSUB statement wherever the instructions are to be repeated. This type of situation is illustrated in Fig. 8.3. In this example, the subroutine may be called from two places in the program in response to input queries. If the user responds with a question mark, the subroutine is called and instructions are displayed. When the subroutine is finished, the statement after the GOSUB causes a loop back to the INPUT statement to allow the user another chance to respond to the question.

This technique could also be used to print different instructions for each input. Simply put each set of instructions into a different subroutine and alter the program outline of Fig. 8.3 so that a "?" response calls the appropriate subroutine.

Review: Using Subroutines

- Use a GOSUB statement to begin execution of a subroutine.
- The first line of a subroutine should be a comment line that gives information about the subroutine.
- The last line of a subroutine must be a RETURN statement.
- Subroutines should be separated from the main part of the program (usually at the end). Use a GOTO statement to bypass the subroutine.

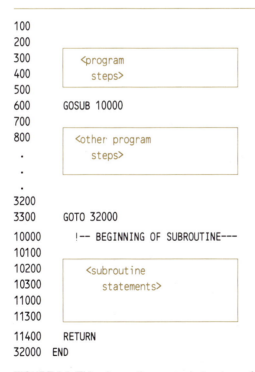

FIGURE 8.2 This shows the general structure of a program that uses a subroutine.

```
100       !*** MAIN PROGRAM LOGIC *****
110       ┌──────────────────────────────────────┐
120       │                                      │
130       │   <usual program                     │
140       │      statements>                     │
150       │                                      │
160       │                                      │
          └──────────────────────────────────────┘
170       PRINT "ENTER THE FOLLOWING INFORMATION"
180       PRINT "ENTER A QUESTION MARK (?) IF YOU NEED HELP"
190       INPUT "TYPE OF SETTING";ST$
200       IF ST$="?"
            THEN
              GOSUB 12000
              GOTO 190
          END IF
210       <other program steps>
             .
             .
             .
250       INPUT "CLARITY"; CL$
260       IF CL$="?"
            THEN
              GOSUB 12000
              GOTO 250
          END IF
270       <other program steps>
             .
             .
             .
300       GOTO 32000
12000     !***** SUBROUTINE TO PRINT INSTRUCTIONS ***
12100     ┌──────────────────────────────────────┐
12200     │   <subroutine                        │
12300     │      statements>                     │
12400     │                                      │
12500     │                                      │
          └──────────────────────────────────────┘
12600     RETURN
32000     END
```

FIGURE 8.3 The same subroutine may be called from different places in the program.

8.2 The ON-GOSUB Statement and Menus

The ON-GOSUB statement is something like a SELECT statement for subroutines. Using it, we can instruct the computer to carry out a particular subroutine that has been selected from a number of different options.

A typical situation is illustrated in Fig. 8.4. When the computer reaches step 200, it tests the value of a control variable—in this case the variable L—and carries out the appropriate subroutine. The ON-GOSUB statement at line 200 has the form:

```
200 ON L GOSUB 500, 800, 1200
```

When line 200 is executed, the value of L determines which subroutine is to be carried out. If L is 1, the subroutine beginning at line 500 is executed; if L

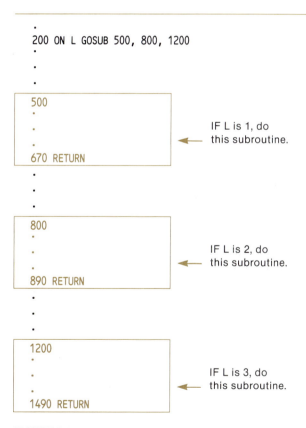

FIGURE 8.4

is 2, the subroutine at line 800 is executed; and if L is 3, the subroutine at line 1200 is executed. When the subroutine is finished, the program continues with the next statement after the ON-GOSUB statement.

A variation of the ON-GOSUB construct allows for the use of a subroutine to handle exceptional cases. The term OTHERWISE is used to indicate the line number of a subroutine or program step that executes whenever the control variable is out of range.

```
200    ON L GOSUB 500, 800, 1200 OTHERWISE 2000
```

As before, a value of 1, 2, or 3 results in the execution of the subroutine at 500, 800, or 1200, respectively. If L is anything other than 1, 2, or 3, the subroutine at line 2000 is called.

The **ON-GOSUB** statement is commonly used in conjunction with a list of options called a *menu* (see Fig. 8.5). The menu, or list of options, is displayed on the terminal screen, and the user is asked to select one by typing in a number.

Here is an outline of the procedure:

> Display the menu.
>
> Get the number that indicates the desired option.
>
> Carry out the appropriate subroutine.

Each option listed in a menu may correspond to a block of steps in a subroutine. For example, a program might contain the six subroutines listed in Table 8.1. The numbers in parentheses correspond to the options listed in the menu.

The outline of Fig. 8.6 shows a possible arrangement of program steps. In this example, the main program loop consists of lines 1800 through 2200. Each time the loop is executed, the menu is printed (**GOSUB 10000**) and an option input is requested. This assigns the value of the control variable L. If L is between 0 and 4, the **ON-GOSUB** statement is executed and the program branches to the appropriate subroutine. The loop repeats until option 4 is selected.

```
CHOOSE AN OPTION USING THE FOLLOWING NUMBERS:
   1 - ENTER NEW DATA
   2 - CHANGE DATA
   3 - DISPLAY CURRENT DATA
   4 - FINISH
```

FIGURE 8.5 A typical menu.

8.2 THE ON-GOSUB STATEMENT AND MENUS

TABLE 8.1 A program might be divided into six subroutines as shown.

Purpose of Subroutine	Begins at Line Number
Print the menu	10000
Obtain new data from the user (1)	11000
Change the data (2)	12000
Display the current data (3)	13000
End the program (4)	14000
Handle exceptional cases	19000

FIGURE 8.6 This program uses a menu and several subroutines.

```
1700    LET L = 0
1800    UNTIL L=4
1900      GOSUB 10000    !-- print menu ---
2000      INPUT "WHAT OPTION"; L
2100      ON L GOSUB 11000, 12000, 13000, 14000 &
              OTHERWISE 19000
2200    NEXT
2300    .
          .
          .
9900    GOTO 32000
10000         !--- subroutine to print menu -----
10100   PRINT " CHOOSE AN OPTION USING THE FOLLOWING NUMBERS:"
10200   PRINT "   1 - ENTER NEW DATA "
10300   PRINT "   2 - CHANGE DATA "
10400   PRINT "   3 - DISPLAY CURRENT DATA "
10500   PRINT "   4 - FINISH "
10600   RETURN

11000         !--- subroutine to enter new data -----
11100
11200     <subroutine
11300       statements>
11970
11980   RETURN
```

(Continued)

FIGURE 8.6 Continued

```
12000          !--- subroutine to change data -----
12100
12200     <subroutine
12300        statements>
12950
12960   RETURN

13000          !--- subroutine to display current data --
13010
13020     <subroutine
12100        statements>
13900
13910   RETURN

14000          !--- subroutine or statements to finish
14100
14200   RETURN

19000          !--- subroutine to handle exceptions ---
19100
19200   RETURN

31000          !
32000   END
```

8.3 User-Defined Functions

If it is necessary to carry out the same type of calculation several times in a program, a special *function* may be defined. The function definition prescribes what operations are to be carried out. For example, the function definition:

```
15000 DEF FNCUBE(X)
15010   FNCUBE = X ** 3
15020 FNEND
```

defines the `FNCUBE( )` function to compute the cube of a number. The first line names the function `FNCUBE` and gives the argument `X`. The second line describes the operation to be carried out with the variable `X`. This prescribes that the value of the function is the cube of the argument. The last line marks

8.3 USER-DEFINED FUNCTIONS

```
DEF FN<name> ( <list of arguments> )
    < statements to
      define the
      function >
FNEND
```

FIGURE 8.7 The format of a multiline function definition.

```
350   LET Z = FNCUBE(2)
400   LET W = FNCUBE(3*Z+2)
500   ! ---------
15000 DEF FNCUBE(X) = X ** 3
32000 END
```

FIGURE 8.8 A single-line function definition and some statements that use the function.

---

the end of the function definition. Functions may be defined anywhere in a program, but it is customary to put them near the end as suggested in the program template of Appendix G.

The general form of a function definition is shown in Figure 8.7. The first line of the definition begins with `DEF` followed by the function name and a list of arguments. A function name is similar to a regular variable name except that it must begin with the letters `FN`. The function name is followed by a list of arguments enclosed within parentheses and separated by commas. The arguments are given in terms of local variables that are used in the function definition only and are not related to other variables in the program.

The next lines of the function definition give the operations that are to be carried out to determine the value of the function. These operations are described in terms of the local variables listed as arguments in the first line of the function definition.

When there is only one line in the function definition, it may be abbreviated as shown in line `15000` of Fig. 8.8.

Once the `FNCUBE` function has been defined in a program, it may be used anywhere to compute the cube of a number. For example, in line 350 of Fig. 8.8, the value 8 is assigned to the variable `Z`. Note that the argument of the `FNCUBE` function can be any valid expression. In particular, in line 400 of Fig. 8.8, the computer evaluates the argument and uses this to determine the value of the FNCUBE function. Because `Z` has the value 8, `W` will be given a value equal to the cube of 26.

Example: Swimming Exercise Value

Assume that we have been given the following formula to calculate the exercise value of swimming a distance of d yards in t minutes:

$$\text{Exercise value} = \left[\left(\frac{d}{6t} + 4\right)\left(\frac{d}{240}\right)\right] - 10.$$

PROGRAM STRUCTURE

```
15000 DEF FNSWIM(D,T)
15010   R = D/T
15020   FNSWIM = (R/6+4)*D/240-10
15030 FNEND

15000 DEF FNSWIM(D,T)=(D/T/6+4)*D/240-10
```

FIGURE 8.9 Two methods of defining a function to calculate the exercise value of a swim.

The exercise value depends on both the distance and the time. The formula can be incorporated into a function FNSWIM(D,T) that calculates the exercise value. Figure 8.9 shows two ways to define the function.

8.4 Building a Program with Subroutines

This section illustrates the process of combining several related programs into a larger one. The finished program will allow the user to input a variety of different exercise activities—for example, a swim, a run, and two sessions of racquetball—and will then produce an evaluation of the overall exercise level.

We have already seen separate programs that calculate the exercise value of a run or walk (Fig. 4.12) and the exercise value of a swim (Fig. 8.9). The following program will contain subroutines that are similar to these programs and will also include a subroutine to calculate the exercise value of playing a session of racquetball, basketball, or soccer using the formula shown in Figure 8.10. The program will perform two major tasks:

- Compute the accumulated exercise value for all exercise activities over a period of time.
- Evaluate the exercise activity by comparing it to a standard.

A separate subroutine will be used for each type of exercise activity, and the program will keep track of the total number of exercise units (TOT-EXVAL)

Exercise value = $40t - 3$.

FIGURE 8.10 The formula for computing the exercise value of a racquetball, basketball, or soccer session. The total time in hours of continuous exercise activity is represented by t.

8.4 BUILDING A PROGRAM WITH SUBROUTINES

that have been accumulated. It will also have a subroutine to obtain the time span in days over which the activity took place. If DAYS is the number of days of this time span, then the ratio

$$\text{EXERCISE RATE} = \frac{\text{TOT\_EXVAL}}{\text{DAYS}}$$

represents the average number of exercise units obtained per day. The standard of 100 exercise units per week is the same as an average of 100/7 units per day. Thus the exercise rate may be evaluated as a percent of this standard by computing the ratio

$$\frac{\text{EXERCISE RATE}}{100/7} * 100 = \text{EXERCISE RATE} * 7.$$

Figure 8.11 contains an outline of the program. The numbers at the right indicate the starting point of a subroutine to carry out the task. The list of variables includes:

EXVAL	the exercise value of a given activity
TOT_EXVAL	the cumulative total exercise value
DAYS	the time span in days for the exercise
EX_RATE	the rate of exercise in units/day
EX_PCT	the exercise rate as a percent of the 100/7 norm

Repeat the following steps until option 4 is selected:
- Display a menu that has the following options:
  1 - Compute exercise value of playing racquetball, basketball or soccer. ---> 3000
  2 - Compute the exercise value of a walk or a run. ---> 4000
  3 - Compute the exercise value of a swim. ---> 5000
  4 - Evaluate the total exercise value. ---> Continue with main PROGRAM.
- Add the newly computed exercise value (EXVAL) to the cumulative total (TOT_EXVAL).

When option 4 has been selected:
- Obtain the time span (DAYS) over which the exercise has taken place. ---> 9000
- Compute the exercise rate using
  LET EX_RATE = TOT_EXVAL/DAYS
- See how this compares to the 100/7 benchmark,
  $$\text{EX\_PCT} = \frac{\text{EX\_RATE}}{100/7} * 100 = \text{EX\_RATE} * 7$$

FIGURE 8.11 An outline of the example program.

PROGRAM STRUCTURE

Figure 8.12 contains a "skeleton" program that does not yet have finished subroutines for options 2 and 3.

FIGURE 8.12 At this stage only options 1 and 4 are operational.

```
200   UNTIL SELECTION = 4
210     LET EXVAL = 0
220         !--print the menu ------
230     PRINT 'SELECT ONE OF THE FOLLOWING OPTIONS'
240     PRINT '1 - Compute the exercise value of playing'
250     PRINT '    racquetball, basketball, or soccer.'
260     PRINT '2 - Compute the exercise value of a walk'
270     PRINT '    or a run.'
280     PRINT '3 - Compute the exercise value of a swim.'
290     PRINT '4 - Evaluate the total exercise value.'
300         !--select and execute an option--
310     INPUT 'WHAT OPTION'; SELECTION
320     ON SELECTION GOSUB 3000,4000,5000,9000 &
              OTHERWISE 19000
330     LET TOT-EXVAL = TOT-EXVAL + EXVAL
340   NEXT
700         !--- compute and print the results--
710         !--rate in exercise units per day--
720   LET EX-RATE = TOT-EXVAL/DAYS
730         !--compare to 100/7 benchmark--
740   LET EX-PCT = EX-RATE*7
750   PRINT 'YOUR EXERCISE LEVEL IS'; EX-PCT;
760   PRINT 'PERCENT OF THE RECOMMENDED LEVEL'
2990  GOTO 32000
3000        !--- subroutine for racquetball, etc.--
3010  PRINT 'THIS CALCULATES THE EXERCISE VALUE OF'
3020  PRINT 'A CONTINUOUS SESSION OF RACQUETBALL,'
3030  PRINT 'BASKETBALL OR SOCCER'
3040  PRINT 'YOU SHOULD COUNT ONLY TIMES OF ';
3050  PRINT 'CONTINUOUS ACTIVITY'
3060  INPUT 'TOTAL TIME (HOURS)'; TOT.TIME
3070  LET EXVAL = 40*TOT.TIME - 3
3080  IF EXVAL<0 THEN EXVAL=0
3090  PRINT 'THIS IS WORTH';EXVAL; 'UNITS'
3100  RETURN
4000        ! --- subroutine for the run value--
4010  PRINT 'RUN IS TO BE ADDED'
4020  RETURN
```

8.4 BUILDING A PROGRAM WITH SUBROUTINES

```
5000          ! ---subroutine for swim ------
5010   PRINT 'SORRY THIS SELECTION IS NOT YET AVAILABLE'
5020   RETURN
9000          !--- subroutine to compute totals--
9110   INPUT 'HOW MANY DAYS'; DAYS
9120   RETURN
19000         !--- subroutine to handle exceptions--
19010  PRINT 'ERRONEOUS SELECTION'
19020  RETURN
32000  END
```

Using The APPEND Command to Combine Programs

The APPEND command may be used in BASIC mode to transfer a copy of a program from disk memory into main memory. The command is similar to the OLD command, except that the OLD command erases the previous contents of main memory, whereas the APPEND command does not (see Fig. 8.13). Therefore you can use the APPEND command to take a program from disk memory and add it to an existing program in main memory. The line numbers in each program will determine the arrangement of the resulting program steps. You should avoid situations with duplicate or overlapping line numbers.

In this section, we will use the APPEND command to combine a slightly modified version of the RUNVAL program of Fig. 4.12 with the skeleton EXVAL program of Fig. 8.12.

The RUNVAL program will be included in the EXVAL program as a subroutine beginning at line 4000 (see Fig. 8.14). In order to do this, a spot will have to be created for the subroutine by eliminating lines 4000, 4010,

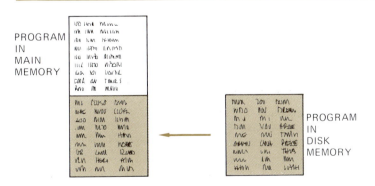

FIGURE 8.13 The APPEND command combines a program from disk memory with the program in main memory.

154
PROGRAM STRUCTURE

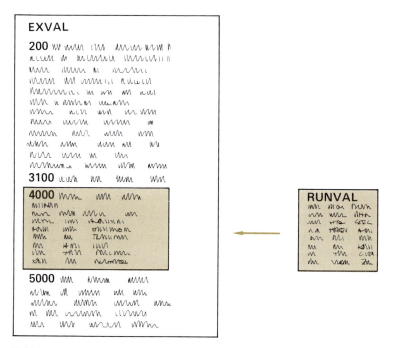

FIGURE 8.14 The RUNVAL and EXVAL programs may be combined as shown.

and 4020 from the EXVAL program, and the lines of the RUNVAL program will have to be renumbered so that they begin at line 4000.

Here is a step-by-step procedure for combining the programs as shown in Fig. 8.14. We begin with the computer in BASIC mode and with the EXVAL program of Fig. 8.12 in main memory.

First, remove all lines numbered from 4000 to 4999 using the `DELETE` command. After this has been done, save the program (see Fig. 8.15).

FIGURE 8.15 Lines 4000 through 4999 are removed from EXVAL.

8.4 BUILDING A PROGRAM WITH SUBROUTINES

```
OLD RUNVAL
Ready

DELETE 100-150
Ready

DELETE 270-280
Ready

290    RETURN

RESEQUENCE   160-290 4000 STEP 10
Ready
```

FIGURE 8.16 The RUNVAL program is converted into a subroutine.

Next, retrieve the RUNVAL program using the OLD command, and remove unwanted lines using the commands DELETE 100-150 and DELETE 270-280. The program will become a subroutine, so replace the END statement with a RETURN statement. Finally, renumber the lines using the RESEQUENCE command (these steps are shown in Fig. 8.16). The RESEQUENCE command tells the computer to renumber lines 160 through 290 with new numbers starting at 4000 and going up in steps of 10.

Now the two programs are ready to be combined. Because the RUNVAL program is already in main memory, the EXVAL program will be combined with it using the APPEND command (see Fig. 8.17). The order in which the two programs are combined will not matter, because we have been careful to avoid duplicate line numbers. Finally, the combined program is renamed EXVAL (otherwise it will have the name RUNVAL).

The result is shown in Fig. 8.18. We can do several things to improve this version of the program. For example, we can improve the instructions to the user and expand the output.

```
APPEND EXVAL
Ready

RENAME EXVAL
Ready
```

FIGURE 8.17 EXVAL and RUNVAL are combined.

FIGURE 8.18 The result of joining the EXVAL program and the RUNVAL program.

```
200     UNTIL SELECTION = 4
210       LET EXVAL = 0
220            !--print the menu ------
230       PRINT 'SELECT ONE OF THE FOLLOWING OPTIONS'
240       PRINT '1 - Compute exercise value of playing '
250       PRINT '    racquetball, basketball, or soccer.'
260       PRINT '2 - Compute the exercise value of a walk'
270       PRINT '    or a run.'
280       PRINT '3 - Compute the exercise value of a swim.'
290       PRINT '4 - Evaluate the total exercise value.'
300            !--select and execute an option--
310       INPUT 'WHAT OPTION'; SELECTION
320       ON SELECTION GOSUB 3000,4000,5000,9000 &
                  OTHERWISE 19000
330       LET TOT_EXVAL = TOT_EXVAL + EXVAL
340     NEXT
700            !--- compute and print the results--
710            !--rate in exercise units per day--
720     LET EX_RATE = TOT_EXVAL/DAYS
730            !--compare to 100/7 benchmark
740     LET EX_PCT = EX_RATE*7
750     PRINT 'YOUR EXERCISE LEVEL IS'; EX_PCT;
760     PRINT 'PERCENT OF THE RECOMMENDED LEVEL'
2990    GOTO 32000
3000           !--- subroutine for racquetball, etc.--
3010    PRINT 'THIS CALCULATES THE EXERCISE VALUE OF'
3020    PRINT 'A CONTINUOUS SESSION OF RACQUETBALL,'
3030    PRINT 'BASKETBALL, OR SOCCER'
3040    PRINT 'YOU SHOULD COUNT ONLY TIMES OF ';
3050    PRINT 'CONTINUOUS ACTIVITY'
3060    INPUT 'TOTAL TIME (HOURS)'; TOT.TIME
3070    LET EXVAL = 40*TOT.TIME - 3
3080    IF EXVAL<0 THEN EXVAL=0
3090    PRINT 'THIS IS WORTH';EXVAL; 'UNITS'
3100    RETURN
4000    INPUT 'HOW FAR DID YOU RUN (MILES)'; DIST
4010    PRINT 'HOW LONG DID IT TAKE (HOURS AND MINUTES)'
4020    INPUT 'HOW MANY HOURS'; TIME.HR
4030    INPUT 'HOW MANY MINUTES'; TIME.MIN
4040    LET TOT.TIME = TIME.HR + TIME.MIN/60
4050    LET RATE = DIST/TOT.TIME
```

```
4060  IF RATE < 6
          THEN
              LET EXVAL = 10/3*(DIST*(RATE-1) -1)
          ELSE
              LET EXVAL = 10/3*(DIST*(5+2/3*(RATE-6)) -1)
      END IF
4070  IF EXVAL < 0 THEN EXVAL = 0
4080  IF RATE > 15 OR EXVAL > 800
          THEN
              PRINT 'WHO DO YOU THINK YOU ARE, BILL ROGERS?'
              GOTO 4110
          !
      END IF
4090  PRINT 'YOUR RUN HAD AN EXERCISE VALUE OF';
4100  PRINT EXVAL; 'UNITS. '
4110  RETURN
5000          ! ---subroutine for swim ------
5010  PRINT 'SORRY THIS SELECTION IS NOT YET AVAILABLE'
5020  RETURN
9000          !--- subroutine to compute totals
9110  INPUT 'HOW MANY DAYS'; DAYS
9120  RETURN
19000         !--- subroutine to handle exceptions--
19010 PRINT 'ERRONEOUS SELECTION'
19020 RETURN
32000 END
```

An improved version of the EXVAL program is shown in Fig. 8.19. A header has been added, the INPUT and PRINT statements have been expanded, and a new subroutine has been added at line 3500 to obtain the value of TOT.TIME from the user. This variable is required in both the "run" and the "racquetball" subroutines. The statement GOSUB 3500 at lines 3060 and 4020 allows the same detailed instructions to be used in both subroutines without having to type the program lines twice. This also provides an example of a subroutine that calls another subroutine.

The revised program also incorporates a SELECT statement in line 770. The variable EX-PCT expresses the exercise rate as a percent of the 100/7 norm. This is used in the SELECT statement to choose a print statement appropriate for the exercise activity. If the percent is greater than 150, the first statement is printed; if it is between 130 and 150, the second statement is printed; and so on.

FIGURE 8.19 An improved version of the EXVAL program.

```
100   ! **************************************************
110   ! PROGRAM: E X V A L
120   ! ------------------------------------------
130         ! PROGRAM TO DETERMINE THE EXERCISE
140         ! VALUE OF A VARIETY OF EXERCISES
150         !
160   !
170
200   UNTIL SELECTION = 4
210     LET EXVAL = 0
220           !--print the menu ------
230     PRINT 'SELECT ONE OF THE FOLLOWING OPTIONS'
240     PRINT '1 - Compute exercise value of playing '
250     PRINT '    racquetball, basketball, or soccer.'
260     PRINT '2 - Compute the exercise value of a walk'
270     PRINT '    or a run.'
280     PRINT '3 - Compute the exercise value of a swim.'
290     PRINT '4 - Evaluate the total exercise value.'
300           !--select and execute an option--
310     INPUT 'WHAT OPTION'; SELECTION
320     ON SELECTION GOSUB 3000,4000,5000,9000 &
                  OTHERWISE 19000
330     LET TOT-EXVAL = TOT-EXVAL + EXVAL
340   NEXT
350   !----------------------------------------
700         !--- compute and print the results--
710         !--rate in exercise units per day--
720   LET EX-RATE = TOT-EXVAL/DAYS
730         !--compare to 100/7 benchmark
740   LET EX-PCT = EX-RATE*7
750   PRINT 'YOUR EXERCISE LEVEL IS'; EX-PCT;
760   PRINT 'PERCENT OF THE RECOMMENDED LEVEL'
770   SELECT   EX-PCT
        CASE >150
            PRINT 'SEE YOU AT THE BOSTON MARATHON'
        CASE 130 TO 150
            PRINT 'QUITE A NOTEWORTHY ACHIEVEMENT'
        CASE 110 TO 130
            PRINT 'THIS INDICATES A BETTER THAN '
            PRINT 'AVERAGE AEROBIC CAPACITY'
        CASE 90 TO 110
            PRINT 'YOU ARE RIGHT ON THE MARK'
```

```
              CASE 50 TO 90
                   PRINT 'GRADUALLY INCREASE YOUR ';
                   PRINT 'LEVEL OF ACTIVITY'
              CASE < 50
                   PRINT 'THIS IS NOT ENOUGH ACTIVITY'
         END SELECT
 780     !----------------------------------------
2990     GOTO 32000
3000              !--- subroutine for racquetball, etc.--
3010     PRINT 'THIS CALCULATES THE EXERCISE VALUE OF'
3020     PRINT 'A CONTINUOUS SESSION OF RACQUETBALL,'
3030     PRINT 'BASKETBALL, OR SOCCER'
3040     PRINT 'YOU SHOULD COUNT ONLY TIMES OF ';
3050     PRINT 'CONTINUOUS ACTIVITY'
3060     GOSUB 3500   !--- get the total time ---
3070     LET EXVAL = 40*TOT.TIME - 3
3080     IF EXVAL<0 THEN EXVAL=0
3090     PRINT 'THIS IS WORTH';EXVAL; 'UNITS'
3100     RETURN
3500              ! --- subroutine to get the total time -
3520     PRINT 'ENTER THE TOTAL TIME (HOURS PLUS MINUTES)'
3530     PRINT 'EXAMPLE: ENTER 0 HOURS PLUS 90 MINUTES '
3540     PRINT '              OR 1 HOUR PLUS 30 MINUTES '
3550     PRINT '              OR 1.5 HOUR PLUS 0 MINUTES'
3560     INPUT 'HOW MANY HOURS'; TIME.HR
3570     INPUT 'HOW MANY ADDITIONAL MINUTES'; TIME.MIN
3580     LET TOT.TIME = TIME.HR + TIME.MIN/60
3590     RETURN
4000              !--- subroutine for the run value--
4010     INPUT 'HOW FAR DID YOU RUN (MILES)'; DIST
4020     GOSUB 3500   !-- get the total time ---
4050     LET RATE = DIST/TOT.TIME
4060     IF RATE < 6
            THEN
               LET EXVAL = 10/3*(DIST*(RATE-1) -1)
            ELSE
               LET EXVAL = 10/3*(DIST*(5+2/3*(RATE-6)) -1)
         END IF
4070     IF EXVAL < 0 THEN EXVAL = 0
4080     IF RATE > 15 OR EXVAL > 800
            THEN
               PRINT 'WHO DO YOU THINK YOU ARE, BILL ROGERS?'
               EXVAL=0
               RETURN
         END IF
```

(Continued)

FIGURE 8.19 Continued

```
4090  PRINT 'YOUR RUN HAD AN EXERCISE VALUE OF';
4100  PRINT EXVAL; 'UNITS. '
4110  RETURN
5000           ! ---subroutine for swim ------
5010  PRINT 'SORRY THIS SELECTION IS NOT YET AVAILABLE'
5020  RETURN
9000           !--- subroutine to compute totals
9010  PRINT 'NOW YOU NEED TO FIGURE OUT THE NUMBER OF'
9020  PRINT 'DAYS THAT THIS ACTIVITY WAS SPREAD OUT OVER'
9030  PRINT 'YOU SHOULD COUNT ALL IDLE DAYS AS WELL AS'
9040  PRINT 'THE DAYS YOU EXERCISED. ALSO COUNT THE IDLE'
9050  PRINT 'DAYS BEFORE THE EXERCISE IN THIS TALLY'
9060  PRINT 'FOR EXAMPLE, IF YOU WERE IDLE FOR 2 DAYS'
9070  PRINT 'THEN EXERCISED FOR 2 DAYS, RESTED 1 AND'
9080  PRINT 'EXERCISED 1, THEN YOU COUNT THE THREE DAYS'
9090  PRINT 'THAT YOU DID NOT EXERCISE AS WELL AS THE '
9100  PRINT 'THREE THAT YOU DID FOR A TOTAL OF 6 DAYS'
9110  INPUT 'HOW MANY DAYS'; DAYS
9120  RETURN
19000          !--- subroutine to handle exceptions--
19010 PRINT 'ERRONEOUS SELECTION'
19020 RETURN
32000 END
```

8.5 Exercises

8.1 Analyze the following program to determine the output:

```
100 PRINT "AT LINE 100"
200 GOSUB 600
300 GOTO 800
400 PRINT "AT LINE 400"
500 RETURN
600 PRINT "AT LINE 600"
700 RETURN
800 PRINT "AT LINE 800"
900 END
```

8.2 Write a program that uses the FNSWIM function of Fig. 8.9 to compute the exercise value of a swim. Your program should ask the user for the distance in yards and the time in minutes, and it should display the computed exercise value.

8.3 Swimmers normally keep track of the distance of a swim in terms of laps and not yards. Find out how long your local pool is (or use the length of a standard Olympic pool) and modify the program of Problem 8.2 so that the user is asked for the distance in terms of laps. Your program should clearly define the required input (that is, that swimming from one end to the other and returning is one lap).

8.4 The function FNSWIM of Fig. 8.9 has a couple of "bugs." The first problem occurs when a value of 0 is used for T. Admittedly, it does not make sense to swim a distance in no time, and so this problem should not arise in normal use.

Another type of problem comes up if you swim a very short distance or take a very long time. In either of these cases, the function may return a negative value. Most people agree that some exercise is better than none, and that it is not reasonable to assign a negative exercise value.

a) Modify the function definition. The new function should ensure that both D and T are positive numbers. If not, the function should return a value of −1. If D and T are positive, the function should calculate the exercise value using the same formula, but return a value of 0 if the formula comes up with a negative number. This ensures that the exercise value is always at least 0 for positive values of D and T.

b) Use the function you wrote in part (a) in a program. Your program should ask the user for the values of D and T and calculate the exercise value using the new FNSWIM function. Under normal conditions, your program should print the exercise value of the swim. However, if the function returns a value of −1, your program should instead print a message to indicate "erroneous input."

8.5 Write a program to convert temperatures between degrees Celsius and Fahrenheit. Your program should allow conversion in either direction (°F to °C or °C to °F) and should contain at least two subroutines.

8.6 Finish the EXVAL program of Fig. 8.19 by adding a "swim" subroutine at line 5000. (Your instructor should be able to provide you with a copy of the program.)

8.7 Add a subroutine to the EXVAL program for computing the exercise value of a bicycle trip using the formula

$$EXVAL = \frac{D * R}{3} - 5,$$

where D is the distance in miles and R is the rate in miles per hour.

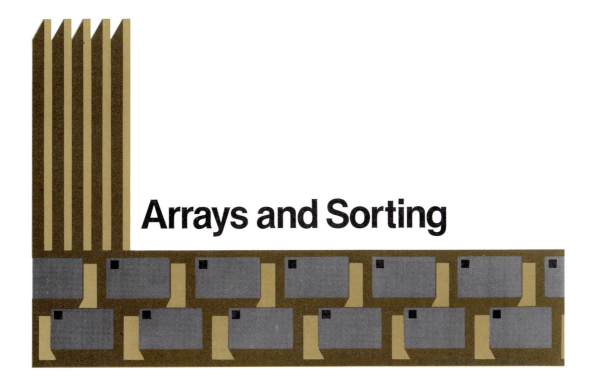

Arrays and Sorting

9.1 Subscripted Variables

Different variables can be given names that are similar except for a number. This was done in Exercise 1.1 for the temperatures H1, H2, H3, H4, and H5. If the numbers are placed inside parentheses, H(1), H(2), H(3), H(4), and H(5), they then become *subscripts*. Subscripted variables like H(1), H(2), and so on, with the same variable name but with different subscripts are collectively called an *array*. In this case, we would collectively refer to all of these variables as the array H.

If you do not specify otherwise, the computer will assume that the subscripts of an array will run from 0 to 10. In particular, when a subscripted variable like H(1) is first used in a BASIC program, the computer will normally set up storage blocks for all the variables H(0) through H(10).

There are some important advantages to using a subscripted variable like H(1) or H(7), rather than separate variable names like H1 or H7. The most important of these is that the control variable in a FOR loop may be used to determine the subscript. This

ARRAYS AND SORTING

```
200 FOR N = 1 TO 10
210    PRINT H(N)
220 NEXT N
```

FIGURE 9.1 The use of a loop to display the values H(1) through H(10) of the array H.

allows different subscripted variables to appear in a repeated statement or calculation. A simple example is shown in Fig. 9.1.

Subscripts may also be used with string variables. This is often done with a list of names. Figure 9.2 shows a program that stores the names of the days of the week in a string array D$ and then prints a list of the days using a FOR loop.

Review: Subscripted Variables

■ Whenever a subscripted variable like H(2) is mentioned in a BASIC program, the computer normally sets up storage blocks for H(0) through

```
200 LET D$(1) = "SUNDAY"
210 LET D$(2) = "MONDAY"
220 LET D$(3) = "TUESDAY"
230 LET D$(4) = "WEDNESDAY"
240 LET D$(5) = "THURSDAY"
250 LET D$(6) = "FRIDAY"
260 LET D$(7) = "SATURDAY"
280 !
300 FOR N = 1 TO 7
310    PRINT D$(N)
320 NEXT N
```

OUTPUT

```
SUNDAY
MONDAY
TUESDAY
WEDNESDAY
THURSDAY
FRIDAY
SATURDAY
```

FIGURE 9.2 The use of a string array to print a list of the days of the week.

through H(10). That is, 11 variables are automatically created and are available for calculations.
- The subscript itself can be determined by the value of another variable. For example, H(N) refers to H(2) if N has the value 2, H(3) if N has the value 3, and so on.
- A subscripted string variable has the form AA$(5).

9.2 The Dimension Statement

The DIMENSION, or DIM, statement may be used to create an array of a specified size or type. If no DIMENSION statement is provided, the computer will set up storage blocks with room for subscripts up to 10. Use the DIMENSION statement if you wish to use larger (or smaller) arrays. It should appear at the beginning of the program, before the array is used. The statement begins with the word DIMENSION or the abbreviation DIM followed by the array name and the maximum value of the subscript. The maximum value of the subscript is also called the *dimension* of the array. For example, the statement pair

```
100 DIM H(3)
102 LET H(2)= 10.3
```

creates the array H with dimension 3 (that is, the variables have subscripts up to 3) and assigns the value 10.3 to the variable H(2). When these statements are executed in a program, a storage block with three slots for data is set up in the computer (ignoring the zero subscript). This is shown diagramatically in Fig. 9.3.

	name	
	H	
subscripts	1	0	values
	2	10.3
	3	0

FIGURE 9.3 Storage for the array H can be visualized as a vertical row of three storage blocks. The subscript is used to identify the row number.

More than one array can be created in the same `DIM` statement if commas are used to separate the array specifications. Here is an example:

```
110 DIM L(5) , X(3)
```

When this statement is executed in a program, the array `L` is created with dimension 5 and the array `X` is created with dimension 3.

Arrays to store string values can be created in the same way using a DIMENSION statement. For example,

```
120 DIMENSION Y$(6)
```

creates the string array `Y$` with storage blocks for six strings.

One final note. A variable cannot be used to specify the size of an array in a `DIMENSION` statement. The maximum value of a subscript must be a specific "literal" number, like 7; that is, `DIMENSION X(N)` is not allowed.

9.3 Using Arrays with Lists

A subscripted variable is often used to keep track of a list of names or numbers. For example, the six numbers shown in the DATA list of Fig. 9.4 can be associated with the six subscripted variables `L(1)` through `L(6)`. After the numbers have been stored in an array (steps 100 to 120), there is a great deal of flexibility in displaying them. For example, they can be displayed in a vertical column (steps 200 to 220), or they can be displayed in reverse order (steps 300 to 320). The output is shown at the bottom of the figure.

There are many situations in which it is desirable to rearrange a list of names or numbers. For example, a class roster may be rearranged so that the names are in alphabetical order; or a list of scores may be rearranged with the highest score first, the second highest score second, and so on. The process of rearranging a list of names or numbers and putting them in a specific order is called *sorting*.

9.4 Finding The Largest Number in a List

If it is necessary to rearrange a list of numbers so that the largest number is listed first and the smallest number is listed last, we might start out by finding the largest number.

9.4 FINDING THE LARGEST NUMBER IN A LIST

```
100 FOR N = 1 TO 6
110    READ L(N)
120 NEXT N
200 FOR N = 1 TO 6
210    PRINT L(N)
220 NEXT N

300 FOR N = 6 TO 1 STEP -1
310    PRINT L(N);
320 NEXT N

330 DATA 23,56,16,78,95,45
```

OUTPUT

```
23
56
16
78
95
45
45 95 78 16 56 23
```

FIGURE 9.4 Putting data into an array and then listing it in two ways.

Before discussing the algorithm for doing this, let us consider the following situation: You have a long list of numbers and want to determine the largest number in the list. You look through the list: 23, 56, 16, 78, 95, 45, and so on. Almost without conscious effort, you begin the process of finding the largest number. This process must be formalized into a step-by-step procedure, or algorithm, in order to instruct the computer to do the same thing. Here is an outline of the procedure:

> Start with the first number and call it the largest number.
>
> Read through the list one number at a time to find a number that is larger than the one supposed to be the largest. If such a number is found, then it becomes the largest number.

ARRAYS AND SORTING

Let us check this algorithm by trying it out on the same list of numbers:

```
23
56
16
78
95
45
```

As we begin, we consider 23 to be the largest number, and we read down the list until a larger number is encountered. This happens immediately, and so 56 becomes the new largest number. This process continues, with 78 and then 95 as the largest number.

Apparently, the process of finding the largest number is a gradual one. At each stage of the process, we have a value that represents the largest number *so far*. Of course, the list has to be read all the way through to ensure that the largest number so far is actually the largest number in the list.

We must use two variables for this process: the largest number (so far) LGST and the number X being considered. Here is a second outline of the algorithm:

> Start with LGST equal to the first number and repeat the following steps until all of the numbers have been read:
>
> ■ Get the next number X.
>
> ■ IF X is bigger than LGST, THEN replace the value of LGST with the value of X.

```
100 READ LGST
110 FOR N = 2 TO 6
120    READ X
130    IF X > LGST THEN LGST = X
140 NEXT N
150 PRINT "THE LARGEST NUMBER IS"; LGST
160 DATA 23, 56, 16, 78, 95, 45
170 END
```

FIGURE 9.5 How to determine the largest number in a data list.

9.4 FINDING THE LARGEST NUMBER IN A LIST

Figure 9.5 shows a program that carries out this algorithm for the six numbers listed above. The loop-control variable N simply counts the number of times that the READ and IF statements are to be repeated. There are six data items, and line 100 reads the first one. Therefore, line 120 must be repeated five more times to read the second through the sixth numbers. Naturally, FOR N = 1 TO 5 would have worked just as well in line 110. We have used the statement FOR N = 2 TO 6 in Fig. 9.5 to emphasize that we are reading the second through the sixth numbers in the data list.

The Selection Sort

Now we want to rearrange the numbers in descending order, so that the largest number is listed first and the smallest number is listed last (see Fig. 9.6). The process of sorting necessitates that the numbers be moved around in the list. This is most easily done by representing the data as an array. The array can be set up using a READ statement in a FOR loop as shown in lines 100 to 120 of Fig. 9.4, or by using an INPUT statement in a FOR loop as shown in Fig. 9.7. In the following discussion, it is assumed that something like this has already been done to establish the values of the array X.

The *selection sort* can be described as follows: Find the largest number in the list and swap it with the number in the top slot in the list, then find the

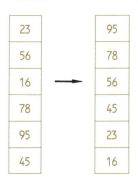

FIGURE 9.6 The list of numbers is to be sorted as shown.

```
100 DIM X(25)
110 LET KMAX = 25
200 FOR K = 1 TO KMAX
210    INPUT 'TYPE A NUMBER'; X(K)
220 NEXT K
```

FIGURE 9.7 A method of using an INPUT statement to obtain values for an array with 25 numbers.

ARRAYS AND SORTING

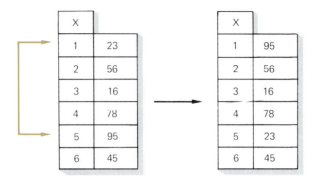

FIGURE 9.8 The first step in the process of arranging the list in descending order using the selection sort. The largest number, at position 5, is swapped with the first number in the list.

second-largest number and swap it with the number in the second slot on the list, and so on.* Figure 9.8 shows the first step in this rearrangement process. The largest number, at position 5, is swapped with the number in position 1. Once the first swap has been accomplished, the second-largest number, at position 4, is swapped with the number in position 2, and so on.

If you think about how to carry out this swapping, it should be apparent that what we really need to know is the position (that is, the subscript) of the largest number, in this case, 5. This really gives us more information: It tells us that the largest number is fifth in the list and that its value is given by X(5).

In the program of Fig. 9.9 the variable SUB.LG keeps track of the subscript of the largest number encountered so far. As before, determining the position of the largest number is a gradual process. SUB.LG starts out with a value of 1 to indicate that X(1) is the largest number encountered so far. In steps 310 to 340, the numbers X(N) are reviewed one at a time and compared with the value X(SUB.LG). If a larger number is encountered, then its subscript becomes the new value of SUB.LG. Using the same numbers as in the previous example, SUB.LG would have the value 5 at the completion of these program steps. The largest number is swapped into the first position using steps 400 to 420 of Fig. 9.9. This swapping process is illustrated graphically in Fig. 9.10.

So far we have shown how the largest number in a list can be swapped with the first number. Once this has been done, the second-largest number can be found by ignoring X(1) and finding the largest number in the remainder of the list. This number is then swapped with X(2). The program of Fig. 9.11 shows how this is done. After this has been carried out, the two largest

*Software that provides an animated illustration of the selection sort is available from the publisher.

9.4 FINDING THE LARGEST NUMBER IN A LIST

```
300 LET SUB.LG = 1
310 FOR N = 2 TO 6
330 IF X(N) > X(SUB.LG)  THEN SUB.LG = N
340 NEXT N

400 LET   Y         = X(1)
410 LET   X(1)      = X(SUB.LG)
420 LET   X(SUB.LG) = Y
```

FIGURE 9.9 The first step in the process of sorting the numbers X(1) to X(6).

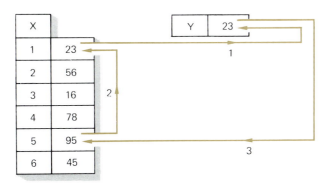

FIGURE 9.10 Swapping the values of X(1) and X(5) is a three-step process. First, the value of X(1) is stored in Y, then the value of X(5) is placed in X(1) and finally, the original value of X(1) is transferred from Y to X(5).

numbers are at X(1) and X(2), and now the third-largest number can be found by looking for the largest number in the remainder of the list starting at X(3). Once found, this number is swapped with X(3). The program of Fig. 9.12 shows how this is done.

```
500 LET SUB.LG = 2
510 FOR N = 3 TO 6
530    IF X(N) > X(SUB.LG)   THEN SUB.LG = N
540 NEXT N
600 LET   Y         = X(2)
610 LET   X(2)      = X(SUB.LG)
620 LET   X(SUB.LG) = Y
```

FIGURE 9.11 Finding the second-largest number in a list.

```
700 LET SUB.LG = 3
710 FOR N = 4 TO 6
730    IF X(N) > X(SUB.LG)   THEN SUB.LG = N
740 NEXT N
800 LET   Y         = X(3)
810 LET   X(3)      = X(SUB.LG)
820 LET   X(SUB.LG) = Y
```

FIGURE 9.12 Finding the third-largest number in a list.

```
LET SUB.LG = K
FOR N = (K+1) TO 6
  IF X(N) > X(SUB.LG)   THEN SUB.LG = N
NEXT N
LET  Y         = X(K)
LET  X(K)      = X(SUB.LG)
LET  X(SUB.LG) = Y
```

FIGURE 9.13 The general form of the previous three figures.

By now the pattern should be apparent. These searches and swaps are the same except for the numbers used in the first, second, fifth, and sixth statements. In fact, the steps to find and swap the Kth largest number all can be put into the form shown in Fig. 9.13. For the sake of simplicity, the second line of Fig. 9.13 can be changed slightly to

```
FOR N = K TO 6
```

This will introduce an unnecessary comparison but makes the algorithm a little more uniform.

The selection sort can be carried out by repeating the steps of Fig. 9.13 with K=1, then K=2, and so on until all of the numbers are rearranged. An example of a program to sort 25 numbers and print the sorted list is given in Fig. 9.14. This program provides a means of rearranging KMAX numbers into decreasing order. With minor modifications, the same program can be used to rearrange numbers into increasing order or to rearrange names into alphabetical order. In particular, if the inequality is reversed in line 270, the program will arrange the numbers in ascending order. Reversing the inequality along with switching to a string array will arrange strings in alphabetical order.

The Bubble Sort

The bubble-sort algorithm provides a different method of sorting a list. To illustrate this algorithm we consider the same list of numbers discussed in the previous section. This time we will rearrange the list so that the numbers are in increasing order.

Any list that is not arranged in the correct order will have at least two adjacent numbers that are out of order. That is, if the list is not in increasing order, then there is at least one place in the list where a number is larger than the one immediately after it. Conversely, if the list is in ascending order, then every number is smaller than the one after it.

The idea of the *bubble sort* is to go through the list and compare adjacent numbers to see if they are in the correct order. If they are not in the correct order, then the numbers are swapped.

9.4 FINDING THE LARGEST NUMBER IN A LIST

```
100 DIM  X(25)
110 KMAX = 25
200 FOR K = 1 TO KMAX
210   INPUT 'TYPE A NUMBER'; X(K)
220 NEXT K
230 !
240 FOR K = 1 TO  KMAX
250    LET SUB.LG = K
260    FOR N = K TO KMAX
270       IF X(N) > X(SUB.LG)  THEN SUB.LG = N
280    NEXT N
290    LET   Y         = X(K)
300    LET   X(K)      = X(SUB.LG)
310    LET   X(SUB.LG) = Y
320 NEXT K
330 PRINT "THE NUMBERS IN DECREASING ORDER ARE"
340 FOR K = 1 TO KMAX
350    PRINT X(K)
360 NEXT K
```

FIGURE 9.14 A program to sort and print 25 numbers by means of the selection sort.

This procedure will be illustrated for the list of six numbers shown at the left of Fig. 9.15. The first two numbers, 23 and 56, are in ascending order, and so they are not swapped. The second number, 56, is larger than the third number, 16. These are not in the correct order, and so they are swapped. The new third number, 56, is smaller than the fourth number, 78, and so they are not swapped. The process continues until the end of the list. The resulting rearrangement, shown at the right of Fig. 9.15, shows that the largest number has settled to the bottom and the small numbers are rising to the top like bubbles.*

The process of going through the list and comparing adjacent numbers may be described informally as follows:

FOR J from 1 TO 5

- check the order of $X(J)$ and $X(J + 1)$
- IF $X(J)$ and $X(J + 1)$ are not in the correct order
- THEN swap them

---

*Software that provides an animation of this sorting process is available from the publisher.

ARRAYS AND SORTING

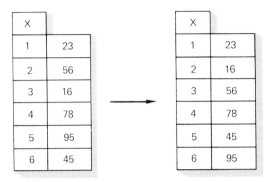

FIGURE 9.15 The bubble sort. On the left are the numbers before the sort; on the right, after one pass through the list.

The process must be repeated a total of five times in order to ensure that a list of six numbers will be fully ordered. The second time, it is not necessary to make the final check in the above algorithm. This is because the largest number will have "settled" to the bottom on the first pass, and so $X(5)$ and $X(6)$ will always be in the correct order. Similarly, the second-largest number will always be in the correct position after the second pass through the list (see Fig. 9.16).

The process of going through the list the third time is the same as before, except that there is no need to check subscript number 4 or 5. This is because the largest two numbers are already in the correct position at the bottom of the list, and so $X(4)$, $X(5)$, and $X(6)$ will always be in the correct order.

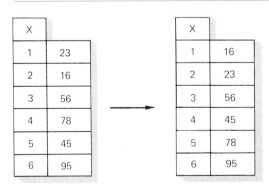

FIGURE 9.16 The second pass through the list brings the numbers closer to the correct ordering. The largest two numbers will always end up in the correct position.

9.4 FINDING THE LARGEST NUMBER IN A LIST

```
150 FOR    I = 1 TO 5
160   FOR    J = 1 TO (6-I)
170      IF  X(J) > X(J+1)
             THEN
                Y      = X(J)
                X(J)   = X(J+1)
                X(J+1) = Y
180   NEXT J
190 NEXT I
```

FIGURE 9.17 The bubble-sort algorithm to put six numbers into increasing order.

The full bubble sort has the form shown in Fig. 9.17. The outside loop-control variable (I) both counts the number of times that the loop is repeated and determines the largest subscript to be checked in the inner loop. The inner loop checks adjacent values in the array and swaps them if they are out of order.

Let us now consider the problem of putting a string array A$(1), A$(2), ... into alphabetical order. A typical string array is shown in Fig. 9.18. We will use the bubble-sort algorithm to go through the list and compare adjacent names to see if they are in the correct alphabetical order. If two names are out of order they are swapped. A program to do this is shown in Fig. 9.19.

Using a "Boolean" Variable to Test for a Sorted List. If the list to be sorted is almost in correct order, then the list may be correctly sorted long before the sorting algorithm is completed. Recall that the bubble-sort algorithm will go

A$(1)	JONES
A$(2)	SMITH
A$(3)	BRAHMS
A$(4)	ABRAHAM
A$(5)	POWELL
A$(6)	AARONSON

FIGURE 9.18 A typical string array. The sorting example will arrange the names in alphabetical order.

ARRAYS AND SORTING

```
100 INPUT 'HOW MANY NAMES'; NMAX
110 IF NMAX>10
       THEN
          PRINT "SORRY, AT MOST 10"
          GOTO 100
       END IF
120 FOR I = 1 TO NMAX
130    INPUT 'TYPE A NAME'; A$(I)
140 NEXT I
150 FOR I = 1 TO NMAX-1
160    FOR J = 1 TO NMAX-I
170       IF A$(J)>A$(J+1)
             THEN
                LET Y$=A$(J)
                LET A$(J)=A$(J+1)
                LET A$(J+1)=Y$
180    NEXT J
190 NEXT I
200 PRINT " HERE IS AN ALPHABETICAL LIST "
210 FOR I = 1 TO NMAX
220    PRINT A$(I)
230 NEXT I
240 END
```

FIGURE 9.19 This program can be used to input up to 10 names. The names are stored in the array A$ and then sorted using the bubble-sort algorithm. Finally, the names are displayed in alphabetical order.

through the list and compare adjacent values to see if they are out of order. To determine if the list has been ordered, we need to answer the YES/NO question, "Were any swaps necessary on the last pass through the list?" An answer of NO will indicate that the list has been sorted and no further checks need to be made.

The following version of the bubble-sort algorithm uses a variable SWAP to indicate whether at least one swap has been made. A value of SWAP=0 will indicate that no swaps have been made, and a value of SWAP=1 will indicate that at least one swap has been made. A variable used in this way to indicate whether a condition is true or not is sometimes called a flag, or a *Boolean* variable. In this case the flag indicates whether one or more swaps were made on the current pass through the list.

9.4 FINDING THE LARGEST NUMBER IN A LIST

Because BASIC makes no explicit provision for a YES/NO or Boolean variable, we will employ a trick: The variables YES and NO will be defined to have the values 1 and 0, respectively. Then `SWAP=NO` is the same thing as `SWAP=0`, and `SWAP=YES` is the same thing as `SWAP=1`. Because the values of YES and NO will never change, they can be set up as constants using the `DECLARE` statement, as shown in the program of Fig. 9.20. This will prevent the values from being altered inadvertently.

Figure 9.20 shows how the program steps between lines 140 and 200 of Fig. 9.19 can be modified to incorporate a variable `SWAP` that acts as a flag to stop the sorting process as soon as the list has been correctly arranged. This program is identical to the program of Fig. 9.19 except for the addition of lines 145, 155, 185, and an additional line in 170. Line 155 sets the value of `SWAP` equal to `NO (0)` to begin with. If any of the values in the list are swapped, the value of `SWAP` is changed to `YES (1)`. If `SWAP` is equal to `NO (0)` at the end of the inner (J) loop, then no values have been swapped and the list is sorted.

```
    .
    .
    .
145 DECLARE CONSTANT YES = 1, NO = 0     ! <--
150 FOR I = 1 TO NMAX-1
155    SWAP = NO                         ! <--
160    FOR J = 1 TO NMAX-I
170       IF A$(J)>A$(J+1)
             THEN
                LET Y$=A$(J)
                LET A$(J)=A$(J+1)
                LET A$(J+1)=Y$
                SWAP = YES                ! <--
180    NEXT J
185    IF SWAP = NO THEN GOTO 200         ! <--
190 NEXT I
200 PRINT "HERE IS A LIST OF THE NAMES"
    .
    .
    .
```

FIGURE 9.20 Some modifications that can be made to the bubble-sort algorithm of Fig. 9.19 in order to check for a sorted list.

ARRAYS AND SORTING

Tandem Sort

It is often necessary to sort a list containing both names and numbers. For example, the following list of student names and grades,

NAME	GRADE
JONES	83
SMITH	79
BRAHMS	93
ABRAHAM	72
POWELL	88
AARONSON	76

might be stored in the computer as two arrays, a string array and a numerical array, as shown in Fig. 9.21.

Assume that this list of names and grades is to be put into alphabetical order. If two of the names are swapped, then the grades must also be swapped so that each line contains the correct grade after each name. In other words, we must modify the selection-sort algorithm of Fig. 9.14 so that the numbers are swapped along with the names. We will have to make similar modifications if the list is to be arranged with the highest grade listed first and the lowest grade listed last. In this case, the names will have to be swapped each time a grade is swapped.

Figure 9.22 shows a program to sort 25 names and grades into alphabetical order. The variable **K-FIRST** is used to keep track of the subscript of the first name in alphabetical order. The comparison on line 270 checks adjacent names in the list to see if they are in the correct order. Lines 290 to 310 have been modified so that the grades are swapped along with the names.

A$(1)	JONES		G(1)	83
A$(2)	SMITH		G(2)	79
A$(3)	BRAHMS		G(3)	93
A$(4)	ABRAHAM		G(4)	72
A$(5)	POWELL		G(5)	88
A$(6)	AARONSON		G(6)	76

FIGURE 9.21 A list of names and grades can be represented as two arrays.

9.4 FINDING THE LARGEST NUMBER IN A LIST

```
100 DIM A$(25), G(25)
110 LET KMAX = 25
200 FOR K = 1 TO KMAX
210   INPUT 'TYPE THE NAME'; A$(K)
220   INPUT 'TYPE THE GRADE'; G(K)
230 NEXT K
240 FOR K = 1 TO  KMAX
250   LET K-FIRST = K
260   FOR N = K TO KMAX
270     IF A$(N) < A$(K-FIRST)  THEN K-FIRST = N
280   NEXT N
290   B$ = A$(K)           \ Y = G(K)
300   A$(K) = A$(K-FIRST) \ G(K) = G(K-FIRST)
310   A$(K-FIRST) = B$    \ G(K-FIRST) = Y
320 NEXT K
330 PRINT "NAME"; TAB(19); "GRADE"
340 FOR K = 1 TO KMAX
350   PRINT A$(K); TAB(20); G(K)
360 NEXT K
```

FIGURE 9.22 The tandem version of the selection-sort algorithm of Fig. 9.14.

* Index Arrays

Consider the list of stocks shown in Fig. 9.23. At different times it may be desirable to have a ranking in terms of yield, in terms of price, or in terms of the price-to-earnings ratio, P/E. Rather than actually rearrange the list for each ranking, we could indicate the ranking in terms of the current position in the array.

	NAME	P/E	YIELD	PRICE
1	ACME	5.2	12	23.5
2	DUDD	7	4	12.0
3	LEAK	23	5	76.5
4	PROM	17	8	34.0
5	SOMY	19	6	29.5

FIGURE 9.23

ARRAYS AND SORTING

NAME	P/E	YIELD	PRICE
2 DUDD	7	4	12.0
3 LEAK	23	5	76.5
5 SOMY	19	6	29.5
4 PROM	17	8	34.0
1 ACME	5.2	12	23.5

I.YLD

1	2
2	3
3	5
4	4
5	1

FIGURE 9.24 The list has been sorted in ascending order of yield.

For example, suppose we wished to rank the stocks in terms of yield, with the lowest yield listed first. This has been done in Fig. 9.24. All of the information concerning the rearrangement is contained in the index array I.YLD. I.YLD(1) has a value of 2. This indicates that item number 2 of the original list has the lowest yield. I.YLD(2) has a value of 3, indicating item 3 of the original list has the second lowest yield, and so on, with I.YLD(5) indicating the position of the stock with the highest yield. As an alternative to actually rearranging the list, the index array I.YLD can be used to specify the ranking. Other index arrays can be used to indicate the rankings according to P/E and price (see Fig. 9.25).

To see how an index array can be used, consider the array I.PR of Fig. 9.25. If ST$( ) is an array that contains the list of stock names given in Fig. 9.23 and PRICE( ) is the corresponding price, then statements 250 to 270 of Fig. 9.26 will display the stocks and prices in the original alphabetical order, and program steps 300 to 320 will display them ranked according to price.

I.P_E

1	3
2	5
3	4
4	2
5	1

I.PR

1	3
2	4
3	5
4	1
5	2

FIGURE 9.25 Index arrays I.P_E and I.PR that indicate the ranking from highest to lowest P/E and price, respectively. The numbers refer to the position in the original list of Fig. 9.23.

9.4 FINDING THE LARGEST NUMBER IN A LIST

```
250 FOR I = 1 TO 5
260   PRINT ST$(I), PRICE(I)
270 NEXT I

300 FOR I = 1 TO 5
310   PRINT ST$(I.PR(I)) , PRICE(I.PR(I))
320 NEXT I
```

FIGURE 9.26 The array I.PR is used to print the list ranked according to price.

Here is an algorithm for setting up the index array I.PR for the stocks and prices given in Fig. 9.23:

> Start with an index array that gives the normal ordering [I.PR(1) = 1, I.PR(2) = 2, I.PR(3) = 3, etc.].
>
> For each value of J from 1 to 4:
>
> ■ check to see if PRICE(I.PR(J)) and PRICE(I.PR(J + 1)) are in the correct order. If not, then swap the index values I.PR(J) and I.PR(J + 1).

FIGURE 9.27 A program that uses an array I.PR to indicate the ordering according to price. The bubble-sort algorithm is used to arrange the values in the index array I.PR.

```
10            !-- set up the arrays --
100  FOR N = 1 TO 5
110    READ ST$(N), PRICE(N)
120    LET I.PR(N)=N
130  NEXT N
140  NMAX = 5
145           ! -- sort the index array --
150  FOR I = 1 TO NMAX-1
160    FOR J = 1 TO NMAX-I
170      IF PRICE(I.PR(J)) < PRICE(I.PR(J+1))
             THEN
               LET Y=I.PR(J)
               LET I.PR(J)=I.PR(J+1)
               LET I.PR(J+1)=Y
180    NEXT J
190  NEXT I
195           ! -- print the results -----
```

(Continued)

FIGURE 9.27 Continued

```
200 PRINT "HERE IS A LIST OF THE STOCKS"
210 FOR I = 1 TO NMAX
220   PRINT ST$(I)
230 NEXT I
240 PRINT
250 PRINT "HERE IS A RANKING BY PRICE"
260 FOR I = 1 TO NMAX
270   PRINT ST$(I.PR(I))
280 NEXT I
1000 DATA ACME 5.2  12   23.5, 23.5
1010 DATA DUDD 7    4    12.0, 12.0
1020 DATA LEAK 23   5    76.5, 76.5
1030 DATA PROM 17   8    34.0, 34.0
1040 DATA SOMY 19   6    29.5, 29.5
2000 END
```

OUTPUT

```
HERE IS A LIST OF THE STOCKS
ACME  5.2  12   23.5
DUDD  7    4    12.0
LEAK  23   5    76.5
PROM  17   8    34.0
SOMY  19   6    29.5

HERE IS A RANKING BY PRICE
LEAK  23   5    76.5
PROM  17   8    34.0
SOMY  19   6    29.5
ACME  5.2  12   23.5
DUDD  7    4    12.0
```

The previous algorithm is similar to the bubble-sort algorithm, except that the index values are being swapped instead of the data values. A program to do this is given in Fig. 9.27.

9.5 Exercises

9.1 The program given in Fig. 9.14 to illustrate the selection sort uses the value KMAX as the loop's ending value in line 240 and K as the loop's starting value in line 260. Show that these values can be replaced by KMAX − 1 and K + 1, respectively, thus eliminating unnecessary comparisons in two different situations.

9.2 Will the bubble-sort algorithm of Fig. 9.19 work if line 160 is replaced by FOR J = 1 TO NMAX − 1?

9.3 Can we swap the values of X(1) and X(SUB.LG) using the following steps?

```
400 LET X(1)      = X(SUB.LG)
410 LET X(SUB.LG) = X(1)
```

9.4 Write a program to INPUT an array of 10 numbers at the terminal, sort the numbers, and print them out so that the smallest number is printed first, and the largest number is printed last. Use a modification of the bubble-sort algorithm to sort the numbers.

9.5 Write a program to READ an array N$( ) of 20 names from a DATA list and then print the names in alphabetical order. Your program should work correctly with different names in the DATA list.

9.6 Modify the sort program of Fig. 9.19 so that up to 25 names can be sorted and printed in alphabetical order.

9.7 Revise the tandem sort program of Fig. 9.22 so that the list is arranged according to grade with the highest grade listed first and the lowest grade listed last. Test your program using the six names and grades given in the example.

9.8 Modify the program of Fig. 9.27 so that the list is also arranged according to the price–earnings ratio using an index array I.P_E. The output of your program should look like the output of the example, but should also display a third listing according to P/E.

More Operations with Strings

10.1 Built-In String Functions and Constants

The term *string function* denotes a function that uses strings in some way. String functions are similar to the other functions we have been using. Each requires one or more arguments and returns a value using a prescribed rule. The arguments and the values may be strings or numbers depending on the particular function.

For example, the LEN function requires a string as its argument and returns a number as its value; whereas the CHR$ function requires a number as its argument and returns a string as its value. Notice that the name of the function is an indication of the data type that the function *returns*. If the name ends with a dollar sign, then the function returns a string value. Table 10.1 contains a list of the functions that we will be discussing in this chapter. A more complete list appears in Appendix E.

The CHR$ Function

The CHR$ function requires an integer variable or expression as its argument and returns a single character as its value. The character is the ASCII equiva-

TABLE 10.1 Some of the most common string functions.

CHR$	Converts a number to a character using the ASCII code (given in Appendix F).
DATE$	Displays a date in the form 06-Feb-85. This can be used to display the current date.
EDIT$	Reformats a given string.
FORMAT$	Displays a number in a specified form.
LEN	Determines the number of characters stored in a given string variable.
POS	Finds a letter or a character string within a given string.
SEG$	Extracts a substring from a given string.
STR$ or NUM$	Converts a number to a string.
VAL	Converts a string to a number.

lent of the argument. Figure 10.1 shows how the CHR$ function may be used in a LET or a PRINT statement. The number 63 is the ASCII code for the question mark character, and 77 is the ASCII code for the letter M.

The program in Fig. 10.2 can be used to print the alphabet across the screen. A loop converts the numbers from 65 to 90 to the equivalent letters of the alphabet. CHR$(65) is A and CHR$(90) is Z

The computer can also handle characters that are not displayed. For example, the "bell" character, CHR$(7), is not displayed on the screen but causes an audible "beep" at the terminal. You can demonstrate this by typing PRINT CHR$(7) in BASIC mode.

```
1000 LET A$ = CHR$(63)
1100 LET N = 35
1100 PRINT CHR$(2*N+7); A$
```

OUTPUT

M?

FIGURE 10.1 The CHR$ function used in LET and PRINT statements.

```
100 FOR I = 65 TO 90
110   PRINT CHR$(I);
120 NEXT I
130 PRINT
140 END
```

OUTPUT

ABCDEFGHIJKLMNOPQRSTUVWXYZ

FIGURE 10.2 Use of a loop to convert the numbers from 65 to 90 to the equivalent letters of the alphabet.

TABLE 10.2 The DATE$ function returns a date that depends on the value of the argument.

Argument				Date
	02	003	--->	DATE$(02003) is 03-Jan-72
	11	125	--->	DATE$(11125) is 05-May-81
	15	230	--->	DATE$(15230) is 18-Aug-85
	17	635	--->	DATE$(17365) is 31-Dec-87
	/	\		
years after 1970		day of the year		

In addition, all of the "extra" keys on the terminal keyboard have representations in terms of the ASCII code. This includes the "cancel button" or control/c character, CHR$(3); the backspace character, CHR$(8); the escape character, CHR$(27); and the delete character, CHR$(127).

The DATE$ Function

The DATE$ function returns a date as a string in the form 06-Sep-86. The date is determined using the following rules:

1. If the argument is 0, DATE$ returns the current date.

    ```
    100 PRINT "TODAY'S DATE IS "; DATE$(0)
    ```

2. If the argument is another integer, then the computer calculates a date starting with 00001 as 01-Jan-70. Other dates are calculated as shown in Table 10.2.

The EDIT$ Function

The EDIT$ function may be used to reformat a string in various ways. We will have occasion to use the two forms of the function shown in Table 10.3. The latter is used for word processing. Figure 10.3 shows how the the EDIT$ function might be used in a program. The EDIT$ function in line 110

TABLE 10.3 Two uses for the EDIT$ function.

EDIT$(A$,32)	Converts all lowercase letters in A$ into uppercase letters.
EDIT$(S$,152)	Converts the string S$ into "standard sentence" form. That is, if S$ is a string that consists of a number of words separated by spaces and/or tabs, then all of the "extra" spaces and tabs will be removed. The result will be a string with exactly one space between each word and no leading or trailing spaces.

MORE OPERATIONS WITH STRINGS

```
100 LET M$ = "Jan"
110 LET MM$ = EDIT$(M$,32)
120 PRINT MM$

200 LET IN$ = "  Note the spacing   in this   sentence. "
210 LET OUT$ = EDIT$(IN$,152)
220 PRINT OUT$
```

OUTPUT

```
JAN
Note the spacing in this sentence.
```

FIGURE 10.3 Some typical uses of the EDIT$ function to reformat a string.

```
IN$  |   Note the spacing   in this   sentence. 
```

```
OUT$ | Note the spacing in this sentence.
```

FIGURE 10.4 The storage blocks created by statements 200 and 210 of the program of Fig. 10.3. The `EDIT$` function converts the string into standard sentence form.

converts the letters "Jan" to uppercase, and the `EDIT$` function in line 210 converts the string `IN$` into standard sentence form. The storage blocks for the strings `IN$` and `OUT$` are shown in Fig. 10.4.

10.2 Building Strings Up

Strings can be combined to form longer strings by using the "+" operation. When two strings are "added" they are combined to form a longer string that contains the characters in the first string followed by the characters in the

FIGURE 10.5 String addition, or concatenation. Two strings are combined to form a longer string.

second string. The process of combining strings in this way is known as *concatenation*. Concatenation is illustrated in Fig. 10.5.

String addition is illustrated in line 300 of the example in Fig. 10.6. Note that the values of DMY$ and DAY$ are not changed when the computer forms the new string DD$. The storage blocks created by this program are illustrated in Fig. 10.7.

In the example of Fig. 10.8, a string **ALPHABET$** that contains all the letters of the alphabet is built up one letter at a time. Line 100 ensures that **ALPHABET$** starts out empty. (Strictly speaking, this is an optional step because string variables are null to begin with.) The output of Fig. 10.8 is simi-

```
100 LET   DMY$ = "18-Aug-85"
200 LET   DAY$ = "Sunday, "
300 LET   DD$ = DAY$ + DMY$
400 PRINT DD$
```

OUTPUT

```
Sunday, 18-Aug-85
```

FIGURE 10.6 A program to illustrate string addition, or concatenation.

| DAY$ | Sunday, | | DMY$ | 18-Aug-85 |

| DD$ | Sunday, 18-Aug-85 |

FIGURE 10.7 The storage blocks created by the program of Fig. 10.6.

MORE OPERATIONS WITH STRINGS

```
100 LET ALPHABET$ = ""
110 FOR I = 65 TO 90
120    LET ALPHABET$ = ALPHABET$ + CHR$(I)
130 NEXT I
140 PRINT ALPHABET$
```

OUTPUT

```
ABCDEFGHIJKLMNOPQRSTUVWXYZ
```

FIGURE 10.8 This program builds up a long string that contains all the letters of the alphabet.

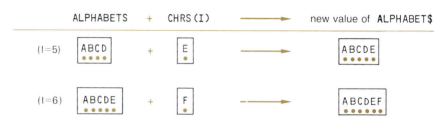

FIGURE 10.9 The fifth and sixth repetitions of statement 120 of the example in Fig. 10.8.

lar to that of Fig. 10.2, but the methods are quite different. In Fig. 10.8, each time line 120 is repeated, one letter is added to the value of **ALPHABET$**; thus building up a long storage block. Figure 10.9 depicts the fifth and sixth repetitions of line 120. Upon each repetition, the next letter of the alphabet is added to ALPHABET$ to form the new value of ALPHABET$. In Fig. 10.2, however, the output is sent directly to the terminal screen one character at a time.

10.3 Taking Strings Apart

In many applications, information is supplied in one form, but we wish to use it in another form. For example, the data on a university registration card may contain a social security number and a name, arranged as shown in Fig. 10.10. Spaces 2 through 10 are reserved for the social security number, the

10.3 TAKING STRINGS APART

```
| SSN    || LAST NAME || FIRST NAME |---other data--->
```

FIGURE 10.10 The arrangement of data on a typical registration card.

next 13 spaces are reserved for the last name, and the following 13 spaces for the first name.

The information on the card can be read into the computer using a card reader, and it can eventually be stored as the value of a string variable in a BASIC program. However, you may wish to use only part of this information; for example, the first and last name only. This requires that the string be broken down into smaller parts and rearranged.

The SEG$ Function

The SEG$ or segment function may be used to duplicate a portion of a given string to form a new string. To use the SEG$ function, you need to supply a string and two numbers as arguments. The string contains the original information to be broken down, and the numbers specify the starting and ending position for the substring to be formed. For example, if STUDAT$ is a string that contains student information arranged as shown in Fig. 10.10, then the student's last name L.NAM$ can be extracted using the statement

```
400 LET L.NAM$ = SEG$(STUDAT$,11,23)
```

This statement instructs the computer to form a new string that contains characters 11 through 23 of the string STUDAT$. This pulls out the last name and stores it in L.NAM$. The process does not change the information contained in the variable STUDAT$ (see Fig. 10.11).

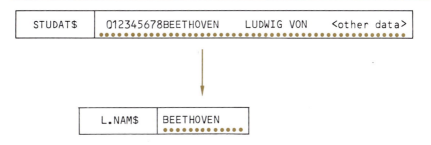

FIGURE 10.11 How the segment function creates a new string that duplicates a portion of a given string.

MORE OPERATIONS WITH STRINGS

```
100 LET D$ = DATE$(0)
110 LET M$ = SEG$(D$,4,6)
120 PRINT "It's great to be alive in the month of "; M$
130 END
```

FIGURE 10.12 How to extract the month from the string returned by the DATE$(0) function.

Figure 10.12 shows how to use the `SEG$` function to extract the month from the string returned by the `DATE$(0)` function. `DATE$(0)` returns the current date in the form `dd-Mmm-yy`, and so the month can be extracted as characters 4, 5, and 6 of the date string.

The program of Fig. 10.13 shows how the SEG$ function may be used to extract a single letter of a string. In this case, the string ALPH$ consists of the letters of the alphabet, and the program will extract letter number N using SEG$(ALPH$,N,N).

The LEN Function

The `LEN` function may be used to determine the length of the storage block for a given string. For example, the statement pair

```
100 LET D$ = "18-Aug-85"
200 LET L = LEN(D$)
```

would assign the value 9 to the variable L. Of course, the quotation marks are delimiters and are not included in the string `D$`, and hence they do not contribute to the count of the length.

The length function is often used in conjunction with the segment function to extract a portion of a string when the length of the string is not known in advance. In the program of Fig. 10.14 an input name, in this case, DAVID, is broken down one letter at a time, and each letter is stored in a subscripted string variable `B$( )`.

```
100 LET ALPH$ = "ABCDEFGHIJKLMNOPQRSTUVWXYZ"
110 INPUT 'TYPE A NUMBER BETWEEN 1 AND 26'; N
120 LET L$ = SEG$(ALPH$,N,N)
130 PRINT L$; ' IS LETTER NUMBER'; N; 'IN THE ALPHABET'
140 END
```

FIGURE 10.13 The SEG$ function in the form SEG$(ALPH$,N,N) creates a one character string starting at the Nth and ending at the Nth letter of ALPH$.

10.3 TAKING STRINGS APART

```
100  INPUT "WHAT IS YOUR FIRST NAME"; A$
200  LET L = LEN(A$)
300  FOR N = 1 TO L
400     LET B$(N) = SEG$(A$, N, N)
500  NEXT N
600  PRINT "THE LETTERS OF YOUR NAME: "
700  FOR N = 1 TO L
800     PRINT B$(N)
900  NEXT N
1000 END
```

OUTPUT

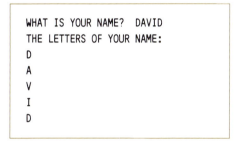

```
WHAT IS YOUR NAME?  DAVID
THE LETTERS OF YOUR NAME:
D
A
V
I
D
```

FIGURE 10.14 The name DAVID is typed in response to the INPUT query. There are 5 letters, so L gets the value 5 and line 400 assigns a letter to B$(1) through B$(5).

Because there is no way of knowing the number of letters in the name, a variable L must be used. After the name has been typed in, the value of L is determined using the LEN function. The program assumes that the name has no more than 10 letters. Statement 400 is repeated L times, once for each letter of A$. Line 400 simply picks out letter number N from the string A$ and stores it in B$(N). The FOR loop beginning at line 700 displays the letters one at a time down the left side of the output screen.

The LEN function may also be used together with the TAB function to center text. Figure 10.15 shows the number of spaces to tab in order to center an M-character string on an 80-column display.

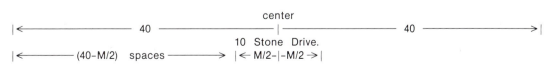

FIGURE 10.15 Centering text.

```
100 LINPUT "WHAT IS YOUR NAME"; A$
200 LINPUT "ADDRESS (NUMBER AND STREET)"; B$
300 LET N = INT(40-LEN(A$)/2)
400 PRINT TAB(N); A$
500 LET M = LEN(B$)
600 PRINT TAB( INT(40-M/2) );B$
```

FIGURE 10.16 The two-line output of this program will be centered on the 80-column display.

The program of Fig. 10.16 centers a name and street address on an 80-column display. This program will ask for the name and address of the user and determine the amount to tab in order to correctly display the information. The LINPUT statement is used because it is possible that the name or address may contain a comma.

For purposes of illustration, we have used two methods to center the text. In line 300 the number of spaces to tab over is computed and assigned to N. This value is used in the tab function of line 400. In line 500, the length of the address string is assigned to the variable M, and this is used in the TAB function on the next line.

The POS Function

The position function can be used to search through a given string for a specific letter or substring. For example, the statement

```
400 LET N = POS(A$,"E",1)
```

instructs the computer to search through the string A$ to find the letter E. The number 1 tells the computer to start the search at the first character of the string. The POS function returns a number that indicates where the letter E first appears in the string. For this search, upper- and lowercase letters are treated as different characters. A value of zero indicates that the search was not successful.

The POS function can be used to determine if a string contains a given letter or word. For example, we may wish to know if the sequence "ON" appears in a string D$. The function POS(D$,"ON",1) causes the computer to search through the string D$ for the first occurrence of the two-character sequence "ON". The value of M1 in the statement

```
500 LET M1 = POS(D$,"ON",1)
```

indicates where ON was found. If M1 is not zero then "O" is at position M1 and "N" is at position M1 + 1 in the string.

10.3 TAKING STRINGS APART

If desired, the string `D$` can be checked for the next occurrence of the character sequence `"ON"` by using the statement

```
600 LET M2 = POS(D$,"ON",M1+2)
```

This statement begins a search at position `M1 + 2`, just after the first occurrence `"ON"`. If `M2` is not zero, then `ON` appears again at positions `M2` and `M2 + 1` in the string `D$`. This process can be repeated until the POS function returns a zero, indicating that the search has failed.

In conducting a search for a given substring, the computer treats uppercase and lowercase letters as different characters. If we wish to find all occurrences of `"ON"`, counting both upper- and lowercase letters, we can use the `EDIT$` function first to convert the letters of D$ to uppercase and then the POS function as indicated above.

Example: Obtaining the First Word of a Sentence. Here we will show how an input string can be put into standard form and divided into two smaller strings, one containing the first word and the other containing the rest of the sentence (see Fig. 10.17). Here is a preliminary outline of a program to do this:

> Obtain the input string IN$.
>
> Convert the input string into a string S$ in standard sentence format.
>
> Split the sentence into two smaller strings, the first word W$ and the rest R$.

The preliminary outline is almost enough to write a program. We need to use the `LINPUT` statement to get the input string (because it may contain a comma), the `EDIT$` function to convert the string into standard sentence format, and the `SEG$` function to split the sentence. After a little thought, it can be seen that the `POS` function in the form:

```
POS(S$," ",1)
```

can be used to find the first space in `S$`, and hence the position where the string should be split. Here is a more detailed outline:

> Obtain the input string `IN$` using the `LINPUT` statement.
>
> Convert the input string into a string `S$` in standard sentence format using the `EDIT$` function.
>
> Determine the position F of the first space in `S$` and the length L of `S$`.
>
> Split the sentence into two smaller strings, the first word W$ and the rest R$ using the `SEG$` function. The first word is the segment from the first letter up to character F − 1, and the rest is the segment from character F + 1 to character L.

A program that will do this is given in Fig. 10.18.

MORE OPERATIONS WITH STRINGS

```
This    is   the   sentence or sentence    fragment.
                        ↓
This is the sentence or sentence fragment.
  ↓                    ↓
This         is the sentence or sentence fragment.
```

FIGURE 10.17 The input string is converted to standard sentence form and the first word is separated to form two new strings.

```
100 ! *****************************************
110 ! PROGRAM: G E T W O R D
120 ! *****************************************
130        !
140 ! This program separates the first word from
150 ! a sentence that you type in.
160 ! LIST OF VARIABLES:
170 !   IN$ - the input string
180 !   S$  - the input string converted to
190 !         standard sentence format
200 !   W$  - the first word of S$
210 !   R$  - the remainder of S$
220 !   F   - the position of the first space in S$
230 !   L   - the length of S$
240 !
250        ! --- obtain the input string ---
260 LINPUT "TYPE A SENTENCE"; IN$
270        ! --- convert to standard sentence ---
280 LET S$ = EDIT$(IN$,152)
290        ! --- split the sentence ----
300 LET L = LEN(S$)
310 LET F = POS(S$," ",1)
320 LET W$ = SEG$(S$,1,F-1)
330 LET R$ = SEG$(S$,F+1,L)
340        ! --- print the results --
350 PRINT S$; " SPLITS INTO:"
360 PRINT W$
370 PRINT R$
380 END
```

FIGURE 10.18 A program to separate the first word from the rest of a sentence.

10.4 Converting Numbers to Strings

The computer uses different methods to store strings and numbers (see Fig. 10.19). If you wish to store a number as the value of a string variable, it must be converted from binary to ASCII form. This section describes ways to do this.

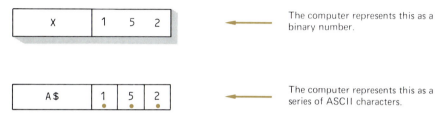

FIGURE 10.19 Numbers and strings are stored in different ways. In one case, 152 is represented as a number; in the other, it is represented in terms of the ASCII code for each of the individual characters.

The NUM$ and STR$ Functions

When the computer carries out a PRINT statement for a numeric variable, such as

    400 PRINT X

it obtains the value of X and displays this on the terminal screen as a sequence of symbols, that is, a string. The NUM$(X) function tells the computer to take the value of X and, instead of displaying the symbols, create a string that contains the characters that would have been displayed on the screen by the PRINT X statement. That is, if PRINT X would have displayed the number 152, then A$ = NUM$(X) creates the five-character string " 152 " (see Fig. 10.20).

FIGURE 10.20 The statement LET A$ = NUM$(X) creates a five-character string that represents the value of X.

MORE OPERATIONS WITH STRINGS

The STR$ function is almost exactly the same as the NUM$ function. Both functions convert a number into a numeric string. The STR$ function, however, does not add a space either at the end of a string or at the beginning of a string created from a positive number (see Fig. 10.21).

The FORMAT$ Function

The FORMAT$ function also converts a number into a string but uses a prescribed method of conversion. For example, you can tell the computer to convert the number 0032.3000 into a string using "dollars-and-cents" format. In this case the computer would create the string "$32.30".

In order to use the FORMAT$ function, you must supply the number to be converted together with a *format string* that provides instructions for conversion. The format string uses the pound sign (#), the double dollar sign ($$), and other special symbols to specify the exact form of the string to be created.

For example, a format string like "$$###.##" would be used for dollars-and-cents format; whereas the format string "####.###" tells the computer to create a storage block for a string that has eight characters: four spaces or digits followed by a decimal point and three digits. When converting a number to a specified format, the computer will add the required number of spaces and/or a dollar sign at the beginning and will either round off or add zeros at the end (see Fig. 10.22).

Note: If the number to be converted is too large or too small for the format you have specified, your format instructions will be ignored and a string will be created following the usual rules for printing numbers. When this happens, the computer will also print a percent sign (%) in front of the number as a warning symbol to indicate that your format instructions have not been used.

```
1400 LET Y = 23.854293
1500 LET BB$ = STR$(Y)
1600 LET CC$ = NUM$(0032.3000)
```

| BB$ | 23.8543 |

| CC$ | 32.3 |

FIGURE 10.21 The use of the STR$ and the NUM$ functions to create strings from numbers. The value of Y has been rounded to six digits and the resulting number has been used to produce the storage block for BB$. The leading and trailing zeros of (0032.3000) have been ignored in creating the storage block for CC$.

10.4 CONVERTING NUMBERS TO STRINGS

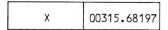

```
400 LET ZZ$ = FORMAT$( X , "####.###" )
500 LET WW$ = FORMAT$( X , "$$###.##" )
```

FIGURE 10.22 The FORMAT$ function will set up a storage block as shown, based on the format strings "####.###" and "$$###.##". The value of X will be rounded, or zeros will be added at the end, to make it fit into the storage block. If X has the value shown, then the leading zeros are dropped, a space and/or a dollar sign is inserted at the beginning, and the number is rounded.

TABLE 10.4 Format strings for use in the FORMAT$ statement to convert and display money amounts.

#####.##	This produces a string with two digits after the decimal point.
$$####.##	This puts a dollar sign in front of the string.
$$####.##−	This places the negative sign at the end of a negative number.

The FORMAT$ function is often used when dealing with monetary calculations. In this situation, numbers are normally displayed with two digits after the decimal point (see Table 10.4).

The program of Fig. 10.23 calculates a sales tax of 5.5% and adds it to the 678.85 price of a new coat. The FORMAT$ statement in line 700 converts TOT.COST, 716.18675, into a string that shows the cost rounded to the nearest cent. The result in Fig. 10.23 could have been printed with a dollar sign in front of it by using a format string that starts with the double dollar sign symbol. That is, if line 500 were changed to

```
500 LET AA$ = "$$#####.##"
```

then TOT.COST would have been printed as $716.19.

Review: Converting Numbers to Strings

- The FORMAT$, NUM$, and STR$ functions may be used to convert a number to a string that represents the value of the number.

MORE OPERATIONS WITH STRINGS

```
100 READ  PRICE.OF.COAT
200 PRINT "THE PRICE OF THE COAT IS "; PRICE.OF.COAT
300 LET TAX = PRICE.OF.COAT * .055
400 LET TOT.COST = PRICE.OF.COAT + TAX
500 LET AA$ = "######.##"
600 PRINT "THE TOTAL COST OF THE COAT IS " ;
700 PRINT FORMAT$(TOT.COST,AA$)
800 DATA 678.85
900 END
```

OUTPUT

```
THE PRICE OF THE COAT IS  678.85
THE TOTAL COST OF THE COAT IS     716.19
```

FIGURE 10.23 The use of the FORMAT$ function to round and display the results of a monetary calculation.

- NUM$ and STR$ create strings that look like the number that would be displayed by a PRINT statement. STR$ does not add leading or trailing spaces; NUM$ does.
- The FORMAT$ function converts a number to a string using rules that you specify in a special format string. Format strings such as "###.##", "$$###.##", or "$$##.##-" are used to convert money amounts.

10.5 Converting a String to a Number

A string that looks like a number is called a *numeric string*. Even though a numeric string looks like a number when displayed, it is actually stored as a series of ASCII characters and therefore cannot be used directly for

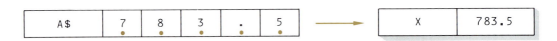

FIGURE 10.24 The conversion that results when the statement X = VAL(A$) is carried out.

10.5 CONVERTING A STRING TO A NUMBER

arithmetic calculations. Use the VAL function to convert a numeric string to a number (see Fig. 10.24).

The argument of the VAL function must be a string that looks like a number. An extra character in the string, such as a dollar sign, will cause an error message when the computer attempts to carry out the conversion.

The program of Fig. 10.25 illustrates some features of the VAL function. In line 120, the numeric string "45.6" is converted to a number, and then the number is added to 23.36 to determine the value of X. In line 130, the strings AB$ and "32" are concatenated, and the result is converted to a number.

Example: Rounding a Number. We have already seen that the FORMAT$ function can be used to convert a number to a string with a specified format. When the computer does this conversion, the number is rounded, if necessary, so that it has the form prescribed by the format string. For example, the statement

```
300 LET A$ = FORMAT$(X, "####")
```

will create a string from the number obtained by rounding X to the nearest four-digit integer. If the rounded numeric string is to be used in a calculation, it can then be converted to a number using the VAL function.

Rounding is often used in monetary calculations to avoid dealing with fractions of a cent. In the following statement, I is rounded to the nearest cent to obtain the new value of I.

```
400 LET I = VAL(FORMAT$(I,"#####.##"))
```

This method of rounding will be used in the INTR program of Fig. 10.39.

```
100 LET AA$ = "45.6"
110 LET AB$ = "63"
120 LET X = 23.36 + VAL(AA$)
130 LET N = VAL(AB$ + "32" )
140 PRINT X, N
```

▼ OUTPUT

68.96	6332

FIGURE 10.25 An illustration of some uses of the VAL function.

MORE OPERATIONS WITH STRINGS

10.6 The PRINT USING Statement

The PRINT USING statement allows you to specify the arrangement of an entire line of output. It is especially useful for printing lists or tables that have text or numbers lined up in vertical columns. Figure 10.26 shows a typical application. Each line of output has the same form; the stock name and price changes from line to line. The top line shows the format string that specifies the arrangement of the output.

A special format string is used with PRINT USING to specify the arrangement of the output. The format string contains the text that is to be displayed with each line of output together with special symbols that designate spots for text or numbers that will change from line to line.

In the format string at the top of Fig. 10.26, the special symbol 'LLL reserves a place in the output for a string. The L denotes left justification, but we can think of each L as simply reserving a spot for printing a letter. Similarly, each # reserves a spot for a digit of a number.

The program statements in Fig. 10.27 will produce the output shown in the lower part of Fig. 10.26. Notice that PRINT USING is followed by the string variable F$, which determines the arrangement of the output. This particular format string contains two *fields* ('LLL and ###.##) that are to be

```
"STOCK: 'LLL    PRICE: ###.##"     ←    format string

 STOCK: IBM    PRICE: 127.00
 STOCK: ATT    PRICE:  57.50       ←    typical output
 STOCK: GTE    PRICE:  89.75
        .             .
        .             .
        .             .
```

FIGURE 10.26 A situation in which the PRINT USING statement is useful.

```
100 LET F$ = " STOCK: 'LLL    PRICE: ###.## "
200 PRINT USING F$, "IBM" , 127
300 PRINT USING F$, "ATT" , 57.5
400 PRINT USING F$, "GTE" , 89.75
```

FIGURE 10.27

10.6 THE PRINT USING STATEMENT

FIGURE 10.28 A typical PRINT USING statement. The format string F$ provides the arrangement of the output; the rest of the statement provides the information required to fill in the blanks.

filled in with a string and a number. The last part of the PRINT USING statement supplies the information necessary to fill in these fields. This is illustrated in the diagram of Fig. 10.28.

One PRINT USING statement can generate several lines of output. PRINT USING F$, will keep producing output until the rest of the information in that statement has been used up. For example, the statement

```
200 PRINT USING F$,  "IBM",127,  "ATT",  57.5
```

will produce two lines of output. The program of Fig. 10.29 will produce the same three-line output as will the program of Fig. 10.27.

More about the PRINT USING Statement

The rest of this section contains detailed information about the PRINT USING statement. You may wish to skip it now and come back to it later.

```
100 LET F$ = " STOCK: 'LLL    PRICE: ###.## "
200 PRINT USING F$, "IBM",127, "ATT",57.5, "GTE",89.75
```

OUTPUT

```
STOCK: IBM     PRICE: 127.00
STOCK: ATT     PRICE:  57.50
STOCK: GTE     PRICE:  89.75
```

FIGURE 10.29

MORE OPERATIONS WITH STRINGS

TABLE 10.5 Special symbols for use in the format string to specify the form of numerical output.

#	Reserves a place for a digit.
$$	Reserves a place for a dollar sign and one digit.
.	Indicates the position of the decimal point in a number.
-	Specifies the use of a trailing minus sign and reserves a place for it.
,	Specifies that large numbers be printed with commas to separate the digits in front of the decimal point.

The PRINT USING statement has the general form:

PRINT USING ⟨format string⟩ , ⟨info.⟩ , ⟨info.⟩,...

The ⟨format string⟩ specifies how the printed output is to be arranged. The last part of the PRINT USING statement contains information items ⟨info.⟩, separated by commas. Each piece of information is a number or string that is to be inserted in the output at the appropriate spot.

Reserving Places for Numbers. Table 10.5 shows the special symbols that are used in the format string to specify the arrangement and form of the numbers that appear in the output. The symbols are similar to those used in the FORMAT$ function.

Pound signs (#) are used in the format string to reserve places for printing numbers. A number is rounded or padded to fit the space reserved for it (see Fig. 10.30). The rules are similar to those used in the FORMAT$ function discussed earlier.

If the format string begins with the double dollar sign ($$), the number will be printed with a dollar sign immediately in front of it. The double dollar sign reserves one place for a dollar sign and one place for a digit (see Fig. 10.31).

---

100 PRINT USING "###.#" , 23 , 123.689 , 9.996

▼OUTPUT
```
  23.0
 123.7
  10.0
```

FIGURE 10.30

2000 PRINT USING "$$###.##" , 1523.4689 , 18.2

▼OUTPUT
```
$1523.47
  $18.20
```

FIGURE 10.31

10.6 THE PRINT USING STATEMENT

```
3200 PRINT USING "$$##.##-" , -234.788
```

▼OUTPUT

```
$234.79-
```

FIGURE 10.32

```
4300 PRINT USING "#####,##.##" , 21000.00
```

▼OUTPUT

```
21,000.00
```

FIGURE 10.33

Negative numbers may be printed with the minus sign at the end of the number instead of the beginning. Negative dollar amounts must be printed this way because the dollar sign is printed where the negative sign would normally go (see Fig. 10.32).

Finally, numbers can be printed with commas separating the digits into groups of three: 21,000.00 instead of 21000.00. You can simply include a comma anywhere in the format string (see Fig. 10.33).

Reserving Places for Strings. The symbols used to reserve places for a string in the output of a PRINT USING statement are summarized in Table 10.6. The simplest way to reserve a place for a string is to use a single quote (') followed by one or more Ls. The string is printed starting at the single quote. For example, " 'LLLL " reserves five spaces for printing a string. A string with less than five characters will be left justified in the field; a string with more than five characters will be cut off after the first five characters.

A single quote followed by one or more Rs reserves a field in which the string is printed right justified in the space reserved for it. In the example of Fig. 10.34, the format string F$ reserves two string fields, one left justified and one right justified. Four strings are provided, and so two lines of output will be produced as shown.

TABLE 10.6 Symbols used to reserve places for a string field in a PRINT USING format string.

'	Begins a string field and reserves a place for one character. This single-quote symbol must be followed by one of the symbols below.
L	Specifies a string field in which characters are printed starting at the left of the field (left justified).
R	Specifies a string field in which characters are printed ending at the right edge of the field (right justified).
C	Specifies a string field in which characters are centered in the field.

MORE OPERATIONS WITH STRINGS

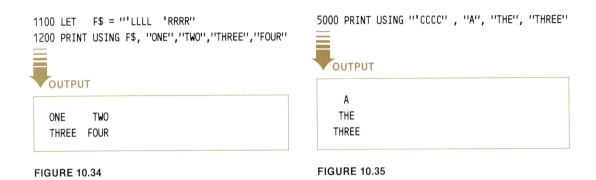

```
1100 LET    F$ = "'LLLL  'RRRR"
1200 PRINT USING F$, "ONE","TWO","THREE","FOUR"
```

▼ OUTPUT

```
ONE     TWO
THREE   FOUR
```

FIGURE 10.34

```
5000 PRINT USING "'CCCC" , "A", "THE", "THREE"
```

▼ OUTPUT

```
  A
 THE
THREE
```

FIGURE 10.35

Strings can also be centered in a field. In this case, the format string consists of a single quote followed by one or more Cs (see Fig. 10.35).

Printing a message along with strings and numbers. The PRINT USING statement allows a format string to contain one or more of the above types of numeric and string fields together with any other strings. Part of the format string represents text that is to be reproduced literally, and part of the string can reserve a place for a string or a number.

For example, we may wish to print out an invoice in the form:

```
ITEM: COAT     QUANTITY: 2    PRICE: $23.50    TOTAL: $47.00
ITEM: HAT      QUANTITY: 3    PRICE:  $4.25    TOTAL: $12.75
ITEM: SHIRT    QUANTITY: 1    PRICE: $17.89    TOTAL: $17.89
```

This can be done using the format string

```
ITEM: 'LLLLLL QUANTITY:##   PRICE:$$###.##   TOTAL:$$####.##
```

Part of this format string uses special symbols, like `'LLLLLL` or `##`, to reserve places for strings or numbers. The rest of the string is reproduced literally.

In a PRINT USING statement, this format string instructs the computer to produce an output of the form represented in Fig. 10.36. When using this format, a string and three numbers are required for each line of output. In this case, PRINT USING requires a total of five pieces of information: the format string, a string representing the ITEM, and three numbers representing QUANTITY, PRICE, and TOTAL.

The program of Fig. 10.37 shows the use of this PRINT USING statement to produce the desired output. Each time that the PRINT USING

```
ITEM: ....... QUANTITY: ..   PRICE: ...$....   TOTAL: .....$..
```

FIGURE 10.36

10.6 THE PRINT USING STATEMENT

```
100 LET F$ = "ITEM: 'LLLLLL  QUANTITY:##   PRICE:$$###.##  "&
            +"  TOTAL:$$####.##"
200 LET A$ = "COAT"
300 LET Q = 2
400 LET P = 23.50
500 LET B$ = "HAT"
600 PRINT USING F$ , A$ , Q , P , Q*P
700 PRINT USING F$ , B$ , 3 , 4.25 , 3*4.25
800 PRINT USING F$ , "SHIRT" , 1 , 17.89 , 17.89
```

OUTPUT

ITEM: COAT	QUANTITY: 2	PRICE: $23.50	TOTAL: $47.00
ITEM: HAT	QUANTITY: 3	PRICE: $4.25	TOTAL: $12.75
ITEM: SHIRT	QUANTITY: 1	PRICE: $17.89	TOTAL: $17.89

FIGURE 10.37

statement is executed, the string F$ is used to format the output with the information supplied in the rest of the statement.

Example: Calculating Compound Interest

Assume that you deposit $1000.00 at a bank that pays interest at 15 percent compounded monthly. The bank pays interest monthly using the formula

```
Interest-payment = Principal * 15 * 0.01 / 12.
```

The annual interest rate of 15 percent is converted to a decimal amount (0.15 = 15 * 0.01) and then converted to a monthly decimal amount (0.01250 = 0.15/12). Therefore, the interest payment for the first month would be $12.50, and the new principal at the beginning of the second month would be $1012.50.

The same process would be repeated for each month. Here is an outline of an algorithm to display a monthly table:

Repeat the following steps for each month:

- Use the current value of the principal P and compute the interest using I = P * (Rate) * 0.01/12.
- Display the current principal and interest payment.
- Compute the new principal using P = P + I.

MORE OPERATIONS WITH STRINGS

```
1000 !*********************************************
1010 !PROGRAM: I N T R A M T
1020 !*********************************************
1030         !
2000 INPUT "PRINCIPAL AMOUNT"; P
2100 INPUT "ANNUAL INTEREST RATE (AS A PERCENT)"; R
2600         !--- set up header and format string ---
2700 PRINT "MONTH        PRINCIPAL       INTEREST "
2800 LET F$=" ##          $$####.##      $$###.## "
3000         !--- compute actual interest ----
3300 FOR N = 1 TO 12
3400    LET I = P * R * .01 / 12
3500         !--- display in dollar format by rounding ---
3600    PRINT USING F$, N , P , I
3700    LET P = P + I
3800 NEXT N
4000 END
```

FIGURE 10.38

Using this calculation, the interest at the end of the second month would be $12.65625. The bank can handle the payment of this interest in at least three ways: It can credit your account with the actual amount of $12.65625; it can round this amount to the nearest cent and credit your account with $12.66; or it can truncate the fractional cents and pay $12.65. (Throwing out digits at the end of a number is called truncation.)

The actual method used may make a difference of only a penny or two at the end of a year. Nevertheless, the methods are different and would be programmed differently. Figure 10.38 shows a program that uses the actual interest payment to compute the new value of the principal. Even though the actual value of the interest payment is used in the calculation, rounded values of the principal and interest amounts are displayed in dollars-and-cents format. This is done using a format string in a PRINT USING statement.

Another version of this program, shown in Fig. 10.39, uses the VAL and FORMAT$ functions to round the monthly interest to the nearest cent before adding it to the principal. The format string B$ is used to display the money amounts with a dollar sign, and the interest is rounded to the nearest cent using A$. It is necessary to use the format string A$ rather than B$ for rounding because the VAL function in line 3700 will not accept a string that contains a dollar sign.

When this program is RUN, values of P and R are obtained from the user and a table of monthly principal and interest amounts is shown at the terminal. A typical run is shown at the bottom of Fig. 10.39.

```
1000 !****************************************************
1100 !   PROGRAM NAME: I N T R
1200 !****************************************************
1300        !
1400        ! LIST OF VARIABLES:
1500        !   P- PRINCIPAL AMOUNT
1600        !   R- ANNUAL INTEREST RATE
1700        !   I- MONTHLY INTEREST
1800        !   A$, B$ - FORMAT STRINGS
1850        !
1860    LET A$ = "######.##"
1870    LET B$ = "$$#####.##"
1900        !--- get values of p and r ---------------
2000    INPUT "PRINCIPAL AMOUNT"; P
2100    INPUT "ANNUAL INTEREST RATE (AS A PERCENT)"; R
2600        !--- set up header --------------------
2700    PRINT "MONTH         PRINCIPAL        INTEREST "
3000        !--- compute interest to nearest cent
3300    FOR N = 1 TO 12
3400      LET I = P * R * .01 / 12
3500      PRINT   N , FORMAT$(P,B$) , FORMAT$(I,B$)
3700      LET P = P + VAL(FORMAT$(I,A$))
3800    NEXT N
4000    END
```

OUTPUT

```
PRINCIPAL? 1000
ANNUAL INTEREST RATE? 15

MONTH        PRINCIPAL        INTEREST
1            $1000.00         $12.50
2            $1012.50         $12.66
3            $1025.16         $12.81
4            $1037.97         $12.97
5            $1050.94         $13.14
6            $1064.08         $13.30
7            $1077.38         $13.47
8            $1090.85         $13.64
9            $1104.49         $13.81
10           $1118.30         $13.98
11           $1132.28         $14.15
12           $1146.43         $14.33

Ready
```

FIGURE 10.39

MORE OPERATIONS WITH STRINGS

Example: A Julian Date Conversion Function

The usual method of describing a date in terms of the day and the month is not convenient for some applications. For example, it is difficult to determine the number of days between say, May 5 and September 23. If, however, the days of the year are numbered starting with 1 for January 1 up to 365 for December 31, (or to 366 on a leap year), then the number assigned to each day is its Julian date. Because Julian dates are consecutive, it is easy to deal with problems like finding the number of days until the end of the year.

For this example, we will assume that it is a leap year and the Julian dates run from 1 to 366. In this way all of the possible dates can be represented. Here is the statement of the problem:

■ Write a function definition to convert a date into a Julian date. The function should have the DAY and the MONTH$ as the inputs and return a Julian date from 1 to 366 that represents the date.

If you were doing this as an exercise, you might need to do some calendar research to determine the Julian dates of the last days of each month. The information is contained in the following table:

LAST DAY OF	IS DAY NUMBER
JANUARY	31
FEBRUARY	60 (on a leap year)
MARCH	91
APRIL	121
MAY	152
JUNE	182
JULY	213
AUGUST	244
SEPTEMBER	274
OCTOBER	305
NOVEMBER	335
DECEMBER	366

This information should give you a clue about a method to determine the Julian date. For example, if the last day of May is day 152, then June 1 is day 153, June 2 is day 154, and so on. Therefore, if the month is June, the Julian date is obtained by adding 152 to the day of the month. A similar rule applies to other months.

The function definition of Fig. 10.40 uses the SELECT statement to calculate the Julian date. The EDIT$ function and the SEG$ function have been used to separate the first three letters of the month and convert them to uppercase. Thus the function will work correctly if the month is given in any form, such as January, JUNE, or Aug.

```
1000 DEF FNJULIAN(DAY, MONTH$)
1010    MON$ = EDIT$(SEG$(MONTH$,1,3) , 32)
1100    SELECT MON$
           CASE = "JAN"
               FNJULIAN = DAY
           CASE = "FEB"
               FNJULIAN = DAY + 31
           CASE = "MAR"
               FNJULIAN = DAY + 60
           CASE = "APR"
               FNJULIAN = DAY + 91
           CASE = "MAY"
               FNJULIAN = DAY + 121
           CASE = "JUN"
               FNJULIAN = DAY + 152
           CASE = "JUL"
               FNJULIAN = DAY + 182
           CASE = "AUG"
               FNJULIAN = DAY + 213
           CASE = "SEP"
               FNJULIAN = DAY + 244
           CASE = "OCT"
               FNJULIAN = DAY + 274
           CASE = "NOV"
               FNJULIAN = DAY + 305
           CASE = "DEC"
               FNJULIAN = DAY + 335
           CASE ELSE
               FNJULIAN = -1
        END SELECT
1200 END DEF
```

FIGURE 10.40 A function to convert a standard date to a Julian date.

Example: The Hangman Game

Hangman is a game in which a word is to be guessed. The computer will select a word and display dashes to represent the letters of the word. The user is asked to guess a letter; if the letter is in the word, the appropriate dash is replaced by the letter. Figure 10.41 illustrates the result of a correct guess of the letter A in the word MARKET. The word to be guessed (MARKET) has been broken down and stored in the string array W$. The array CW$ keeps

MORE OPERATIONS WITH STRINGS

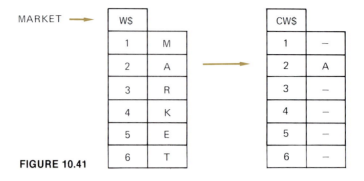

FIGURE 10.41

track of the correct guesses. If a correct guess is made, the dash is replaced by the letter as shown. The computer keeps track of how many incorrect guesses have been made and ends the game at the tenth incorrect guess unless the word is completed sooner.

Here is an outline of the program:

> Get a word at random from the data list.
>
> Break the word down letter by letter, and store each letter in the string array W$. Store dashes in the string array CW$.
>
> Repeat the following steps until 10 incorrect guesses have been made:
>
> - Display the contents of the current word array CW$.
> - Get a one-letter guess and see if the letter is in the word; if so, replace the appropriate dashes; if not, count it as an incorrect guess.
> - Check to see if the correct word has been guessed; if so print a message and end the game.
> - Print a message indicating whether the guess is correct or not. If the guess is not correct, record and display the incorrect guesses.
> - See if the user is close to being hung (nine guesses) and print a warning message.
> - Print the word showing the correct letters guessed and get another guess.

The technique outlined in Fig. 6.9 is used to get a word at random from the data list of 50 words:

> Restore the pointer to the top of the list.
>
> Get a random integer M between 1 and 50.
>
> Repeat M times: Read a word from the data list into the variable GUESSWORD$.

10.6 THE PRINT USING STATEMENT

The main logic of the program is contained in lines 580–620:

```
580 CORRECT-LETTER = NO
585 CORRECT-WORD = YES
590 FOR I = 1 TO L
600    IF GUESS$=W$(I)
          THEN
             CW$(I)=W$(I)
             CORRECT-LETTER = YES
610    IF CW$(I)="-" THEN CORRECT-WORD = NO
620 NEXT I
```

These lines check to see whether the guess is correct and whether the correct word has been guessed. The variables YES and NO have values 1 and 0, respectively.

The guess GUESS$ is incorrect unless it matches at least one value of W$(I). Line 600 checks this. If GUESS$ matches a letter in the word W$(I) then the dash in CW$(I) is replaced by the correct letter and CORRECT-LETTER is set equal to YES (1) to indicate that GUESS$ was a correct guess.

The word is the correct word if there are no dashes left after the current letter has been substituted. This is checked in line 610: if there is at least one dash "-", then the correct word has not been guessed, and so CORRECT-WORD is set equal to NO (0) to indicate this.

The program for Hangman appears in Fig. 10.42.

FIGURE 10.42

```
100 !*****************************************************
110 !PROGRAM NAME: H A N G M A N
120 !*****************************************************
130       !LIST OF VARIABLES:
140       !  GUESSWORD$ - WORD TO BE GUESSED
150       !  L - LENGTH OF THE WORD
160       !  CORRECT-WORD - INDICATES IF WORD GUESSED
170       !  CORRECT-LETTER - IF CORRECT LETTER GUESSED
180       !  GUESS$ - CURRENT LETTER GUESS
190       !  WRONG$ - WRONG LETTERS GUESSED PREVIOUSLY
200       !  BAD-GUESSES - NUMBER OF INCORRECT GUESSES
210       !  M, I - LOOP VARIABLES
220       !
230       !
240       !LIST OF ARRAYS:
250       !  W$ - THE LETTERS OF THE WORD TO BE GUESSED
260       !  CW$ - THE CURRENT LETTERS GUESSED
```

(Continued)

FIGURE 10.42 Continued

```
270          !
280          !
290 DECLARE REAL CONSTANT YES=1, NO=0
300          !
310          ! --- get a word at random from the data ----
320 RANDOMIZE
330 LET M = INT( 50*RND ) + 1
340 FOR I = 1 TO M
350   READ GUESSWORD$
360 NEXT I
370          ! --- put letters into W$ and initialize CW$
380 LET L = LEN(GUESSWORD$)
390 FOR I = 1 TO L
400   LET W$(I) = SEG$(GUESSWORD$,I,I)
410   LET CW$(I) ="-"
420 NEXT I
430          ! -- initialize variables ------------
440 BAD_GUESSES=0
450 WRONG$=""
460          !
470 WHILE  (BAD_GUESSES < 10)
480          ! --- print the current correct guesses ---
490   PRINT \ PRINT "CURRENT WORD: ";
500   FOR I = 1 TO L
510     PRINT CW$(I);
520   NEXT I
530   PRINT \ PRINT
540          !--- get a guess --------------------
550   INPUT "GUESS ";GUESS$
560   IF LEN(GUESS$)<>1
         THEN
            PRINT "GUESS ONLY ONE LETTER"
            GOTO 550
570          !--- check to see if any letters match ---
580   CORRECT_LETTER = NO
585   CORRECT_WORD = YES
590   FOR I = 1 TO L
600     IF GUESS$=W$(I)
           THEN
              CW$(I)=W$(I)
              CORRECT_LETTER = YES
610     IF CW$(I)="-" THEN CORRECT_WORD = NO
620   NEXT I
```

```
630             !--- count and record incorrect guesses ---
640    IF CORRECT-LETTER = NO
          THEN
             BAD-GUESSES = BAD-GUESSES + 1
             WRONG$ = WRONG$ + GUESS$ + " "
650             !---exit loop if word has been guessed ---
660    IF CORRECT-WORD = YES THEN 700
670    IF CORRECT-LETTER = YES
          THEN
              PRINT "THAT WAS A CORRECT GUESS"
          ELSE
              PRINT "THAT WAS AN INCORRECT GUESS"
              PRINT "HERE IS A LIST OF YOUR ";&
              BAD-GUESSES;" INCORRECT GUESSES: ";WRONG$
680    IF BAD-GUESSES = 9
          THEN
              PRINT "CAREFUL, ONE MORE INCORRECT "; &
                    "GUESS AND YOU ARE 'HUNG' "
690 NEXT
700          !
710          !--- see if hung -----------
720 IF BAD-GUESSES >= 10
          THEN
              PRINT "SORRY YOU ARE 'HUNG' "
              PRINT "THE CORRECT WORD WAS "; GUESSWORD$
730          !
740          !--- see if correct word guessed --------
750 IF CORRECT-WORD = YES
          THEN
              PRINT "RIGHT! ";GUESSWORD$;" IS THE WORD"
760          !
770 PRINT \ PRINT
780 INPUT "DO YOU WANT TO PLAY AGAIN (Y/N)";D$
790 IF D$="Y" OR D$="y" THEN RESTORE \ GOTO 330
800 PRINT "HOPE YOU ENJOYED THE GAME"
810          !
820 DATA MACHETE,MAGAZINE,MAFIA,MAINSAIL,MALEVOLENT
830 DATA MARKET,MARLINE,MATERIAL,MEAGER,MATURE,MECHANISM
840 DATA MEDICATION,MERCURY,METABOLISM,MINORITY,MOLASSES
850 DATA MORALISTIC,MUMMIFY,NARCOTIC,NATURAL,NAUGHTY
860 DATA NOVICE,NOXIOUS,OBJECTIVE,OCCLUSION,OCTAVE,ORGANISM
870 DATA OVERTONE,PAYLOAD,PESTILENCE,POISON,PRESSURE
880 DATA PROPONENT,QUAHAUG,RADIATION,RELATIVE,RELEGATE
890 DATA REMUNERATE,RESEARCH,RHYTHM,ROBUST,SCRUTINIZE
900 DATA FINAGLE,EXPLICATE,EXPLICIT,DECONTROL
910 DATA MARGINAL,MELIORATE,MONKEY,NEGATIVE,PRIMARY
920 END
```

MORE OPERATIONS WITH STRINGS

10.7 Exercises

10.1 Analyze the following program to determine the output. Is the "+" operation used the same way in lines 120 and 130? Test your conclusion by running the program.

```
100 LET AA$ = "45.6"
110 LET AB$ = "63"
120 LET XX = VAL( AB$ + AA$ )
130 LET YY = VAL( AB$ ) + VAL( AA$ )
140 PRINT XX, YY
150 END
```

10.2 Write a program to take a word and convert it to simplified "pig latin." This is done by taking the first letter of the word and moving it to the end of the word and then adding "ay." (For example, the word "number" is converted to "umbernay.") Your program should ask the user to type in a word and then display the translated word.

10.3 Write a program to translate from pig latin to English. Your program should contain the strings OMPUTERSCAY, RANSLATETAY and ORDSWAY in a DATA statement and should print a list of the translated words.

10.4 Write a program to display words backward. Your program should ask for a word and then display the word spelled out in reverse order. For example, your program should convert the word NOWHERE to EREHWON.

10.5 Write a program to compute the total cost of a new automobile. The total cost includes the base price, destination charges of $175.00, and a 3.5 percent (0.035) excise tax on the total amount. Your program should ask for the base price and the make of the car and print out the results in the form:

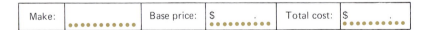

The total cost should be rounded to the nearest cent. Test your program using base prices of $7250.00 for a Rabbit and $10,239.90 for a Pontiac.

10.6 Enter and run the INTRAMT program of Fig. 10.38. Use a principal amount of $1000.00 and an interest rate of 15 percent. Is the final principal amount the same as that obtained from the INTR program of Fig. 10.39? Complete the program by adding a list of variables and comment statements.

10.7 Show that the calculation X=INT(X*100)/100 will result in the removal or truncation of all digits beyond two after the decimal point. Use this method to modify the INTR or the INTRAMT program to compute the interest by ignoring fractional cents. Your program should display a table showing the monthly interest and principal in dollars-and-cents format. Run the program with $1000.00 at 15 percent to compare the end result with that obtained in the INTR program.

10.8 The function FNJULIAN of Fig. 10.40 converts a date expressed as a day and month into the Julian date for a leap year. The DATE$ function can be used to convert a Julian date (for 1970) into a day, month, and year. Write a program to compare the two conversions. Your program should use the FNJULIAN function to convert a day and month into a Julian date and the DATE$ function to convert that Julian date back into a day, month format. (Use the SEG$ function to get rid of the year part of the date string.)

Unfortunately, 1970 was not a leap year, and so the two conversions will not always agree. Modify the program so that the conversions are consistent. *Hint:* 1972 was a leap year, so consider the date generated by DATE$(2000+FNJULIAN(D,M$)).

10.9 The GETWORD program of Fig. 10.18 separates the first word W$ from a string S$ in standard sentence format (see also Fig. 5.14). What happens if S$ consists of a single word?

Revise the program so that a single-word input is transferred to W$. That is, if S$ consists of a single word, then the word is transferred to W$ and R$ ends up blank. The program should work the same as before for other inputs.

10.10 Devise an algorithm to go through an array W$( ) of 10 words and determine the subscript of the longest word in the list. Modify the selection-sort algorithm so that the words are rearranged with the longest word first and the shortest word last. Write a program to test the correctness your algorithm.

Using Standard Data Files

11

Up to now, all of the information used in our program examples has been contained in DATA statements or typed by the user in response to INPUT queries. In some cases, however, information may already have been stored in a data file and is available for use in a program.

This chapter deals with the methods used to retrieve information from a data file and use it in a program and, conversely, the methods used to store information, such as the result of a calculation, in a data file for future use. That is, we will be discussing how data can be moved between a disk file and a program.

The files discussed here are called *terminal format* files. Terminal format files are easy to visualize because information is stored in the file exactly as it would be written on the terminal screen. In addition, the contents of a terminal format data file can be examined using the DCL TYPE command.

USING STANDARD DATA FILES

11.1 Writing Output to a Data File

Before information can be transferred from a program to a data file, the file name must be specified in the program and an output channel established. This is done using the OPEN statement:

```
100 OPEN "TYPICAL.DAT" FOR OUTPUT AS FILE #3
```

In this example, the data file TYPICAL is opened on channel 3. Notice that the file name must be enclosed in quotes and that the word OUTPUT refers to output *from the program*, not output from the data file.

Once a file has been opened and a channel assigned, information can be transferred to the file using a variation of the PRINT statement that includes the channel number. A PRINT statement with a channel number sends output to the file that is open on that channel (see Fig. 11.1). For example, the statements

```
200 LET X = 12
300 PRINT #3, "X = "; X
```

will cause the line

```
X =    12
```

to be printed in the file `TYPICAL.DAT`.

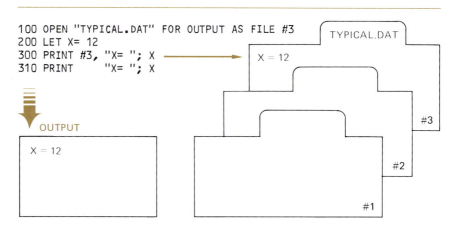

FIGURE 11.1 The PRINT statement sends output to the terminal screen. The PRINT #3 statement, on the other hand, sends output to the data file that has been opened on channel 3.

11.1 WRITING OUTPUT TO A DATA FILE

```
10  ! *********************************************
20  ! PROGRAM: S R O O T
30  ! *********************************************
40           !
50  OPEN "SROOT.DAT" FOR OUTPUT AS FILE #1
100 FOR N = 1 TO 100
200    PRINT     N, SQR(N)
250    PRINT #1, N, SQR(N)
300 NEXT N
350 CLOSE #1
400 END
```

FIGURE 11.2 Lines 50, 250, and 350 will produce a table in the file SROOT.DAT that is identical to the one displayed at the terminal when the program is run.

The CLOSE statement is used when there is no further need for the file:

```
9000 CLOSE #3
```

After you run a program that sends output to a data file, a permanent copy of the file is retained in disk memory.

The program of Fig. 11.2 produces a file SROOT.DAT that contains a square root table similar to the one produced in Fig. 5.2. When this program is RUN, a new data file called SROOT.DAT is opened and assigned to channel 1 (see line 50). Lines 200 and 250 are repeated 100 times to create the square root tables. Each time line 200 is executed, the value of N and its square root is printed at the terminal. When line 250 is executed, an identical line is added to the file SROOT.DAT. When the program is finished, the data file is closed and the program ends. The data file will contain a permanent copy of the same square root table that was printed at the terminal.

After the program is run, the contents of the data file can be examined using the DCL TYPE command:

```
$TYPE SROOT.DAT
```

This will produce a display similar to the output seen when the program was run.

If a line sent to a data file is more than 72 characters in length, it may be split into two or more lines containing 72 characters or less. To avoid this problem, the right margin of the file may be set at column 80 or 132 by using the MARGIN statement:

```
120 MARGIN #1, 132
```

USING STANDARD DATA FILES

Other values may be used for the right margin, but 80 and 132 are the most common because a standard video terminal displays 80 columns and a standard high-speed printer can print 132 columns.

Review: Writing Data to a File

Use the open statement in the form:

```
OPEN "<filename.type>" FOR OUTPUT AS FILE #<chnl>
```

- The file specification is enclosed in quotes.
- A new (blank) file is always created with a different version number if necessary.
- The word OUTPUT refers to program output.
- The channel number ⟨chnl⟩ can be any integer from 1 to 99.
- More than one file may be open at a time provided different channel numbers are assigned.
- The PRINT #⟨chnl⟩ statement is used to transfer data from the program to the file.
- The MARGIN #⟨chnl⟩ statement may be used to set the maximum length of a line in the data file.

11.2 Obtaining a Copy of a Program and the Output

Methods for obtaining copies of your programs were discussed in Chapter 1. At that point it was necessary to use the DEC-writer or a special DOPRINT command to obtain a copy of the program together with the output of the program. We can now use an alternative method using a data file. The output from a program can be printed to a data file, and then the program and the data file can be printed using the high-speed printer.

Of course, this method requires that you modify the program so that it sends the appropriate output to a data file. For example, consider the program SROOT.BAS of Fig. 11.2. Without lines 30, 250 and 350, this program would display a table of numbers and square roots on the terminal screen. By adding lines 30, 250, and 350, an identical table is printed to the file SROOT.DAT when the program is run. After the program has been run and saved, a copy of the program and the data file can be obtained by using the DCL PRINT command,

```
$PRINT SROOT.BAS, SROOT.DAT
```

This is a variation of the standard `PRINT` command where two files are printed, one after the other. The program file is printed, and then the data file containing the program's output is printed on the next page.

11.3 Getting Data from a File

Information that has been placed in a data file can be retrieved using a variation of the INPUT statement. Before this can happen, the data file must be specified and an input channel established. This is done using an OPEN statement, such as,

```
10 OPEN "TYPICAL.DAT" FOR INPUT AS FILE #1
```

Here again, a word of caution is in order. The word INPUT refers to program input not data file input.

After the file has been opened, numbers or other data can be read from the file by using an INPUT statement that specifies a channel number. Figure 11.3 illustrates both kinds of INPUT statement.

The file `NUMBERS.DAT` is opened on channel 1, and then line 200 is executed. This is a normal `INPUT` statement that causes the message,

```
WHAT NUMBER?
```

to be printed on the terminal screen. The number that the user types is assigned to the variable X.

When line 300 is executed, the computer goes to the *first line* of the file `NUMBERS.DAT.` If the first line consists of a number only, that number is assigned to the variable Y. If the first line of the data file has several numbers or strings separated by one or more commas, the program reads from the beginning of the line up to the first comma. The resulting value is assigned to the variable Y.

```
100 OPEN "NUMBERS.DAT" FOR INPUT AS FILE #1
200 INPUT "WHAT NUMBER";X
300 INPUT #1, Y
400 INPUT #1, Z, A$, N%, W
```

FIGURE 11.3

Note that the first line of the data file must begin with a number. If there is anything else on the line, the number must be followed by a comma. For example, the first line of the data file might look like

```
23.76
```

or

```
23.76, 67.2, A STRING
```

In both of these cases the variable Y will be assigned the value 23.76. In the second case, the extra information after the first comma is ignored. If the file contains letters or other punctuation at the beginning of the first line, then an error message will be produced when the program attempts to input the extraneous characters.

When the second INPUT #1, statement (line 400) is executed, the computer looks at the *second line* of the data file for input. This second INPUT statement contains four variables, and so the second line of the input file should contain at least four data items separated by commas. In addition, the *type* of data supplied must agree with the variable type. For example, the second line of the file NUMBERS.DAT might look like

```
67.453, #####.##, 6, .056, <anything else>
```

In this case, the value 67.453 would be assigned to Z; #####.## would be assigned to A$; 6, assigned to N%; and .056, assigned to W.

LINPUT from a File

The `LINPUT` statement is used to assign a value to a string variable. When a channel number is specified, the computer reads the next line of the file open on that channel and assigns the contents to the string variable specified in the `LINPUT` statement. The `LINPUT` statement reads the *entire line* of the data file, including commas and quotation marks.

Figure 11.4 illustrates the distinction between the `INPUT` and `LINPUT` statements when reading a data file. When the INPUT statement of line 20 is executed, the first line of the file INFILE.DAT is used to assign the value `ABCD` to the variable `A$`. Here, the commas are interpreted as data separators and the quotation marks, as delimiters for the string. In contrast, when the `LINPUT` statement of line 30 is executed, the entire second line of the file is assigned to the variable `B$`. This is the same thing that would happen if these strings were typed at the terminal in response to an `INPUT` and a `LINPUT` statement, respectively (see Table 6.2).

The `LINPUT` statement is useful in reading files that may contain data stored in a way that is not convenient for the use of an INPUT statement. For instance, a file may contain a number and a name on each line but no comma

11.3 GETTING DATA FROM A FILE

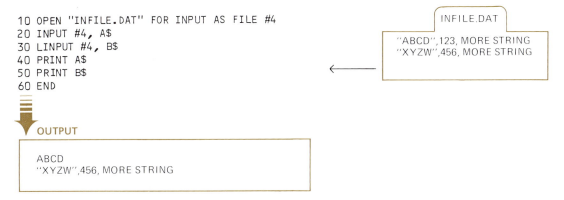

FIGURE 11.4 The action of the INPUT and LINPUT statements when used with a data file.

separating them. The `LINPUT` statement may be used to obtain the entire line of text, and then the `SEG$` and `VAL` functions may be used to split the line and convert the numeric string to a number for use in a program.

Review: Getting Data from a File

Use the OPEN statement in the form

```
OPEN "<filename.type>" FOR INPUT AS FILE #<chnl>
```

- The file specification is enclosed in quotes. The channel number ⟨chnl⟩ can be any integer from 1 to 99.
- Use the `INPUT #`⟨chnl⟩ and `LINPUT #`⟨chnl⟩ statements to transfer data from the file to the program.
- When the computer gets information from the file, the first `INPUT #`⟨chnl⟩ or `LINPUT #`⟨chnl⟩ statement will read the first line of the file, the second `INPUT` (or `LINPUT`) `#`⟨chnl⟩ statement will read the second line of the file, and so on.
- More than one file may be open at a time, provided different channel numbers are assigned.

Creating the Data File Used for Input

So far in our discussion, we have assumed that there is already a data file that can be used for input to a program. If there is not, then the data file itself must be created. This can be done by using the methods discussed in Section

USING STANDARD DATA FILES

```
100 OPEN "NUMBERS.DAT" FOR OUTPUT AS FILE #1
200 READ Y, Z, A$, N, W
300 DATA 23.76, 67.453, "#####.##", 6, .056
400 PRINT #1, Y
500 PRINT #1, Z ; "," ; A$; "," ; N ; "," ; W
600 CLOSE #1
```

```
NUMBERS.DAT
23.76
67.453 , #####.##, 6 , .056
```

FIGURE 11.5 The PRINT #1 statement in line 500 contains quoted commas to insert the data separators into the file. When this program is run, the file NUMBERS.DAT is created containing the lines shown.

11.1. That is, the file may be created by writing and running a program that sends its output to the data file. The text editor may also be used to create the file, as shown in Appendix H.

Because of the special requirements of the INPUT statement, some advance planning is often required when creating a data file. In particular, if commas are required to separate data items, they must be inserted into the data file when the output is written. For example, the program of Fig. 11.5 will store the values of Y, Z, A$, N, and W in the file NUMBERS.DAT so that they can be read by the program of Fig. 11.3.

11.4 Testing for the End of a File

If a program attempts to read beyond the end of a file the computer issues error message number 11,

    ENDFILDEV, End of file on device

This will normally cause the program to stop.

However, there may be times when a file is deliberately read all the way through until the end is encountered. In this case the end-of-file error can be anticipated and the computer can be instructed to ignore the error and resume running at a specified line. This is done with the ON ERROR statement.

The ON ERROR statement directs the computer to go to a specified line and carry out instructions to deal with an error condition. Figure 11.6 outlines the program steps that should be added to take care of an end-of-file error. In many programs, the error handling IF statement is given a line number of 19000 as shown (see Appendix G).

```
100 ON ERROR GOTO 19000
  ...

18900 GOTO 32000
19000 IF ERR = 11
        THEN RESUME <line#>
        ELSE ON ERROR GOTO 0
  ...
32000 END
```

FIGURE 11.6 An error "trap" that intercepts the "end-of-file" error and instructs the program to resume at a specified line. If properly implemented, the program will continue without displaying an error message.

ERR is a special variable that is used to keep track of the type of error that caused a problem. In this case, if the error was caused by attempting to read past the end of a file, then ERR has the value 11 and the error handling IF statement will cause the program to resume at the line number specified. If some other error has been made, then ERR will have a value different from 11, and "`ON ERROR GOTO 0`" will cause the computer to use the usual procedure for that other error.

11.5 Adding to a Data File

Output from a program may also be added to the end of an existing data file. This is done by using the OPEN statement in the following form:

```
100 OPEN   "<filename>" AS FILE #<chnl>, ACCESS APPEND
```

The "`FOR OUTPUT`" clause should not be included because this instructs the computer to open a new file. For example, the statement

```
100 OPEN "HIGHTEMP.DAT" AS FILE #1, ACCESS APPEND
```

followed by a PRINT #1 statement will add lines to the end of the file `HIGHTEMP.DAT`. If there is no such file, the computer will create a new one.

Example: Displaying the Contents of a File

The contents of a file can be displayed by using the DCL TYPE command. As an alternative, the following program can be used to display the contents of a file from BASIC mode.

```
100   ! ***********************************************
110   ! PROGRAM: P F I L E
120   ! ***********************************************
130   ON ERROR GOTO 19000
140   INPUT "WHAT FILE DO YOU WISH TO SEE "; A$
150   OPEN A$ FOR INPUT AS FILE #1
160   WHILE 1
170      LINPUT #1, D$
180      PRINT D$
190   NEXT
200   CLOSE #1
18900 GOTO 32000
19000 IF ERR = 11    &
         THEN RESUME 200      &
         ELSE ON ERROR GOTO 0
32000 END
```

FIGURE 11.7 A program to read and display the contents of a data file. The file is read and displayed line by line until the end of the file is encountered.

Here is an outline of the program.

Get the name of the file.

`OPEN` the file for `INPUT`.

Repeat the following steps until the end of the file is encountered:

get a line of the file (using `LINPUT`);

`PRINT` the line.

The program of Fig. 11.7 has an interesting feature: the name of the file is stored in the string variable `A$`, and the variable `A$` is used in the `OPEN` statement instead of a quoted string. A valid filename and filetype must be specified by the user in response to the `INPUT` query. The statement

`WHILE 1`

begins a never-ending loop in which the condition "1" is never false. Each line is read from the file and displayed at the terminal until the end-of-file error stops the process.

Example: Text Analysis

In some situations, it is necessary to go through a file to look for some particular word or character. For example, we might wish to analyze a grammar school reader to determine the percentage of "easy" words in the book.

11.5 ADDING TO A DATA FILE

```
1000   !*******************************************
1100   ! PROGRAM: E C O U N T
1200   !*******************************************
1300   !
1400   ON ERROR GOTO 19000
1500   OPEN "TEXT.DAT" FOR INPUT AS FILE #1
1600   LET ECOUNT = 0
1700   WHILE 1
1800     LINPUT #1, IN$
1900     FOR I = 1 TO LEN(IN$)
2000       LET L$ = SEG$(IN$,I,I)
2100       IF L$ = "E" OR L$ = "e" THEN ECOUNT = ECOUNT + 1
2200     NEXT I
2300   NEXT
2400   CLOSE #1
2500   PRINT "THE FILE HAS "; ECOUNT ; " E's IN IT "
2600   !
18900  GOTO 32000
19000  IF ERR = 11    &
           THEN RESUME 2400 &
           ELSE ON ERROR GOTO 0
32000  END
```

FIGURE 11.8

The program of Fig. 11.8 will read through a file and count the number of times the letter E is used. This type of program might be useful in determining the frequency of use of the different letters of the alphabet.

Here is the outline of the program:

> OPEN the file for INPUT.
>
> Copy a line of the file into IN$.
>
> Break IN$ down one character at a time, and add one to ECOUNT each time an E is encountered.
>
> Get the next line of the file, and repeat the procedure until the file is read through.
>
> When finished:
>   CLOSE the file;
>   PRINT the value of ECOUNT.

The string IN$ is broken down letter by letter using a FOR loop. A more detailed outline of this procedure is given by

USING STANDARD DATA FILES

> FOR I going from 1 up to the number of characters in IN$:
>   copy the Ith letter of IN$ into L$;
>   test if L$ is an E ?
>   yes: add one to ECOUNT;
>   no: no action.
> NEXT I.

We assume that the length of the file is unknown, so it must be read until the end-of-file is encountered. The program of Fig. 11.8 uses a never-ending `WHILE` loop, set up in lines 1700 and 2300, to read through the file and count the number of E's on each line. When the end-of-file error is generated, the error handler causes the program to resume at line 2400. Then the file is closed and the results are printed.

11.6 The RESTORE Statement for a File

Terminal format files are read one line at a time, starting at the beginning. That is, each time an `INPUT #1` or `LINPUT #1` statement is executed, the next line of the file open on channel 1 is read. The `RESTORE #1` statement can be used to start over at the beginning of the file. Figure 11.9 shows how the `ECOUNT` program of Fig. 11.8 can be modified first to count the number of E's in the file and then to go back and find the first line containing an E.

> ### Example: Cryptograms
>
> A cryptogram is a message that has been translated using a code or cipher. The process of translating a message is called encryption. Once a message has been encrypted, it can no longer be read unless the code is known or can be figured out.
>
> The simplest form of encryption uses a code in which the usual letters of the alphabet are switched around. This is called a simple substitution code. For example, the letter D might be substituted for the letter A, R substituted for B, and so on. In this way, each letter in the original message gets replaced by a different one. Here is an example of a complete substitution, or encode, table:
>
> A B C D E F G H I J K L M N O P Q R S T U V W X Y Z
> | | | | | | | | | | | | | | | | | | | | | | | | | |
> D R T L O W Q S X B N U I P A Z E C V F G H Y J M K

11.6 THE RESTORE STATEMENT FOR A FILE

```
1000
    .
    .   (the same as before)
    .
2300  NEXT
2400  !
2500  PRINT "THE FILE HAS "; ECOUNT ; " E's IN IT "
2600  RESTORE #1
2700  IF ECOUNT = 0 THEN GOTO 32000
2800  WHILE 1
2900    LINPUT #1, IN$
3000    FOR I = 1 TO LEN(IN$)
3100      LET L$ = SEG$(IN$,I,I)
3200      IF L$ = "E" OR L$ = "e" THEN 3500
3300    NEXT I
3400  NEXT
3500  PRINT "THE FIRST LINE CONTAINING AN E IS: "
3600  PRINT IN$
18900 GOTO 32000
19000 IF ERR = 11    &
         THEN RESUME 2400 &
         ELSE ON ERROR GOTO 0
32000 END
```

FIGURE 11.9

Actually, it is not necessary to have the whole table in order to know the code. We already know the unscrambled alphabet, so it is only necessary to know the second line, which gives the scrambled alphabet.

Using the above substitution table, the message,

MY HEART LEAPS UP WHEN I BEHOLD
A RAINBOW IN THE SKY

is changed into the encoded message,

IM SODCF UODZV GZ YSOP X ROSAUL
D CDXPRAY XP FSO VNM

Of course, if a system such as this is used to code messages, there must be a way to decode them. This is done by setting up a decode table.

Here is a decode table corresponding to the above substitution table:

A B C D E F G H I J K L M N O P Q R S T U V W X Y Z
| | | | | | | | | | | | | | | | | | | | | | | | | |
O J R A Q T U V M X Z D Y K E N G B H C L S F I W P

USING STANDARD DATA FILES

Notice that it is easy to obtain the decode table from the encode table. For example, looking for A in the bottom row of the encode table, we observe that O becomes A in the encryption process, and so A must be changed to O in order to decode the message.

The XLATE function, discussed below, can be used to make the above type of substitution. As we have seen, a scrambled alphabet is used to make the substitution, but the XLATE function requires a substitution table for all of the 128 ASCII characters that the computer can recognize. Of course, this includes uppercase letters, lowercase letters, symbols, punctuation marks, and so on; so it is possible to make a very complicated substitution table.

Here is an example of a substitution table for the 94 printable ASCII characters from number 33 through 126:

```
! " # $ % & ' ( ) * + , - . /
| | | | | | | | | | | | | | |
! " # $ % & ' ( ) * + , - . /

0 1 2 3 4 5 6 7 8 9 : ; < = > ? @
| | | | | | | | | | | | | | | | |
0 1 2 3 4 5 6 7 8 9 : ; < = > ? @

A B C D E F G H I J K L M N O P Q R S T U V W X Y Z
| | | | | | | | | | | | | | | | | | | | | | | | | |
D R T L O W G S X B N U I P A Z E C V F G H Y J M K

[ \ ] ^ _ `
| | | | | |
[ \ ] ^ _ `

a b c d e f g h i j k l m n o p q r s t u v w x y z
| | | | | | | | | | | | | | | | | | | | | | | | | |
d r t l o w g s x b n u i p a z e c v f g h y j m k

{ | } ~
| | | |
{ | } ~
```

This substitution table switches letters only. A more complicated code can be generated by switching letters, numbers, and symbols.

The XLATE Function

The XLATE function has the form:

`<output-str> = XLATE(<input-str>,<look-up-str>)`

where ⟨input-str⟩ is the input string to be encoded, ⟨look-up-str⟩ is the string giving the scrambled alphabet, and ⟨output-str⟩ is the scrambled version of the input string. For example, if IN$ is the string to be encoded, OUT$

11.6 THE RESTORE STATEMENT FOR A FILE

is the encoded string, and **TABLE$** is the look-up string, the **XLATE** function has the form

```
2150  OUT$ = XLATE(IN$,TABLE$)
```

The string **IN$** is translated, or encrypted, using the scrambled alphabet specified in the string **TABLE$**. The resulting coded string is assigned to the variable **OUT$**.

The program of Fig. 11.10 is an example of the use of the **XLATE** function to encode text and store it in the file **MESSAGE.DAT**.

```
1000     ! **************************************************
1010     !      PROGRAM:         C R Y P T O
1020     ! **************************************************
1030           !  THIS PROGRAM ENCODES A MESSAGE AND STORES
1040           !  IT IN THE FILE "MESSAGE.DAT"
1050           !
1060           ! LIST OF VARIABLES:
1070           !   TABLE$ - LOOK-UP TABLE FOR SUBSTITUTIONS
1080           !   IN$    - INPUT STRING TO BE ENCODED
1090           !   OUT$   - ENCODED OUTPUT STRING
1100           !
1110           !--- set up substitution table ------------
1120 TABLE$="                                           "
1130 TABLE$=TABLE$ + '!"#$%&' + "'()*+,-./"
1140 TABLE$=TABLE$ + "0123456789" + ":;<=>?@"
1150 TABLE$=TABLE$ + "DRTLOWQSXBNUIPAZECVFGHYJMK" + "[\]^_'"
1160 TABLE$=TABLE$ + "drtlowqsxbnuipazecvfghyjmk" + "{|}~"
1170           !
1180           !--- open file and print header ---
1190 OPEN "MESSAGE.DAT" FOR OUTPUT AS FILE #1
1200 PRINT "TYPE YOUR MESSAGE "
1210 PRINT "THE LAST LINE SHOULD BE THE WORD:  END"
1220           !
               !--- begin loop to encode message ----
1230 WHILE IN$<>"END" AND IN$<>"end"
1240    LINPUT IN$
1250    OUT$=XLATE(IN$,TABLE$)
1260    PRINT #1,OUT$
1270 NEXT
1280           !
1290 END
```

FIGURE 11.10

The message can be decoded in a similar way by using a decode table and the XLATE function. The program DECODE reads the file MESSAGE.DAT, decodes each line, and prints the decoded message. In the following version of the program shown in Fig. 11.11, a subroutine has been used to set up the decode string.

```
1000    ! ****************************************************
1010    !        PROGRAM:          D E C O D E
1020    !****************************************************
1030         !   THIS DECODES A MESSAGE STORED IN
1035         !   THE FILE  "MESSAGE.DAT"
1040         !
1050         ! LIST OF VARIABLES:
1060         !   TABLE$ - DECODE-TABLE STRING
1070         !   IN$ - INPUT STRING FROM ENCODED FILE
1080         !   OUT$ -DECODED STRING
1090         !
1100         ! --- set up decode string ----------
1120 GOSUB 2000
1130         !
1150         ! --- get message and decode --------
1160 OPEN "MESSAGE.DAT" FOR INPUT AS FILE #2
1170 WHILE OUT$<>"END"  AND OUT$<>"end"
1180    LINPUT #2, IN$
1190    OUT$=XLATE(IN$,TABLE$)
1200    PRINT OUT$
1210 NEXT
1220 GOTO 3000
1230         !
2000 !******** subroutine to set up decode string *****
2010 TABLE$ = SPACE$(33)
2020 TABLE$ = TABLE$+ '!"#$%&'  +  "'()*+,-./"
2030 TABLE$ = TABLE$+ "0123456789" + ":;<=>?@"
2040 TABLE$ = TABLE$+ "OJRAQTUVMXZDYKENGBHCLSFIWP"+ "[\]^_`"
2050 TABLE$ = TABLE$+ "ojraqtuvmxzdykengbhclsfiwp"+ "{|}~"
2060 RETURN
2070         !
3000 END
```

FIGURE 11.11

Note that the `SPACE$` function has been used in line 2010 instead of quoted spaces. `SPACE$(33)` is equivalent to a string of 33 spaces.

11.7 Exercises

11.1 Write a program to copy data from one file into a new file. Your program should go through the file and copy all of the lines that are not blank lines. That is, the new file should be the same as the original file except that blank lines have been removed.

11.2 Write a program `AMPERSAND.BAS` that will go through a file to remove all characters after an ampersand character (&) on a text line. That is, each line of the output file will be the same as the corresponding line of the input file except where an ampersand character has been used. Each of those lines will end with the ampersand character.

11.3 The file `DTMP1.DAT` contains 31 lines of data. Each line contains three numbers separated by commas. Write a program to read through the file and determine the largest number in the file.

11.4 Modify the `INTR` program of Fig. 10.39 so that the interest table is printed to the data file `MONEY.DAT`.

11.5 Write a program that will create a data file containing employment information, including
   a) employee name, 15 characters;
   b) age, `###`;
   c) address, 10 characters;
   d) hourly salary, `####.##`

11.6 Using the data file from Exercise 11.5, print an employee payroll list. Read the employee data file, `PRINT` the name, `INPUT` from the terminal the hours worked (hours worked is not on the file), and then display a line of information,

   NNNNNNNNNNNNNNN ####.## ####.##

where N represents a letter in the employee's name, the first number is the hourly salary, and the second number is the gross pay. The gross pay is calculated as the hours worked times hourly wage up to 40 hours, and 1.5 times hourly wage for hours over 40.

11.7 The file `"BLACKBOOK.DAT"` contains 30 names and telephone numbers. Each line in the file contains a name and telephone number arranged as follows.

1,2, ..., 10	11	12,13, ..., 20	21	22,23,24	25	26,27, ..., 32
LAST NAME		FIRST NAME		AREA CODE		TELEPHONE NUMBER

Spaces 1–10 contain the last name; 12–20, the first name; 22–24, the area code; 26–32, the telephone number; and spaces 11, 21, and 25 are blank.

Write a program to find and print all of the NAMES in the file with Arlington, Mass., exchange telephone numbers (that is, with an area code of 617 and a telephone number beginning with 646).

11.8 Write a program to change all of the letters in a file to uppercase. Your program should open the original file for input, the new file for output, read the input file one line at a time, and use the EDIT$ function to change all of the letters to uppercase before writing the string to the output file.

11.9 The file BALL.DAT contains the lifetime statistics of some of the players elected to the baseball hall of fame. Each line contains eight data items arranged in the following way:

NAME, TOTAL GAMES, AT BATS, HITS, HOME RUNS, RUNS, RBI, BATTING AVERAGE

For example, the following is one line of data in the file:

COBB_TYRUS   , 3034, 11437, 4192, 118, 2245, 1933, .367

Note that data items are separated by commas, and the batting averages are rounded to three places after the decimal point. The file is terminated with the line,

ENDDATA , 0, 0, 0, 0, 0, 0, .0

a) Write a program to go through the file and determine the player or players with the highest total of hits plus home runs. Your output should look something like,

HIGHEST TOTAL NUMBER OF HITS PLUS HOME RUNS: <. . .>
PLAYER(S): <. . .>
       <. . .> (More than one player is listed if there is a tie.)

b) Write a program to read through the file and place the name and the batting average of each player into arrays NP$( ) and BA( ). Then use an index array P(N) (or a tandem sort) to determine the ranking according to batting average. Print this ranking into a file BATAVE.DAT.

c) Read through the file and compute the "scoring index" for each player. The scoring index is given by the formula,

SC_IND = (HITS/AT_BATS)*(RUNS+RBI) + HOME_RUNS

Put the name and the scoring index of each player into arrays `NP$( )` and `SC_IND( )`, and then rank the players according to scoring index. Print the ranking in a file `SCORE.DAT`.

11.10 Use the `CHR$( )` function to construct the nonscrambled portion of the substitution table used in the CRYPTO and DECODE programs.
(`TABLE$=SPACE$(33)+CHR$(33)+CHR$(34)`, etc.)

Block-Structured Programming Methods

We have already discussed the use of subroutines and user-defined functions to group sections of a program into blocks. VAX-BASIC has a variety of other enhancements that enable the introduction of even more structure into a program. For example, program statements can be grouped together into sections with a single line number for each section. In addition, descriptive labels can be inserted anywhere in the program. Each label provides a name for a program location and can be used instead of a line number as the destination for a GOTO or GOSUB statement.

Because some knowledge of the use of the EDT editor is required to make full use of these methods, we recommend that you read Appendix H before beginning this chapter.

12.1 Omitting Line Numbers

Line numbers may be omitted from a VAX-BASIC program everywhere except for the very first line and for lines that follow DATA statements. In addition, certain statements, such as the destination of a RESUME clause in an error handler, require line numbers.

BLOCK-STRUCTURED PROGRAMMING METHODS

The general rules for line numbers are as follows:

- The program must begin with a line number.
- All line numbers must begin in column 1.
- If a program line begins with a space or tab character in column 1, it is assumed to be a continuation line or a descriptive label.
- Except for the REM statement and the IF-THEN, IF-THEN-ELSE, and SELECT-CASE structures, continuation lines should be complete program statements.
- If you wish to split one program statement (other than REM, IF, or SELECT) into two text lines, you must type the ampersand character at the end of the first line.
- The END IF clause must be used to mark the end of an IF-THEN or IF-THEN-ELSE structure when the next line contains no line number.
- A REM statement is continued automatically until you type a line number.
- DATA statements should start with a line number and should be followed by a statement with a line number.

Although many programs require only one line number, it is a good idea to use a line number at the beginning of each program block or section.

12.2 Using Labels

A label is a cross between a variable name and a line number. It looks like a variable name, but it acts like a line number in the sense that it defines a location in a program. Unlike a variable, labels are not assigned values. You simply put the label at a specific location in your program, and then you can refer to it elsewhere in the program as if it were a line number.

When a label is used to define a location, it ends with the colon character (`find_e:`); when a label is referred to, it is written without the colon (`GOTO find_e`). Remember, because only line numbers may begin in column 1, labels must be preceded by one or more spaces when you define them in a program. Once you have defined a label, it may be used instead of a line number in a `GOTO`, `GOSUB`, or `ON-GOSUB` statement.

Labels may also be used at the beginning of an `IF`, `FOR`, `WHILE`, `UNTIL`, or `SELECT` program block to identify the entire program block. Once a program block has been labeled, the `EXIT` statement may be used to leave the program block.

Example: The ECOUNT Program. Here we are going to modify the `ECOUNT` program from Chapter 11, using some of the features discussed in

12.2 USING LABELS

```
        find_e:
            WHILE 1
                .
                .
                .
                IF L$ = "E" OR L$ = "e"
                    THEN
                        EXIT find_e  ───────────────┐
                END IF                              │
            NEXT                                    │
3000    PRINT "THE FIRST LINE CONTAINING AN E IS: " ◄┘
        PRINT
```
FIGURE 12.1

this chapter. We will remove line numbers and use labels instead of line numbers in many of the `GOTO` statements. Since line numbers are eliminated, all of the IF statements must be modified by adding `END IF` clauses.

In Fig. 12.1, we have used the label `find_e:` to identify the WHILE/NEXT program block. When EXIT `find_e` is executed, the program jumps to the statement after the WHILE/NEXT block and continues there.

FIGURE 12.2 The revised `ECOUNT` program (see Figs. 11.8 and 11.9).

```
1000    !*******************************************
        ! PROGRAM: E C O U N T 2
        !*******************************************
        !
        ON ERROR GOTO error_handler
        INPUT 'WHAT FILE'; F$
        OPEN F$ FOR INPUT AS FILE #1

1500            !--- count the e's -----
        LET ECOUNT = 0
        WHILE 1
            LINPUT #1, IN$
            FOR I = 1 TO LEN(IN$)
                LET L$ = SEG$(IN$,I,I)
                IF L$ = "E" OR L$ = "e"
                    THEN
                        ECOUNT = ECOUNT + 1
                END IF
            NEXT I
        NEXT
```
(Continued)

BLOCK-STRUCTURED PROGRAMMING METHODS

FIGURE 12.2 Continued

```
2000              !--- print the results ------
         PRINT "THE FILE HAS "; ECOUNT ; " E's IN IT "
2500              !--- go back to find first e ---
         RESTORE #1
         IF ECOUNT = 0
           THEN GOTO finish
         END IF
    find-e:
         WHILE 1
           LINPUT #1, IN$
           FOR I = 1 TO  LEN(IN$)
             LET L$ = SEG$(IN$,I,I)
             IF L$ = "E" OR L$ = "e"
                THEN
                    EXIT find-e
             END IF
           NEXT I
         NEXT

3000     PRINT "THE FIRST LINE CONTAINING AN E IS: "
         PRINT
         PRINT IN$

         GOTO finish
    error-handler:
         IF ERR = 11
           THEN RESUME 2000
           ELSE ON ERROR GOTO 0
         END IF
    finish:
         END
```

The revised ECOUNT program appears in Fig. 12.2. The **RESUME** statement in the error handler must refer to an actual line number. This is one of the few instances in which a label may not be used instead of a line number.

Example: The Aerobic Exercise Program. The program of Fig. 12.3 is a revision of the **EXVAL** program we discussed in Chapter 8 (Fig. 8.19). It uses labels to identify the various subroutines. User instructions and some input checking have been added. Additional subroutines have been added, and the subroutines have been moved around to clarify the organization of the program.

This version of the program also illustrates some variations on the use of subroutines.

- Subroutines do not have to be at the end of the program. User instructions have been included in a subroutine at the beginning of Fig. 12.3 because this helps document the program.

- A subroutine may call itself. The get_time subroutine at line 8000 will call itself until a nonzero time is entered.

- A GOSUB call does not have to have a matching RETURN in order to work. In this case, the effect is similar to a GOTO. In particular, when option 4 (GOSUB evaluate-results) is selected, the net effect is to leave the input loop and begin the process of evaluating the results. The program is ready to return to the input loop and would do so if another RETURN statement were encountered. In this case, however, the program ends before this happens. (This also illustrates that programs will often run if a RETURN statement is inadvertently omitted.)

FIGURE 12.3 The revised EXVAL Program (see Fig. 8.19).

```
100     REM ********************************************
           PROGRAM: E X E R C I S E
           --------------------------------------------
           The following program section is actually a
           subroutine that may be used to describe this
           program to the user. It is placed at the beginning
           because it also describes the program listing.
120     GOTO input-loop

150             ! -- program description --------------
  description:
  print' This program may be used to determine the aerobic'
  print' exercise value of a variety of activities.'
  print' These include: '
  print'      1 - a session of racquetball, basketball or'
  print'          soccer'
  print'      2 - a run or walk'
  print'      3 - a swim'
  print'   Your total exercise activity for a period of'
  print' time may be evaluated at once. The program computes'
  print' an exercise rate to see if you are active enough.'
  print' '
  print' You need to keep track of the times and distances'
  print' (where appropriate) of your exercise activities.'
  print' '
  RETURN
```

(Continued)

FIGURE 12.3 Continued

```
200               !-- loop to input exercise information --
  input-loop:
        INPUT 'DO YOU NEED INSTRUCTIONS (Y/N)';ANS$
        IF ANS$="Y" OR ANS$="y"
          THEN GOSUB description
        END IF
        WHILE 1
          LET EXVAL = 0
          GOSUB show-menu

              !-- select and execute an option --
          INPUT 'WHAT OPTION'; SELECTION
          ON SELECTION GOSUB ball-val, run-val, swim-val,&
           evaluate-results OTHERWISE exceptions
          LET TOT-EXVAL = TOT-EXVAL + EXVAL
        NEXT

300               !-- compute the exercise rate and
                  ! compare to the 100/7 benchmark ------
  evaluate-results:
        GOSUB get-days
        IF DAYS = 0
          THEN PRINT "YOU NEED TO COUNT AT LEAST ONE DAY"
               GOTO evaluate-results
        END IF
        LET EX-RATE = TOT-EXVAL/DAYS
        LET EX-PCT = EX-RATE*7
        PRINT 'YOUR EXERCISE LEVEL IS'; EX-PCT;
        PRINT 'PERCENT OF THE RECOMMENDED LEVEL'
        GOSUB show-response
        GOTO finish
```

```
     !--------------------------------------------------
     ! SUBROUTINES:
     !--------------------------------------------------

1000           !-- subroutine to print the menu ----
  show-menu:
       PRINT 'SELECT ONE OF THE FOLLOWING OPTIONS'
       PRINT '1 - Compute exercise value of playing '
       PRINT '    racquetball, basketball or soccer.'
       PRINT '2 - Compute the exercise value of a walk'
       PRINT '    or a run.'
       PRINT '3 - Compute the exercise value of a swim.'
       PRINT '4 - Evaluate the total exercise value.'
    RETURN

1500             ! -- select an appropriate response ---
  show-response:
       SELECT  EX-PCT
          CASE >150
                PRINT 'SEE YOU AT THE BOSTON MARATHON'
          CASE 130 TO 150
                PRINT 'QUITE A NOTEWORTHY ACHIEVEMENT'
          CASE 110 TO 130
                PRINT 'THIS INDICATES A BETTER THAN '
                PRINT 'AVERAGE AEROBIC CAPACITY'
          CASE 90 TO 110
                PRINT 'YOU ARE RIGHT ON THE MARK'
          CASE 50 TO 90
                PRINT 'GRADUALLY INCREASE YOUR ';
                PRINT 'LEVEL OF ACTIVITY'
          CASE < 50
                PRINT 'THIS IS NOT ENOUGH ACTIVITY'
       END SELECT
    RETURN
```

(Continued)

FIGURE 12.3 Continued

```
2000                !--- subroutine for racquetball, etc.--
   ball-val:
       PRINT 'THIS CALCULATES THE EXERCISE VALUE OF'
       PRINT 'A CONTINUOUS SESSION OF RACQUETBALL,'
       PRINT 'BASKETBALL, OR SOCCER'
       PRINT 'YOU SHOULD COUNT ONLY TIMES OF ';
       PRINT 'CONTINUOUS ACTIVITY'
       GOSUB get-time
       LET EXVAL = 40*TOT.TIME - 3
       IF EXVAL<0
        THEN EXVAL=0
       END IF
       PRINT 'THIS IS WORTH';EXVAL; 'UNITS'
   RETURN

4000              ! --- subroutine for the run value--
   run-val:
       INPUT 'HOW FAR DID YOU RUN (MILES)'; DIST
       GOSUB get-time
       LET RATE = DIST/TOT.TIME
       IF RATE < 6
          THEN
             LET EXVAL = 10/3*( DIST*(RATE-1) -1 )
          ELSE
             LET EXVAL = 10/3*( DIST*(5+2/3*(RATE-6)) -1 )
       END IF
       IF EXVAL < 0
         THEN EXVAL = 0
       END IF
       IF RATE > 15 OR EXVAL > 800
          THEN
             PRINT 'WHO DO YOU THINK YOU ARE, BILL ROGERS?'
             EXVAL=0
             RETURN
       END IF
       PRINT 'YOUR RUN HAD AN EXERCISE VALUE OF';
       PRINT EXVAL; 'UNITS. '
   RETURN

5000             ! --- subroutine for swim ------
   swim-val:
       PRINT 'SORRY THIS SELECTION IS NOT YET AVAILABLE'
   RETURN
```

12.2 USING LABELS

```
8000              ! --- subroutine to get the total time -
  get-time:
      PRINT 'ENTER THE TOTAL TIME (HOURS PLUS MINUTES)'
      PRINT 'EXAMPLE: ENTER 0 HOURS PLUS 90 MINUTES '
      PRINT '            OR 1 HOUR PLUS 30 MINUTES '
      PRINT '            OR 1.5 HOUR PLUS 0 MINUTES '
      INPUT 'HOW MANY HOURS'; TIME.HR
      INPUT 'HOW MANY ADDITIONAL MINUTES'; TIME.MIN
      LET TOT.TIME = TIME.HR + TIME.MIN/60
      IF  TOT.TIME = 0
        THEN
           PRINT "YOU NEED TO ENTER A NON-ZERO TIME"
        END IF
  RETURN

9000              !--- subroutine to get the total days --
  get-days:
      PRINT 'NOW YOU NEED TO FIGURE OUT THE NUMBER OF'
      PRINT 'DAYS THAT THIS ACTIVITY WAS SPREAD OUT OVER'
      PRINT 'YOU SHOULD COUNT ALL IDLE DAYS AS WELL AS'
      PRINT 'THE DAYS YOU EXERCISED. ALSO COUNT THE IDLE'
      PRINT 'DAYS BEFORE THE EXERCISE IN THIS TALLY.'
      PRINT 'FOR EXAMPLE, IF YOU WERE IDLE FOR 2 DAYS'
      PRINT 'THEN EXERCISED FOR 2 DAYS, RESTED 1 AND'
      PRINT 'EXERCISED 1, THEN YOU COUNT THE THREE DAYS'
      PRINT 'THAT YOU DID NOT EXERCISE AS WELL AS THE '
      PRINT 'THREE THAT YOU DID FOR A TOTAL OF 6 DAYS'
      INPUT 'HOW MANY DAYS'; DAYS
  RETURN

15000             !--- subroutine to handle exceptions --
  exceptions:
      PRINT 'ERRONEOUS SELECTION'
  RETURN
32000
  finish:
         END
```

Example: FORMTXT—A Word Processing Program. Before we consider the actual program to take a file and reformat it, we will consider the following related problem. Assume that we are given a string `IN$` that is a "standard" sentence. That is, `IN$` contains words arranged so that there is exactly one space between each word and there are no spaces in front of the first word or after the last word. (If this is not true, the `EDIT$` function can be used to create a "standard" sentence from the given string.)

BLOCK-STRUCTURED PROGRAMMING METHODS

FIGURE 12.4 The string `IN$` is to be split so that it fits into `MAXLINE` spaces. In this case, it must be split at the space between the words "fit" and "into."

Suppose the string `IN$` is too long to display on one line. The string may be split using the SEG$ function into two or more shorter strings that will fit in the allowed space. Because IN$ is a sentence, it is better to split it between words rather than in the middle of a word.

Here is a statement of the problem: If one line of display will fit at most `MAXLEN` characters, then without splitting words, find the longest substring of `IN$` that will fit on one line (Fig. 12.4).

Here is a first outline of a procedure to find where to split the string:

> Ensure that the string `IN$` is too long.
>
> Find the position of the first space.
>
> Find the position of the next space.
>
> Repeat the last step until the next space is beyond position `MAXLINE` in the string.

Admittedly, it's hard to see much of a program in this, but the procedure should be clear. We want to hop from one space to the next as long as we do not go beyond `MAXLINE` characters.

What additional variables do we need? At first it may seem that the computer must keep track of the positions of all the spaces. Actually, only two variables are required:

- L, the position of a space, and
- K, the position of the next space beyond L.

The algorithm becomes a little clearer when it is expressed in terms of L and K.

> Start at space L = 0.
>
> From the current position L, find K (the position of the next space after space L).
>
> As long as K < MAXLINE do the following:
>
>> "advance to space K" (that is, the current value of K becomes the new value of L) and find a new value for K (the position of the *next* space).

12.2 USING LABELS

When the process stops, K is too big but L is not, and so the string should be split at space L.

Here is an implementation of this algorithm.

```
LET L = 0
LET K = POS(IN$," ",1)
WHILE K<MAXLEN+1  AND  K>0
   LET L = K
   LET K = POS(IN$," ",L+1)
NEXT
```

This is used in the following program to create an output string OUT$ that will fit into a 40-column display. First the input string is obtained and converted into standard sentence format. Then the string is checked to see if it is less than 40 characters. The program ends quickly in that case. Otherwise, the algorithm we have just presented is used to determine the value L where the string should be split.

```
100 INPUT "TYPE A LONG SENTENCE"; IN$
    LET IN$ = EDIT$(IN$,152)
    LET MAXLEN = 40

    IF LEN(IN$)<MAXLEN
      THEN
        LET OUT$ = IN$
        LET IN$=""
      ELSE
        LET L = 0
        LET K = POS(IN$," ",1)
        WHILE K<MAXLEN+1  AND  K>0
          LET L = K
          LET K = POS(IN$," ",L+1)
      NEXT
      LET OUT$=SEG$(IN$,1,L-1)
      LET IN$=SEG$(IN$,L+1,LEN(IN$))
    END IF

    PRINT OUT$
    END
```

The word processing program FORMTXT does a similar thing. FORMTXT reads through an input file and reformats it so that text is filled in to the maximum line length (see Fig. 12.5).

BLOCK-STRUCTURED PROGRAMMING METHODS

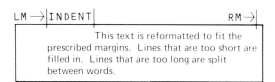

FIGURE 12.5 The FORMTXT program will take input text as shown above and reformat it to fit within prescribed margins. It will also indent the first line of a new paragraph.

```
WHILE IN$<>BLANK
   IF LEN(OUT$)+LEN(IN$)< RM-LM -INDENT
      THEN   OUT$ = OUT$+IN$+SP
             IN$ = BLANK
      ELSE   LET K = POS(IN$,SP,1)
             LET L=0
             WHILE (LEN(OUT$)+K<RM-LM-INDENT+1)AND(K>0)
                   LET L = K
                   LET K = POS(IN$,SP,L+1)
             NEXT
             IF L>1
                THEN
                   OUT$=OUT$+SEG$(IN$,1,L)
                   IN$=SEG$(IN$,L+1,LEN(IN$))
             END IF
             GOSUB put-line
   END IF
NEXT
```

FIGURE 12.6 This WHILE loop is used in the FORMTXT program to build the output string OUT$.

12.2 USING LABELS

The algorithm used in the FORMTXT program is similar to the one we saw earlier. The program builds up an output string OUT$ by reading an input string IN$ and adding it to the output string until the length of the output string cannot be increased without exceeding the maximum allowed line length (RM-LM-INDENT). The program then passes control to the subroutine put_line, which writes the output string OUT$ to the output file. The program section that does this is shown in Fig. 12.6. This example uses the system constant SP instead of the string literal " ". SP is a pre-defined constant that is equivalent to the space character.

The FORMTXT program (see Fig. 12.7) uses the REM statement to allow a long descriptive comment at the beginning. All text is ignored from REM until the next line number is encountered at line 200.

The DECLARE statements in line 200 specify integer variables and integer and string constants. The DECLARE statement is discussed more fully in Chapter 13.

FIGURE 12.7

```
100    REM    This is a program to reformat the file
              INFILE$ into a form suitable for printing on a
              letter quality printer.
                 The output file name is the same as the input
              file name, with the file type replaced by FMX.
                 The input file can contain commands that are
              used to format the file. Here is a summary of the
              allowable commands (default values are given in
              parentheses).

              .S n  - skip n lines.
              .I n  - indent n characters
              .C; <text> - text is centered
              .LM n - set the left margin to column n (0)
              .RM n - set the right margin to column n (60)
              .LT - text is reproduced literally (except for
                 the inclusion of page numbers and form feeds).
              .EL - end literal reproduction of text.
```

(Continued)

FIGURE 12.7 Continued

A line with a period in column 1 is interpreted to be a command line. The center command .C; is followed by the text to be centered. All other command lines should contain no text. Commands other than those listed above are ignored.

   A blank line, or a line that begins with one or more spaces, begins a new paragraph in the output.

   The commands are consistent with those used in DEC Standard Runoff and the results are similar to using DSR with pages numbered at the bottom and with autoparagraph enabled and right justification disabled.

```
200     DECLARE INTEGER L,M,N,K, LM, RM, INDENT, LINE_COUNT
        DECLARE INTEGER LINES, PAGE_COUNT, NEW_PARAGRAPH
        DECLARE INTEGER CONSTANT YES=1, NO=0
        DECLARE STRING CONSTANT BLANK = ""
                ! -- establish initial values --------------
        LM = 0 \ RM = 60 \ LINES = 50 \ LINE_COUNT = 1
        PAGE_COUNT = 1 \ NEW_PARAGRAPH = NO \ INDENT = 0
        ON ERROR GOTO error_handler

300     ! -- set up input and output files --------
        INPUT "NAME OF FILE TO BE REFORMATTED"; INFILE$
        LET N = LEN(INFILE$)
        LET M = POS(INFILE$,".",N-4)
        IF M<N AND M>0
          THEN LET OUTFILE$=SEG$(INFILE$,1,M) + "FMX"
            OPEN INFILE$ FOR INPUT AS FILE #1
            PRINT 'OUTPUT FILE IS '; OUTFILE$
            OPEN OUTFILE$ FOR OUTPUT AS FILE #2
                PRINT #2,
                PRINT #2,
                PRINT #2,
                PRINT #2,
          ELSE PRINT "ERROR IN FILE SPECIFICATION"
            GOTO 300
        END IF
```

```
500       ! -----------------------------------------------
          ! -- begin loop to process the input file INFILE$
          ! -----------------------------------------------
    WHILE 1         ! - repeat until end of file
      GOSUB get-line
      GOSUB fill-line
    NEXT
    GOTO finish
          ! SUBROUTINES:
700       ! -----------------------------------------------
    get-line:      ! Subroutine to read the input file until
                   ! a nonblank text line is encountered. The
                   ! input string is checked to see if it is a
                   ! command or begins a new paragraph.
                   ! If so, the last output string, if not
                   ! blank, is printed to the output file and
                   ! the input string is processed ---------
      WHILE IN$ = BLANK
          LINPUT #1, IN$
          WHILE SEG$(IN$,1,1)="."
            IF OUT$<>BLANK
                 THEN GOSUB put-line
            END IF
            GOSUB process-command
            LINPUT #1, IN$
          NEXT
          IF SEG$(IN$,1,1)=SP OR IN$=BLANK
            THEN
               IF OUT$<>BLANK
                   THEN GOSUB put-line
               END IF
               NEW-PARAGRAPH = YES
               INDENT = 5
          END IF
          IN$ = EDIT$(IN$,152)    ! -- Remove leading spaces
             !- trailing spaces and extra spaces between words.
      NEXT
    RETURN
```

(Continued)

BLOCK-STRUCTURED PROGRAMMING METHODS

FIGURE 12.7 Continued

```
800      !------------------------------------------------
    fill_line:   ! subroutine to transfer characters from
                 ! the input string IN$ to the output string
                 ! OUT$ until the input string is used up.
                 ! Whenever possible, the output string is
                 ! filled to the maximum allowable length
                 ! (RM-LM-INDENT) and transferred to the
                 ! output file.
                 !------------------------------------------
        WHILE IN$<>BLANK
           IF LEN(OUT$)+LEN(IN$)< RM-LM -INDENT
              THEN   OUT$ = OUT$+IN$+SP
                     IN$ = BLANK
              ELSE   LET K = POS(IN$,SP,1)
                     LET L=0
                     WHILE (LEN(OUT$)+K<RM-LM-INDENT+1)AND(K>0)
                            LET L = K
                            LET K = POS(IN$,SP,K+1)
                     NEXT
                     IF L>1
                        THEN
                             OUT$=OUT$+SEG$(IN$,1,L)
                             IN$=SEG$(IN$,L+1,LEN(IN$))
                     END IF
                     GOSUB put_line
           END IF
        NEXT
     RETURN
```

```
850       ! ----------------------------------------
  put-line:     ! Subroutine to print a line in the output
                ! file. If the output is the first line of
                ! a new paragraph then a blank line is
                ! printed and the output is indented.
                !   A new page is started if the beginning
                ! of a new paragraph is too close to the
                ! bottom of the page.
                !   When a page is full it is ended by
                ! printing the page number centered below
                ! the text.
                ! ----------------------------------------
        IF NEW-PARAGRAPH = YES
           THEN
                IF LINE-COUNT + 3 >= LINES
                    THEN GOSUB end-page
                    ELSE
                         PRINT #2,
                         LINE-COUNT=LINE-COUNT+1
                END IF
                NEW-PARAGRAPH = NO
        END IF
  out-line:
        PRINT #2, TAB(LM+INDENT);OUT$
        OUT$ = BLANK
        INDENT=0
        LINE-COUNT = LINE-COUNT + 1
        IF LINE-COUNT >= LINES
           THEN GOSUB end-page
        END IF
  RETURN
```

(Continued)

FIGURE 12.7 Continued

```
860     ! ----------------------------------------------
        process-command:
                    ! Subroutine to process a format
                    ! command (.S n, .I n, .C; <txt>
                    ! .LM n, .RM n, .LT or .EL )
                    ! Commands are converted to upper
                    ! case before processing.
              CMND$ = EDIT$(SEG$(IN$,2,3),32)
              C1$ = SEG$(CMND$,1,1)
              IF C1$ = "S"
                 THEN L = VAL%(SEG$(IN$,3,10))
                      FOR N = 1 TO L
                         GOSUB out-line
                      NEXT N
              END IF
              IF C1$ = "I"
                 THEN INDENT = VAL%(SEG$(IN$,3,10))
              END IF
              IF CMND$= "C;"
                 THEN ! --discard leading and trailing spaces
                      ! and compute indent to center output--
                      OUT$= EDIT$(SEG$(IN$,4,LEN(IN$)),136)
                      INDENT = INT( (RM+LM-LEN(OUT$)) /2 )
                      GOSUB out-line
              END IF
              IF CMND$ = "LM"
                 THEN LM = VAL%(SEG$(IN$,4,10))
              END IF
              IF CMND$ = "RM"
                 THEN RM = VAL%(SEG$(IN$,4,10))
              END IF
              IF CMND$ = "LT"
                 THEN LINPUT #1, IN$
                      INDENT=0
                      UNTIL EDIT$(SEG$(IN$,1,3),32)=".EL"
                         OUT$=IN$
                         GOSUB out-line
                         LINPUT #1, IN$
                      NEXT
              END IF
        RETURN
```

12.2 USING LABELS

```
870       ! ---------------------------------------------
end-page:       ! -- subroutine to end a page
                ! ---------------------------------------
        FOR M = LINE-COUNT TO LINES + 3
             PRINT #2,
        NEXT M
        LET L = INT( (RM+LM)/2 -2)
        PRINT #2, TAB(L); "-"; NUM$(PAGE-COUNT);"-"
        PRINT #2, CHR$(12)
        PRINT #2,
        PRINT #2,
        PRINT #2,
        PRINT #2,
        LINE-COUNT = 1
        PAGE-COUNT = PAGE-COUNT + 1
    RETURN
        ! --- end of subroutine section -------
        ! *******************************************

1000    ! ---     resume here at end of input file -----
        ! --------------------------------------------
        CLOSE #1
                ! -- print last line and finish page --
        IF OUT$<> BLANK
           THEN GOSUB out-line
        END IF
        GOSUB end-page
                ! -- close the file
        CLOSE #2
        GOTO finish
error-handler:
        IF ERR = 11
           THEN RESUME 1000 ELSE ON ERROR GOTO 0
        END IF
finish:
        END
```

12.3 Exercises

12.1 The algorithm discussed in the example about FORMTXT contains what seems like an extra condition, K>0, in the WHILE statement:

```
LET L = 0
LET K = POS(IN$," ",1)
WHILE K<MAXLEN+1  AND  K>0
  LET L = K
  LET K = POS(IN$," ",L+1)
NEXT
```

Show why this condition is necessary to ensure that the correct result is obtained. (*Hint:* Consider the case when the input string has a length that is one or two characters longer than MAXLEN.)

You will use the FORMTXT program of Fig. 12.7 for Exercises 12.2 and 12.3. There is no need to type the program into the computer. Your instructor should be able to provide you with a copy.

12.2 Modify the FORMTXT program so that a SELECT statement is used to process the commands. The completed program should print an error message if an illegal command is used.

12.3 Modify the FORMTXT program so that output text is "filled." That is, if the output string is shorter than the allowed length of (RM-LM-INDENT), then spaces are added between words so that the right side of the output strings line up with the right margin setting. Of course, text at the end of a paragraph (that is, incomplete lines) should not be filled.

12.4 Take one of your programs and use the methods of this chapter to revise it. Put line numbers only at the beginning of each program block. Use at least one label. Do not forget to include an END IF statement at the end of each IF block.

12.5 Modify the bubble-sort algorithm of Fig. 9.19 so that the label bsort: is used to identify the outside FOR loop (lines 150–190 of the example) and an EXIT statement is used to leave the loop when the list is sorted (that is, IF SWAP=NO THEN EXIT bsort). Do not forget to add END IF clauses if line numbers are not used. Test the algorithm by writing a program to sort a list of 10 names.

You will use the EXERCISE program of Fig. 12.3 for Exercise 12.6. There is no need to type the program into the computer. Your instructor should be able to provide you with a copy.

12.6 Modify the `EXERCISE` program to include a calculation of the exercise value of a swim. Your program should incorporate the `FNSWIM` function of Fig. 8.10.

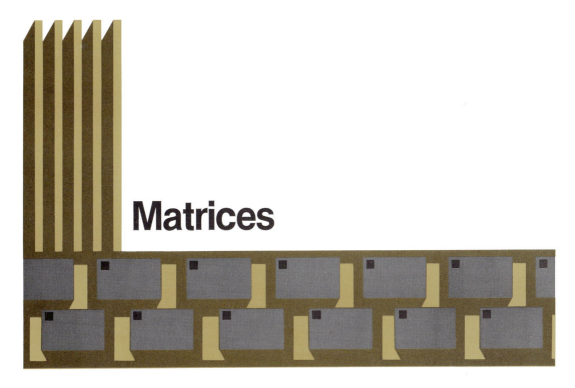

Matrices

A *matrix* is a subscripted variable with two different subscripts. For example, for the subscripted variables X(1,3) and X(8,6), X is the matrix name and 1,3 and 8,6 are the values of the subscripts. A matrix is often represented as a rectangular array of storage blocks (as shown in Fig. 13.1). Each position in the storage block is represented by a row number and a column number as shown. The first subscript of the matrix is the row subscript, and the second is the column subscript.

The first time you use a matrix such as X(1,1) in a program, the computer sets up a matrix storage block with subscripts that can take any nonnegative integer value up to and including 10. Larger or smaller matrices can also be created using the DIMENSION statement. For example, consider the following program steps:

```
100 DIM Z(6,7)
200 LET Z(1,2) = 2.6
300 LET Z(4,3) = 371
```

When statement number 100 is executed, a 6 by 7 matrix storage block is set up just like the one in

MATRICES

	Column numbers						
Z	1	2	3	4	5	6	7
1	0	0	0	0	0	0	0
2	0	0	0	0	0	0	0
3	0	0	0	0	0	0	0
4	0	0	0	0	0	0	0
5	0	0	0	0	0	0	0
6	0	0	0	0	0	0	0

(Row numbers on left)

FIGURE 13.1 The storage block for a matrix, represented as a rectangular array. This depicts the storage block for a 6 by 7 matrix Z.

Fig. 13.1. When statements 200 and 300 are executed, 2.6 is stored in the first row, second column of Z, and 371 is stored in the fourth row, third column of Z (see Fig. 13.2).

There are a number of situations in which a matrix is the most natural way to handle and store information. For example, suppose that we wish to

	Column numbers						
Z	1	2	3	4	5	6	7
1	0	2.6	0	0	0	0	0
2	0	0	0	0	0	0	0
3	0	0	0	0	0	0	0
4	0	0	371	0	0	0	0
5	0	0	0	0	0	0	0
6	0	0	0	0	0	0	0

(Row numbers on left)

FIGURE 13.2 The matrix Z after the values of the variables Z(1,2) and Z(4,3) have been established.

	Test number		
T	1	2	3
1	90	86	70
2	60	58	40
3	80	74	82
4	77	80	71
5	99	90	100
6	70	80	88
7	80	0	60
8	55	70	65
9	64	60	50

(Student number on vertical axis)

FIGURE 13.3 Test scores of nine students, recorded using a 9 by 3 matrix.

keep track of the test scores of a group of nine students. If there are three tests, all of the scores can be recorded in a single 9 by 3 matrix T(9,3) as shown in Fig. 13.3, where each row contains the three test scores of a particular student.

13.1 The MAT Statements

The **MAT** statements make it easy to perform calculations using matrices or arrays. There are four general types of **MAT** statements:

1. the matrix assignment statement (**MAT**... = ...),
2. the matrix PRINT statement (**MAT PRINT**...),
3. the matrix READ statement (**MAT READ**...), and
4. the matrix INPUT statements (**MAT INPUT**... and **MAT LINPUT**...).

These statements are similar to the **LET**, **PRINT**, **READ**, **INPUT**, and **LINPUT** statements for ordinary variables, except that they operate on matrices.

Assigning Values Using MAT

If the matrices W and Z have the same size and shape, we will say that they are similar. A matrix assignment statement is like a LET statement, except that it operates only on matrices of equal size. For example, the matrix assignment statement

250 MAT W = Z

can be used to transfer values from the matrix Z into corresponding locations in a similar matrix W (Fig. 13.4). In these examples we assume that a DIMENSION statement of the form

100 DIM Z(2,3), W(2,3)

has been placed at the beginning of the program.

The VAX-BASIC reserved word ZER is used to denote a matrix with all values set equal to zero. ZER may be used in a MAT statement to set all of the values of a matrix equal to zero.

MAT Z = ZER

Similarly, NUL$ is a null or empty string matrix. The following MAT statement empties the contents of the string matrix A$:

600 MAT A$ = NUL$

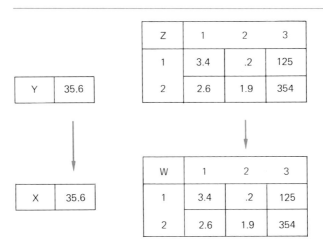

FIGURE 13.4 The assignment statement LET X = Y transfers the value of Y into X. Similarly, the matrix assignment statement MAT W = Z transfers the values from Z into the similar matrix W.

13.1 THE MAT STATEMENTS

```
300 MAT PRINT Z,
350 PRINT
400 MAT PRINT W;
```

OUTPUT

```
3.4         .2        125
2.6        1.9        354

3.4 .2 125
2.6 1.9 354
```

FIGURE 13.5 Two typical uses of the MAT PRINT statement.

These MAT statements are useful for initializing the values of a matrix or array.

The MAT PRINT Statement

The matrix print statement, MAT PRINT, like the usual PRINT statement, can be used to display the values of a matrix. It causes the values of the matrices to be displayed in rectangular form, with each row producing one line of output. Two forms of the matrix print statement are illustrated in Fig. 13.5. The comma and semicolon specify the spacing between the values in each row of output. If a comma is used, each value is written in a different tab zone. If a semicolon is used, each value is written with no extra spacing between the numbers.

The MAT READ Statement

The matrix read statement, MAT READ, assigns values from a DATA list to a matrix or array. Values are assigned to the elements of row 1 beginning with column 1 and continuing to the end of the row, and then to row 2 from column 1 to the end of the row, and so on (see Fig. 13.6). This process continues until all elements of the array are assigned or the DATA list is exhausted. If the DATA list is exhausted before all values of the array are assigned, then the process stops and the remaining array elements are unchanged. No error message is printed.

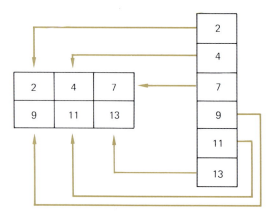

FIGURE 13.6 How the MAT READ statement transfers elements of a DATA list to a matrix.

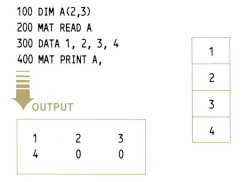

FIGURE 13.7 The MAT READ statement assigns values to four of the six available storage blocks of A.

An example is shown in Fig. 13.7. The MAT READ statement on line 200 will assign the four values A(1,1), A(1,2), A(1,3) and A(2,1). The values A(2,2) and A(2,3) will remain unchanged. The MAT PRINT statement will produce the output shown.

The MAT INPUT Statement

The matrix input statement, MAT INPUT, can be used to input the values of a matrix from a terminal or from a terminal-format data file. In the program of Fig. 13.8, the MAT INPUT statement is used to obtain data for the

13.1 THE MAT STATEMENTS

matrix X. When the **MAT INPUT** statement is executed, a question mark is printed at the terminal while the computer waits for user input. The numbers that are to be inserted in the matrix must then be typed in, separated by commas. The values of the matrix will be assigned starting from the first column of row 1, X(1,1), and continuing across each row until the numbers are used up or the matrix is full.

The **MAT INPUT** statement may also be used to read input from a data file as shown in Fig. 13.9. Line 20 opens the file for input, and then line 30 reads the values from the first line of the file into the array XX.

```
10 DIM X(3,2)
20 MAT INPUT X
30 MAT PRINT X,
```

OUTPUT

```
? 12, 34, 56, 78, 90

12        34
56        78
90         0
```

FIGURE 13.8 The use of the **MAT INPUT** statement to assign the values of the matrix X. All of the input must be typed on one line as shown.

```
10 DIM XX(4,5)
20 OPEN "ARRAY.DAT" FOR INPUT AS FILE #1
30 MAT INPUT #1, XX
```

ARRAY.DAT

1, 2, 3, 4, 5, 10, 20, 30, 40, 50
100, 200, 300, 400, 500
1000, 2000, 3000, 4000, 5000

XX	1	2	3	4	5
1	1	2	3	4	5
2	10	20	30	40	50
3	0	0	0	0	0
4	0	0	0	0	0

FIGURE 13.9 The use of **MAT INPUT** to transfer information from a data file to a matrix.

MATRICES

```
10 DIM XX(4,5)
20 OPEN "ARRAY2.DAT" FOR INPUT AS FILE #1
30 MAT INPUT #1, XX
```

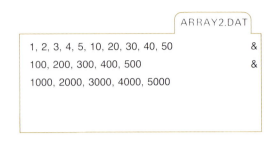

XX	1	2	3	4	5
1	1	2	3	4	5
2	10	20	30	40	50
3	100	200	300	400	500
4	1000	2000	3000	4000	5000

FIGURE 13.10 The MAT INPUT statement will transfer all 20 values from the data file to the matrix storage block XX. In this case, an ampersand must be used at the end of the first and second lines of the data file.

The ampersand character (&) may be used in a data file to indicate a line continuation. If the ampersand is the last character on a line, then the MAT INPUT statement will continue to read data from the next line of the file. This is illustrated in Fig. 13.10.

13.2 Matrix Calculations

We have already seen that the MAT assignment statement, MAT W = Z, may be used to copy values from one matrix into a similar one (Fig. 13.4). This is an example of one of the special matrix operations that can be carried out with similar matrices (that is, matrices that have the same size and shape). Other calculations, such as matrix addition, can be carried out using the MAT statement. Matrix addition is illustrated in Fig. 13.11. The value in the first row and first column of Z is added to value in the first row and first column of W to obtain the value of the first row and first column of Y (and so on across each row). The program of Fig. 13.12 illustrates the use of matrix assignment and addition. It produces storage blocks similar to those shown in Fig. 13.11.

*Advanced Matrix Operations

Other matrix operations can be performed using the MAT statement. These include matrix multiplication, scalar multiplication, and matrix inversion and transposition.

13.2 MATRIX CALCULATIONS

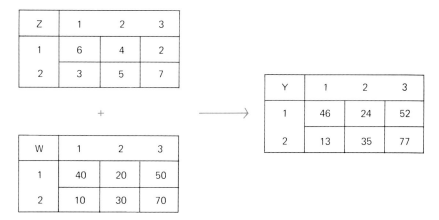

FIGURE 13.11 Illustration of the operation of matrix addition, which may be carried out using the statement MAT Y=Z+W.

```
100 DIM Y(2,3), Z(2,3), W(2,3)
110 MAT READ Z,W
120 PRINT 'THESE ARE THE VALUES OF THE MATRIX {Z}'
130 MAT PRINT Z;
140 PRINT
150 PRINT 'THESE ARE THE VALUES OF THE MATRIX {W}'
160 MAT PRINT W;
170 PRINT
180 PRINT 'THESE ARE THE VALUES OF THE SUM {Z}+{W}'
190 MAT Y = Z + W
200 MAT PRINT Y;
210 DATA 6,4,2,3,5,7,40,20,50,10,30,70
```

FIGURE 13.12 The use of matrix assignment and addition.

These operations require more advanced knowledge of matrices and linear algebra than most readers will have. We will give a brief overview here to illustrate the ease with which such operations can be carried out. The following examples will all use 3 by 3 matrices. Of course, similar results hold for other sizes of square matrices.

The matrix constants shown in Table 13.1 are predefined and are available for use in matrix calculations.

MATRICES

TABLE 13.1 Matrix constants available for use in calculations.

$$\text{CON} = \begin{bmatrix} 1 & 1 & 1 \\ 1 & 1 & 1 \\ 1 & 1 & 1 \end{bmatrix} \qquad \text{IDN} = \begin{bmatrix} 1 & 0 & 0 \\ 0 & 1 & 0 \\ 0 & 0 & 1 \end{bmatrix} \qquad \text{ZER} = \begin{bmatrix} 0 & 0 & 0 \\ 0 & 0 & 0 \\ 0 & 0 & 0 \end{bmatrix}$$

TABLE 13.2 Operational symbols that can be used in a MAT statement.

MAT X = Y + Z	Matrix addition
MAT X = Y − Z	Matrix subtraction
MAT X = Y * Z	Matrix multiplication
MAT X =(C)* Z	Scalar multiplication (C is a scalar quantity)

TABLE 13.3 These operators can be used in the MAT statement to perform the indicated transformations on a square matrix.

MAT X = TRN(Y)	X is the transpose of Y
MAT X = INV(Y)	X is the inverse of Y

Table 13.2 shows the various symbols that can be used to carry out operations in a MAT statement. The usual rules apply for matrix multiplication.

Table 13.3 summarizes the matrix operators that can be used only with square matrices (that is, a matrix with the same number of rows and columns).

The `LINEQ` program of the next section illustrates how some matrix operations can be used to solve a system of linear equations.

13.3 Examples

The following three examples all use matrices in different ways. The `BUSINESS` program uses a matrix to keep track of a large number of data items. No special matrix calculations are carried out. The LIFE program uses a matrix to keep track of the positions of pieces on a game board. This program uses matrix addition. Finally, the `LINEQ` program uses matrix algebra to solve a system of linear equations.

The BUSINESS Program

In some situations, it is necessary to deal with a large quantity of information. For example, the data base used to measure economic activity includes such information as the price of gold, the amount of money in circulation, the price of certain stocks and commodities, and so on. In practice, it is necessary to keep track of these prices for a long enough period of time so that trends can be determined.

Before the data can be analyzed for trends, it must be available in a convenient form. The BUSINESS program is designed to store and retrieve data in the form of a 26 by 14 matrix BW—that is, an array with 26 rows and 14 columns (see Fig. 13.13). The matrix contains up to 26 weeks of data consisting of the values of 14 economic indicators (such as the price of gold, or the amount of money in circulation). A list of the 14 indicators is contained in Table 13.4. The string array IDENT$(14) contains the labels at the left of the table. These strings are used in the BUSI program to identify the contents of the 14 columns of the matrix BW.

Thus a statement of the form,

```
PRINT "THE VALUE OF ";IDENT$(M);" FOR WEEK";N;"IS";BW(N,M)
```

will produce various outputs depending on the values of M and N. For example, the output for M = 2 and N = 4 is of the form,

```
THE VALUE OF GOLD FOR WEEK 4 IS <..>
```

The file **BUSI.DAT** contains the information in a form that can be easily read using a **MAT INPUT** statement. The **BUSINESS** program begins by setting up the matrices and arrays and reading the current data from the file.

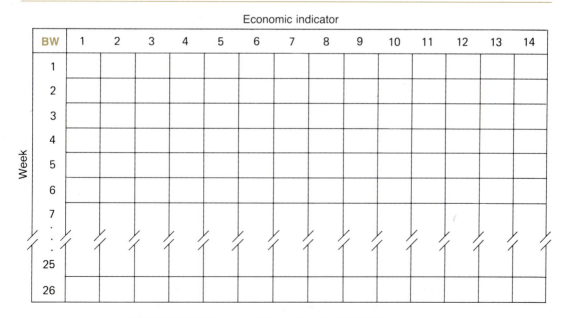

FIGURE 13.13 The matrix BW used in the BUSINESS program.

TABLE 13.4 The 14 economic indicators stored in the BW matrix.

1	B.W. INDEX	A weekly index of economic activity
2	GOLD	The price of gold in international trading
3	RAW_MATLS	The composite price of raw materials
4	FOODS	The average price of food items
5	M1_B	Measures the amount of money in circulation
6	PRIME	The prime interest rate
7	MARK	The value of the German mark
8	YEN	The value of the Japanese yen
9	STOCK_P/E	Price/earnings ratio of common stocks
10	DOW_AV	The Dow-Jones industrial average
11	LIPPER	The Lipper average of stock prices
12	AVE.VOL	The average volume on the N.Y. stock market
13	NO.BLOCKS	The number of large blocks of stocks traded
14	AAA_UTIL	Interest rate on triple-A utility bonds

The program has four major subroutines:

- enter new data or change the current data;
- display the current data;
- store the data in the file BUSI.DAT; and
- produce graphs of the data.

Creating graphs of 14 different data items with 14 different ranges of values presents some special problems. The BUSINESS program sets different scales for each graph using a function FNPLOT. This function has three arguments—X, Y, and Z. The first argument, X, represents the value that is assigned to the left side of the graph, the second argument, Y, is the value assigned to the right side of the graph; and the third argument, Z, is the value to be plotted (see Fig. 13.14). If X is the smallest value and Y is the largest value of the data, then FNPLOT(X,Y,Z) will always return a value between

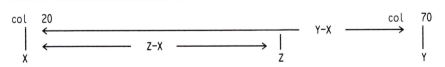

FIGURE 13.14 The method used to determine the scale for plotting each graph.

```
         <----------------- GOLD----------------->
WEEK    465.5              527.29                589.75
 \/      X                   X                     X
  1
  1                                        X--   575.5


         <----------------- MARK----------------->
WEEK    .4615              .483727               .5162
 \/      X                   X                     X
  1
  1                                        X--   .5029
```

FIGURE 13.15 Some typical headers produced for the graphical output of the BUSINESS program. The weekly data points are plotted by printing the symbol X-- in the appropriate column, followed by the actual value associated with the point.

20 and 70. This value is then used with the TAB function to display the value of Z in the correct position.

The graphs are plotted using the FNPLOT function with the values X = MINVAL( ) and Y = MAXVAL( ) for each set of data. Because the scale changes from one graph to the next, a header is printed for each data item showing the minimum value, the maximum value, and the average value. Additional information is included in the display by printing the actual value of each data point. Some typical headers are shown in Fig. 13.15.

The BUSINESS program is shown in Fig. 13.16. It incorporates the use of INTEGER (whole number) variables. These are introduced in the DECLARE statement in line 1100. The computer uses a particular method of storage for an integer variable. See Chapter 15 for more about integer and other types of variables.

FIGURE 13.16

```
1000 REM *****************************************************
              PROGRAM NAME:  B U S I N E S S
         *****************************************************

              BUSINESS DATA STORAGE AND RETRIEVAL
              THIS STORES AND ALTERS DATA IN THE
              FORM OF A 26 X 14 MATRIX STORED IN
              THE FILE "BUSI.DAT"
```

(Continued)

FIGURE 13.16 Continued

```
           LIST OF VARIABLES:
             N - WEEK (INTEGER)
             M - DATA ITEM (INTEGER)
             LAST-WK - LAST WEEK THAT DATA
                   IS AVAILABLE (INTEGER)

           LIST OF ARRAYS:
             BW(N,M) - 26 X 14 DATA ARRAY
             IDENT$(M) - DATA IDENTIFIER STRING
             MAXVAL(M) \
             MINVAL(M) -    DATA MAX, MIN AND
             AVEVAL(M) /       AVERAGE

           LIST OF CONSTANTS:
             MAX-N - MAXIMUM NUMBER OF WEEKS

           LIST OF FUNCTIONS:
             FNMAX(X,Y) - COMPUTES MAX OF X, Y
             FNMIN(X,Y) - COMPUTES MIN OF X, Y
             FNPLOT(X,Y,Z) - PLOTS Z ON A SCALE
                         FROM X TO Y

1100 DECLARE  INTEGER          N, M, LAST-WK
     DECLARE  INTEGER CONSTANT  MAX-N = 26
             !
     DIMENSION MAXVAL(14), MINVAL(14), AVEVAL(14)
     DIMENSION BW(26,14), IDENT$(14)
             !    ^---- value must agree with MAX-N -----

2000 ! *********   MAIN PROGRAM   ********************

             !--- establish values of identifier strings --
     FOR M = 1 TO 14
       READ IDENT$(M)
     NEXT M
2100 DATA  B.W.INDEX, GOLD, RAW-MATLS, FOODS, M1-B
2110 DATA  PRIME, MARK, YEN, STOCK-P/E, DOW-AV
2120 DATA  LIPPER, AVE.VOL, NO.BLOCKS, AAA-UTIL
2130         !
```

```
              ! --- read current weekly data ----------------
      OPEN  "BUSI.DAT"  AS FILE #1
      MAT INPUT #1,  BW
      CLOSE  #1

              ! --- main program loop -------
      WHILE 1
        GOSUB show-menu
        INPUT "OPTION"; N
        ON N GOSUB in-data, show-data, store-data, do-graphs, &
                   OTHERWISE finish
      NEXT
              !
      GOTO 32000
              !
      ! ******************* END OF MAIN PROGRAM ************
              !
10000         ! --- subroutine to print menu ----
  show-menu:
         PRINT\PRINT "CHOOSE AN OPTION: "
         PRINT ,"1-ENTER OR CHANGE DATA"
         PRINT ,"2-PRINT CURRENT DATA MATRIX"
         PRINT ,"3-STORE CURRENT DATA"
         PRINT ,"4-GRAPH CURRENT DATA MATRIX"
         PRINT ,"5-FINISH"
         RETURN

11000   ! -----subroutine to enter or change data ---
  in-data:

              ! --- determine week # for last data entered -
        FOR N = 1 TO MAX-N
          IF BW(N,1) <> 0 THEN   LAST-WK = N
        NEXT N

        PRINT "DATA AVAILABLE UP TO WEEK ";LAST-WK
        PRINT "ENTER THE NUMBER OF THE WEEK THAT YOU"
        INPUT "WISH TO ENTER OR CHANGE DATA FOR"; N
```

(Continued)

FIGURE 13.16 Continued

```
        FOR M = 1 TO 14
          PRINT IDENT$(M);
          IF  BW(N,M) = 0
            THEN
                INPUT BW(N,M)
            ELSE
                PRINT "  CURRENT VALUE IS:"; BW(N,M)
                PRINT "PRESS RETURN TO KEEP THIS VALUE"
                INPUT "OTHERWISE ENTER NEW VALUE"; TMP.VAL
                IF TMP.VAL<>0
                  THEN BW(N,M)=TMP.VAL
                END IF
          END IF
        NEXT M
        RETURN

12000      ! --- subroutine to store the current data --
   show_data:
        PRINT "CURRENT DATA MATRIX:"
        PRINT
        MAT PRINT    BW;
        RETURN

13000         !--- subroutine to show the current data --
   store_data:
        OPEN "BUSI.DAT" FOR OUTPUT AS FILE #2
        MARGIN #2, 132
        FOR N = 1 TO MAX_N
          C$ =STR$(BW(N,1))
          FOR M = 2 TO 14
            C$ = C$ + "," + STR$(BW(N,M))
          NEXT M
          C$ =C$+"&"
          PRINT #2,C$
        NEXT N
        CLOSE #2
        RETURN

14000         ! --- subroutine to print graphs ----
   do_graphs:
```

```
                !--- compute maximum, minimum, and average --
        FOR M = 1 TO 14
          SUM = 0
          ITEMS = 0
          FOR N = 1 TO 26
            SUM = BW(N,M) + SUM
            IF  BW(N,M) <> 0
                THEN  ITEMS = ITEMS + 1
            END IF
            MAXVAL(M) = FNMAX( MAXVAL(M), BW(N,M) )
            MINVAL(M) = FNMIN( MINVAL(M), BW(N,M) )
          NEXT N
          IF ITEMS<>0
             THEN AVEVAL(M) = SUM/ITEMS
             ELSE AVEVAL(M) = 0
          END IF
        NEXT M

14100           !---------------- plot graphs -------------
    plot_graphs:
         FOR M = 1 TO 14
           LET  X = MINVAL(M)
           LET  Y = MAXVAL(M)
           LET  Z = AVEVAL(M)
           PRINT\PRINT

           PRINT  TAB(20); "<---------------- "; IDENT$(M) ; &
                  TAB(30);    "---------------->"
           LET I = FNPLOT( X, Y, Z )
           PRINT  "WEEK"; TAB(19); MINVAL(M); TAB(I-1); &
                  AVEVAL(M); TAB(69); MAXVAL(M)
           PRINT  " \/ "; TAB(20); "X"; TAB(I); "X"; TAB(70);"X"
           FOR N = 1 TO 26
             LET I = FNPLOT( X, Y, BW(N,M) )
             PRINT N
             IF I>0
                 THEN  PRINT N; TAB(I); "X-- "; BW(N,M)
                 ELSE  PRINT N
             END IF
             PRINT N
           NEXT N
         NEXT M
         RETURN
```

(Continued)

FIGURE 13.16 Continued

```
15000   ! *******************************************************
15010   !          FUNCTION DEFINITIONS

        DEF  FNMAX(X,Y)
          IF X > Y
            THEN FNMAX = X
            ELSE FNMAX = Y
          END IF
        FNEND

        DEF  FNMIN(X,Y)
          IF X = 0
            THEN X = Y
          END IF
          IF Y = 0
            THEN Y = X
          END IF
          IF X > Y
            THEN FNMIN = Y
            ELSE FNMIN = X
          END IF
        FNEND

        DEF  FNPLOT(X,Y,Z)
          IF Y=X
            THEN FNPLOT=20
            ELSE FNPLOT = INT(50*(Z-X)/(Y-X)) +20
          END IF
        FNEND

        ! *******************************************************
32000
 finish:
        END
```

*The Game of Life

The game of life is not really a game, but a simulation. It models the behavior of some hypothetical organism that is capable of reproduction and eventually dies. The organisms live in a two-dimensional world that is represented by a rectangular grid (Fig. 13.17). Each square in the grid represents a

13.3 EXAMPLES

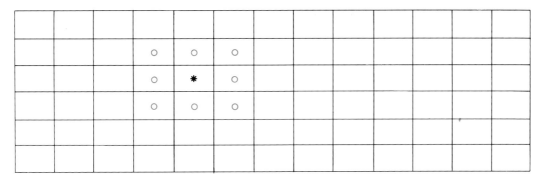

FIGURE 13.17 The two-dimensional world of the organisms in the life simulation.

possible site for an organism and may be occupied by no more than one organism at a time. The presence of an organism is represented by an asterisk (*). Each location has eight neighboring sites as indicated by the circles inside the squares around the occupied site.

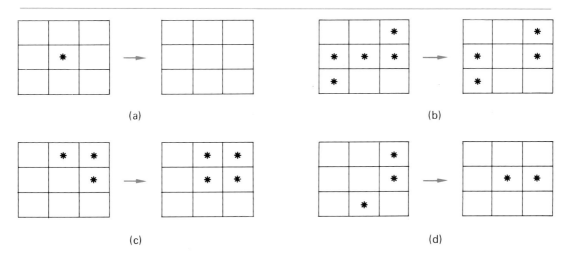

FIGURE 13.18 The rules for survival and reproduction for the organisms in the game of life. If the organism has no neighbors, then it dies from isolation (a). If the organism has four neighbors, then it dies from crowding (b). If a site (here the central site) has exactly three occupied neighboring sites, then a new organism is born on the next generation (c). Births and deaths occur simultaneously (d). A new organism is born in the central square while at the same time the upper and lower organisms each have only one neighbor, and so they die of isolation.

If an organism occupies a site, it may survive to the next generation or it may die, depending on the number of neighboring sites that are occupied by other organisms. In order to survive, the organism must have either two or three neighbors. If it has fewer than two neighbors, it dies of isolation (see Fig. 13.18a). If it has more than three neighbors, it dies of overcrowding (see Fig. 13.18b). If a site is not occupied by an organism, then a new organism may be born there on the next generation if exactly three of the neighboring squares are currently occupied (see Fig. 13.18c). All sites must be analyzed completely before making any changes, and the changes all occur simultaneously (see Fig. 13.18d).

The LIFE program uses a 10 by 10 matrix to keep track of the positions of the organisms. The following illustrations will use 5 by 5 matrices for simplicity, but the operations are identical. The matrix G1 keeps track of the current positions of organisms using zeros to denote unoccupied sites and ones to denote occupied sites. The string matrix SY$ is used to display the configuration (see Fig. 13.19). SY$(N,M) consists of either two space characters (blanks) or a space followed by an asterisk. (The extra space provides a more attractive display.) The MAT PRINT statement is used to display the configuration. The G1 matrix could have been used, but the SY$ matrix produces a pictorial display (see Fig. 13.20).

The matrix SUM is used to tally the number of occupied neighboring cells. The calculation of the value of SUM is perhaps the most intricate part of the LIFE program. This is done in a loop with four layers of nesting. The value of SUM(I,J) is computed for all values of I and J between 1 and 10. For each value of I and J, SUM is calculated by computing a row displacement K and a

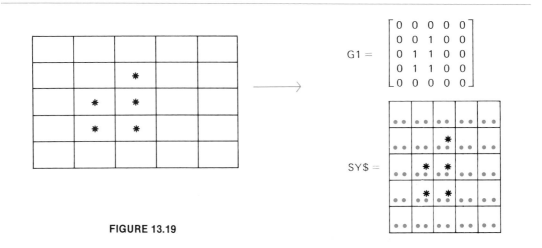

FIGURE 13.19

13.3 EXAMPLES

```
0 0 0 0 0                      0 0 0 0 0        0 1 1 1 0              0 0 0 0 0
0 0 1 0 0          *           0 0 1 0 0        1 3 2 2 0              0 1 1 0 0
0 1 1 0 0         * *    G1 =  0 1 1 0 0  SUM = 2 4 4 3 0   ─→   G2 =  0 0 0 1 0
0 1 1 0 0         * *          0 1 1 0 0        2 3 3 2 0              0 1 1 0 0
0 0 0 0 0                      0 0 0 0 0        1 2 2 1 0              0 0 0 0 0
```

FIGURE 13.20 The output of a MAT PRINT G1; (left) and MAT PRINT SY$; (right) for the configuration shown in Fig. 13.19.

FIGURE 13.21 SUM records how many neighboring cells are occupied.

column displacement L, of −1, 0, or 1, and adding up the values of G1(I+K,J+L) for each of the possible values of the row and column displacements. For example, in Fig. 13.21, the value recorded in, say SUM(2,3), indicates the number of cells around (2,3) that are occupied. This is calculated by adding G1(1,2), G1(1,3), G1(1,4), G1(2,2), G1(2,4), G1(3,2), G1(3,3), and G1(3,4). (The LIFE program also adds G1(2,3) and later subtracts it.) G1 and SUM are used to determine the next generation G2 using the rules given earlier. This method is adequate except at the edges of the 10 by 10 region. To avoid this problem, the board is "reflected" so that G1(11,J) = G1(1,J), G1(I,0) = G1(I,10), and so on.

The program also employs a variable FLAG to detect if there is a change from one generation to the next. The DECLARE statement in line 170 of the first LIFE program, given in Fig. 13.22, has been used to tell the computer to use INTEGER storage because these variables will always be whole numbers.

FIGURE 13.22 The LIFE program and the output produced with the beginning configuration shown in Fig. 13.20. The organisms die out in generation 5. Other beginning setups produce growing or moving configurations or populations that do not die out or change.

```
100  !*************************************************
120  ! PROGRAM: L I F E
140  !*************************************************
150          ! the game of life is set up on a
160          ! 10 by 10 matrix
170  DECLARE INTEGER I,J,K,L,IK,JL,FLAG
180  DIMENSION G1(10,10) , G2(10,10)
190  DIMENSION SUM(10,10) ,SY$(10,10)
210          !
```
(Continued)

FIGURE 13.22 Continued

```
220         ! ----- get initial setup ---
230 PRINT "HOW MANY CELLS DO YOU WISH TO BEGIN WITH";
240 INPUT K
250 PRINT "GIVE THE ROW AND  COLUMN OF EACH CELL"
260 PRINT "EXAMPLE: 3,5  OR  4,7 "
270 PRINT "DO NOT USE THE EDGES (COORDINATE 1 OR 10)"
280 FOR N = 1 TO K
290   INPUT I,J
310   G1(I,J)=1
320 NEXT N
330 INPUT "HOW MANY GENERATIONS DO YOU WISH TO SEE"; G
340 PRINT "" FOR N = 1 TO 25
350         !------ begin loop to compute generations-
400 FOR N = 1 TO G
410         ! --- display setup using SY$ ---
420 FOR I = 1 TO 10
430   FOR J = 1 TO 10
440     IF G1(I,J)=1
            THEN SY$(I,J)=" *" ELSE SY$(I,J)="  "
450   NEXT J
460 NEXT I
470 PRINT \PRINT "GENERATION ";N  \PRINT
480 MAT PRINT SY$;
490   ! -- initialize and compute the number of
500   ! occupied cells around each spot SUM(I,J)
520 MAT SUM = ZER
530   FOR I = 1 TO 10
540     FOR J = 1 TO 10
550       FOR K = -1 TO 1
560         FOR L = -1 TO 1
570           LET IK = I + K
580           LET JL = J + L
590           IF IK > 10 THEN IK = 1
595           IF IK < 1 THEN IK = 10
600           IF JL > 10 THEN JL = 1
605           IF JL < 1 THEN JL = 10
610           SUM(I,J) = SUM(I,J) + G1(IK,JL)
620         NEXT L
630       NEXT K
640     NEXT J
650   NEXT I
660   MAT SUM = SUM - G1
```

```
670          ! --- compute next generation in G2 ---
700    MAT G2 = ZER
705    LET FLAG=0
710    FOR I = 1 TO 10
720      FOR J = 1 TO 10
730        IF G1(I,J) = 0 AND SUM(I,J) = 3
             THEN G2(I,J) = 1
740        IF G1(I,J) = 1 AND (SUM(I,J)=2 OR SUM(I,J)=3)
             THEN G2(I,J) = 1
745        IF G1(I,J)<> G2(I,J) THEN FLAG=1
750      NEXT J
760    NEXT I
765    IF FLAG=0 THEN PRINT "STABLE AFTER"; N ;&
           "GENERATIONS"\GOTO 800
770          !--- transfer the contents of G2 to G1 --
780    MAT G1 = G2
790 NEXT N
800          ! ---- end of loop for each generation --
950 END
```

OUTPUT

```
GENERATION 1

      *
   * *
   * *



GENERATION 2

   * *
      *
   * *



GENERATION 3

    *
      *
    *



GENERATION 4

   * *
```

MATRICES

In another version of the LIFE program (Fig. 13.23), we have used cursor movement to improve the output. (This version will run only on a video terminal that recognizes the standard cursor-control codes discussed in Appendix I.) Instead of having the generations displayed one below the other as in the output of Fig. 13.22, the cursor is moved up so that generations are superimposed. This provides a display that more clearly shows the growth and movement of the organisms. In addition, the output pattern is repeated three times across the screen and twice down the screen to more clearly illustrate the geometry. In this version we have also employed an improved input method where the beginning configuration may be typed in using a pattern of asterisks.

FIGURE 13.23

```
100 !*****************************************************
    ! PROGRAM: L I F E P L O T
    !*****************************************************
              ! THE GAME OF LIFE IS PLAYED ON A
              ! SQUARE BOARD...

200 DIMENSION G1(10,10), G2(10,10), SUM(10,10) ,SY$(10)
    DECLARE INTEGER I, J, K, L, M, N, IK, JL, FLAG
    MAT G1 = ZER

300           ! ----- GET INITIAL SETUP ---
    PRINT "TYPE UP TO 8 LINES OF SPACES AND ASTERISKS"
    PRINT "TO SHOW THE BEGINNING SETUP. "
    PRINT "TRY TO AVOID GETTING TOO CLOSE TO THE EDGES"
    PRINT "FOR EXAMPLE TYPE     *** **  "
    PRINT "                      **  *  "
    FOR N = 2 TO 9
      LINPUT SY$(N)
    NEXT N
    FOR I = 1 TO 10
      FOR N = 1 TO 10
        LET IN$=SEG$(SY$(I),N,N)
        IF IN$="*"
           THEN G1(I,N)=1
        END IF
      NEXT N
    NEXT I
```

```
400 PRINT ESC;"[2J"         !--to clear the screen---
    LET FLAG = 1 \LET N = 0
            ! ------ begin while loop ---------------
    WHILE FLAG=1
      LET N = N + 1
            ! --- display setup using SY$ ---
    FOR I = 1 TO 10
      LET LAST$(I)=SY$(I)
      LET SY$(I) =""
      FOR J = 1 TO 10
        IF G1(I,J)=1
            THEN SY$(I)=SY$(I) + " *"
            ELSE SY$(I)=SY$(I)+" "
        END IF
      NEXT J
    NEXT I
    PRINT ESC;"[23A"  !--- moves cursor up 23 lines --
    PRINT "GENERATION ";N  \PRINT
    FOR J = 1 TO 2
      FOR I = 1 TO 10
        IF LAST$(I)=" " AND SY$(I)=" "
            THEN PRINT
            ELSE PRINT TAB(10);SY$(I);SY$(I);SY$(I)
        END IF
      NEXT I
    NEXT J
500         !--- initialize sum and compute the number
            !    of occupied cells around each spot.
    MAT SUM = ZER
    FOR I = 1 TO 10
      FOR J = 1 TO 10
        FOR K = -1 TO 1
          FOR L = -1 TO 1
            LET IK = I + K
            LET JL = J + L
            IF IK > 10 THEN IK = 1    END IF
            IF IK < 1  THEN IK = 10   END IF
            IF JL > 10 THEN JL = 1    END IF
            IF JL < 1  THEN JL = 10   END IF
            SUM(I,J) = SUM(I,J) + G1(IK,JL)
          NEXT L
        NEXT K
      NEXT J
    NEXT I
    MAT SUM = SUM - G1                              (Continued)
```

FIGURE 13.23 Continued

```
600         ! --- compute the next generation (G2) ---
      MAT G2 = ZER
      LET FLAG=0
      FOR I = 1 TO 10
        FOR J = 1 TO 10
          IF G1(I,J) = 0 AND SUM(I,J) = 3  &
            THEN G2(I,J) = 1
          END IF
          IF G1(I,J) = 1 AND ( SUM(I,J)=2 OR SUM(I,J)=3 )
            THEN G2(I,J) = 1
          END IF
          IF G1(I,J)<> G2(I,J)
            THEN FLAG=1
          END IF
        NEXT J
      NEXT I
700         ! --- transfer the contents of G2 to G1 ----
      MAT G1 = G2
      NEXT
            ! --- this is the end of the WHILE loop ---
      PRINT "STABLE AFTER"; N ;"GENERATIONS"
950 END
```

*Solution of a Linear System of Equations

The following program solves a linear system of two equations of the form:

$3x + 4y = 10;$
$2x - y = 3.$

The coefficients are stored in matrices A and B (Fig. 13.24). The solution of the equations is contained in the 2 by 1 matrix W, where W(1,1) = X and W(2,1) = Y, and is calculated using the following two MAT statements.

```
MAT AINV=INV(A)
MAT W = AINV * B
```

The program of Fig. 13.25 solves such a system of two equations. It also contains an error trap for a noninvertible matrix (that is, a system that does not have a unique solution).

$$A = \begin{bmatrix} 3 & 4 \\ 2 & -1 \end{bmatrix} \qquad B = \begin{bmatrix} 10 \\ 3 \end{bmatrix}$$

FIGURE 13.24 The matrix representation of the coefficients for the given set of equations in the two unknowns *x* and *y*.

FIGURE 13.25

```
100 !*******************************************
110 ! PROGRAM L I N E Q
120 !*******************************************
130 !
140         ! program to solve a system of linear
150         ! equations using matrix arithmetic
160         !
170 DIM A(2,2) , W(2,1) , B(2,1) , AINV(2,2)
180         !
190 ON ERROR GOTO 520      ! in case the matrix
200                        ! has no inverse
210
220 PRINT 'THIS SOLVES A SYSTEM OF LINEAR EQUATIONS'
230 PRINT 'OF THE FORM:'
240 PRINT
250 PRINT ' C X + D Y = E '
260 PRINT ' F X + G Y = H '
270 PRINT
280 PRINT ' FOR EXAMPLE  3 X + 2 Y = 4 '
290 PRINT '              5 X - 3 Y = 6 '
300 PRINT
310 PRINT 'YOU NEED TO ENTER THE NUMBERS ';
320 PRINT      ' C,D,E,F,G AND H:'
330 INPUT 'C:' ; A(1,1)
340 INPUT 'D:' ; A(1,2)
350 INPUT 'E:' ; B(1,1)
360 INPUT 'F:' ; A(2,1)
370 INPUT 'G:' ; A(2,2)
380 INPUT 'H:' ; B(2,1)
390 PRINT
```

(Continued)

FIGURE 13.25 Continued

```
400 PRINT 'HERE ARE THE EQUATIONS TO BE SOLVED:'
410 PRINT   A(1,1); 'X +' ; A(1,2); 'Y =' ; B(1,1)
420 PRINT   A(2,1); 'X +' ; A(2,2); 'Y =' ; B(2,1)
430 PRINT
440 MAT AINV = INV(A)
450 MAT W = AINV * B
460 PRINT 'HERE IS THE SOLUTION:'
470 PRINT '   X= ';W(1,1)
480 PRINT '   Y= ';W(2,1)
490            !
500 GOTO 550
510            ! error trap for noninvertible matrix ----
520 IF ERR=56
       THEN RESUME 530
       ELSE ON ERROR GOTO 0
530 PRINT 'THIS SET OF EQUATIONS DOES NOT HAVE'
540 PRINT '  A UNIQUE SOLUTION '
550 END
```

We now consider a version of the LINEQ program that solves a system of three equations in three unknowns. The program displays the equations in the form shown in Fig. 13.26, and the user simply types in the appropriate number where the question mark is displayed.

This version of the program, shown in Fig. 13.27, uses cursor control to improve the method of data entry, employing many of the cursor-control commands discussed in Appendix I. In particular, the special character sequences shown in Table 13.5 are stored in string variables to make screen and cursor control easier.

```
?_____ X + _____ Y + _____ Z = _____
 _____ X + _____ Y + _____ Z = _____
 _____ X + _____ Y + _____ Z = _____
```

FIGURE 13.26 The program of Fig. 13.27 uses cursor-control codes to create this display and position the question mark. The user simply types in the appropriate number where the question mark is displayed.

13.3 EXAMPLES

TABLE 13.5 The special cursor-control strings and the FNPOS$ function used in the LINEQ2 program.

ERAS$	Erase the screen.
ERAL$	Erase the rest of the line.
REV$	Turn reverse video display on.
NOR$	Turn reverse video display off.
FNPOS$(R,C)	Position the cursor at row number R and column number C.

FIGURE 13.27

```
100  !*******************************************
     ! PROGRAM  L I N E Q 2
     !*******************************************
             !
             ! program to solve a system of linear
             ! equations using matrix arithmetic
             !
150  DIM A(3,3) , X(3,1) , B(3,1) , AINV(3,3)
     DECLARE INTEGER  N, M, R, C

     ERAS$=ESC+"[2J"
     ERAL$=ESC+"[K"
     REV$=ESC+"[7m"
     NOR$=ESC+"[0m"

     DEF FNPOS$(R,C)=ESC+"["+STR$(R)+";"+STR$(C)+"H"
160  ON ERROR GOTO 1000     ! in case the matrix
                            ! has no inverse
170  PRINT ERAS$;FNPOS$(1,1)
     PRINT ESC;"#3";'         LINEAR EQUATION SOLVER'
     PRINT ESC;"#4";'         LINEAR EQUATION SOLVER'
     PRINT
     PRINT TAB(18);'TYPE IN THE COEFFICIENTS '
     PRINT

200  LET FLD$="_____ "
     LET V$(1)=" X  +"
     LET V$(2)=" Y  +"
     LET V$(3)=" Z  ="
```

(Continued)

FIGURE 13.27 Continued

```
250   FOR N = 1 TO 3
         LET R = 6 + 2*N
         FOR M = 1 TO 3
              LET C = 6 + 12*M
              PRINT FNPOS$(R,C);FLD$;V$(M);
         NEXT M
         PRINT FLD$
      NEXT N

300   FOR N = 1 TO 3
         LET R = 6 + 2*N
         FOR M = 1 TO 3
              LET C = 6 + 12*M
              PRINT FNPOS$(R,C);
              INPUT A(N,M)
         NEXT M
         PRINT FNPOS$(R,54);
         INPUT B(N,1)
      NEXT N

350   FOR N = 1 TO 3
         LET R = 6 + 2*N
         PRINT FNPOS$(R,18);
         FOR M = 1 TO 3
            PRINT A(N,M); V$(M);
         NEXT M
         PRINT B(N,1); ERAL$
      NEXT N

400   MAT AINV = INV(A)
      MAT X = AINV * B

500   PRINT \ PRINT
      PRINT TAB(18); 'HERE IS THE SOLUTION:'
      PRINT
      PRINT ,, 'X= '; X(1,1)
      PRINT ,, 'Y= '; X(2,1)
      PRINT ,, 'Z= '; X(3,1)
```

```
1000            ! error trap for noninvertible matrix ----
      IF ERR=56
        THEN
          PRINT 'SORRY THESE EQUATIONS DO NOT HAVE A ';&
              'UNIQUE SOLUTION'
          RESUME 2000
        ELSE ON ERROR GOTO 0
      END IF
2000 END
```

The calculation of the solution is contained in the line

```
400 MAT AINV = INV(A)
    MAT X = AINV * B
```

These are similar to the calculations performed in the LINEQ program except that A and AINV are 3 by 3 matrices.

13.4 Exercises

13.1 If the matrices X, Y, and Z are created using the statement

```
100 DIM X(3,4), Y(9,7), Z(5,8)
```

how many different numbers can be stored in each array? (Ignore the zero subscript.)

13.2 Analyze the following program to determine the output:

```
10 DIM Z(4,3)
20 FOR N = 1 TO 3
30   FOR M = 1 TO 4
40     Z(M,N)= M+N
50   NEXT M
60 NEXT N
70 MAT PRINT Z,
80 END
```

What would the output look like if the comma in line 70 were removed? What would the output look like if line 70 ended with a semicolon?

13.3 Show that the program fragment

```
40 DIM Z(4,3)
50 MAT Z = ZER
```

is equivalent to

```
40 DIM Z(4,3)
50 FOR N = 1 TO 4
51   FOR M = 1 TO 3
52     LET Z(N,M) = 0
53   NEXT M
54 NEXT N
```

The following information applies to Exercises 13.4, 13.5, and 13.6: The file **DTMP1.DAT** contains information recorded at a testing station during the month of December. Each line contains three numbers: the day of the month, the maximum temperature for that day, and the minimum temperature for that day. The first few lines are

1,69,39
2,69,33
3,47,29

and the last line is

31,36,19

The file **DTMP2.DAT** is identical except that there is an ampersand (&) at the end of each line:

1,69,39 &
2,69,33 &
.
.
.
30,51,27 &
31,36,19

13.4 Write a program to
   a) get the high and low temperatures for each day from the file **DTMP1.DAT** and store them in a 31 by 2 matrix;
   b) find the largest maximum temperature and the average maximum temperature;
   c) find the lowest minimum temperature and the average minimum temperature; and
   d) print the results in a file TEMPAVE.DAT.

13.5 Write a program to
   a) get the data from **DTMP2.DAT** and store it in a 31 by 3 matrix; and
   b) display the high and low temperatures graphically. The format of the graph should be similar to the graph done earlier (Exercise 2.8).

13.6 Similar data for January 1981 is available but not stored in a data file. Write a program to store the information in a data file. Your program should
   a) input the maximum and minimum temperature for each day (at the terminal);
   b) store the day number, the maximum temperature, and the minimum temperature for each day in a file called JTMP.DAT. The file should look like the file **DTMP2.DAT** (that is, it should have three numbers on each line, separated by commas and ending with an ampersand).

   Test your program using the following data:

1	33	22
2	37	16
3	38	14
4	18	7
5	35	9
6	36	9
7		
.	⟨make up your
.	own high and
.	low temperature⟩
31		

13.7 Modify the program of Exercise 13.6 so that the input is checked to assure that it is reasonable. Your program should check to see that all temperatures are between -40 and 100. In addition, the program should check to assure that the minimum temperature is less than the maximum temperature for each day. The user should be asked to INPUT new information whenever a problem is detected.

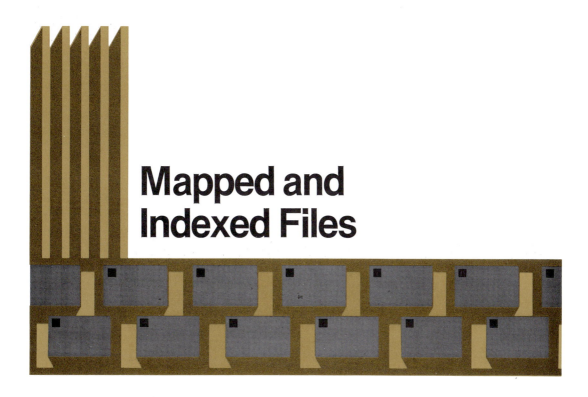

Mapped and Indexed Files

A mapped file uses a "map" to specify the format of each line. Mapped files require some planning to set up, but the data is easier to access and modify.

An indexed file uses a key, such as a name or a social security number, to determine an ordering of the data in the file. The key provides a means of finding information and makes it easy to update or display the contents of the file. If more than one key is used, say the name and social security number, then the information can be displayed either alphabetically according to name or according to social security number.

14.1 The MAP Statement

A **MAP** statement is a means of prescribing the exact format for each line of a data file. Once this format has been prescribed, the process of transferring data back and forth between a program and a data file is greatly simplified.

A typical **MAP** statement is shown in Fig. 14.1. It begins with the key word **MAP** followed by the name of

MAPPED AND INDEXED FILES

```
MAP (PHONE) L.NAM$=10, F.NAM$=9, AREA$=3, &
    TELE$=8, INTEGER PRIORITY
```

FIGURE 14.1 A typical MAP statement.

the map in parentheses. Any unused variable name can be used for the name of the map. This particular MAP statement creates storage for four string variables and one integer variable. Each variable has a fixed length, defined in the MAP statement.

The MAP statement prescribes a format for a data file and also divides each line of the data file into segments that are associated with variables used in the program. Figure 14.2 shows how the MAP statement of Fig. 14.1 pro-

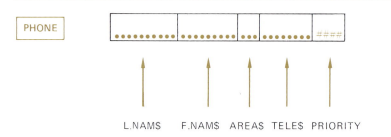

FIGURE 14.2

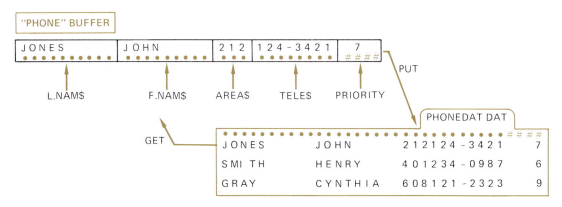

FIGURE 14.3

vides space for the four string variables and the integer variable. The length of each variable is shown schematically. Each dot represents one character of a string and uses one byte (8 bits) of storage. Each number symbol represents one byte used to store a numeric variable.

When a MAP is used, the computer creates a buffer in main memory. The *buffer* is a storage block that contains space for an entire line of the data file. The buffer is divided into segments that correspond to the variable names used in the MAP definition. Figure 14.3 shows that the variable names assigned in the MAP statement of Fig. 14.2 are automatically associated with the appropriate area of the buffer. When information is transferred from a file to the program using a GET statement, a line of the file is inserted into the buffer storage block (see Fig. 14.3). Similarly, when information is written to the file using a PUT statement, the current contents of the map buffer are transferred to a line of the file.

14.2 The OPEN Statement for a Mapped File

If you wish to use a MAP buffer with a file, the OPEN statement must include an ORGANIZATION and a MAP clause to associate the MAP with the file. For example,

```
OPEN "<filename>" [ FOR OUTPUT ] AS FILE #1,  &
     ORGANIZATION SEQUENTIAL, MAP PHONE
```

or

```
OPEN "<filename>" [ FOR INPUT ] AS FILE #1,  &
     ORGANIZATION SEQUENTIAL, MAP PHONE
```

Thus, opening a mapped file is a two-step process:

1. Define the map using a MAP statement.
2. OPEN the file using the ORGANIZATION and the MAP clauses.

Once a mapped file has been opened for OUTPUT, the PUT statement may be used to transfer information from the MAP buffer to the file. Similarly, once an existing mapped file has been opened for input, the GET statement may be used to transfer information from the file to the map buffer. The map buffer used with an existing file must be the same as (or consistent with) the map buffer that was used to create the file.

14.3 The PUT and GET Statements

The PUT statement is used to transfer data from the memory buffer to the data file (see Fig. 14.3). The program of Fig. 14.4 illustrates the use of the PUT statement to write information into a mapped file. The MAP is the same as the one described above. Variables are assigned values using INPUT statements, which place the values in the buffer. Each time the PUT #1 statement is executed, a line is written from the buffer to the data file using the current values of the variables L.NAM$, F.NAM$, AREA$, TELE$, and PRIORITY.

In the program of Fig. 14.5, the contents of the data file created by the program of Fig. 14.4 are displayed at the terminal. The program illustrates

```
100   !***********************************************
      ! P H O N E M A P
      !***********************************************
      ! THIS SHOWS HOW TO CREATE A MAPPED FILE CONTAINING
      ! TELEPHONE INFORMATION IN THE FOLLOWING FORMAT:
      ! |LAST NAME|FIRST NAME|AREA CODE|TELE. NO.|PRIORITY|
      ! |<---10-->|<---9---->|<---3--->|<---8--->| integer|
      !
      ! ------------------------------------------------

200       MAP (PHONE) L.NAM$=10 , F.NAM$=9, AREA$=3,       &
              TELE$=8, INTEGER PRIORITY

300       OPEN "PHONEDAT.DAT" FOR OUTPUT AS FILE #1        &
              , ORGANIZATION SEQUENTIAL, MAP PHONE

400       INPUT "HOW MANY NAMES DO YOU WANT TO LIST";N
          FOR K = 1 TO N
             INPUT "LAST NAME"; L.NAM$
             INPUT "FIRST NAME"; F.NAM$
             INPUT "AREA CODE"; AREA$
             INPUT "PHONE NUMBER ";TELE$
             INPUT "PRIORITY"; PRIORITY
             PUT #1
          NEXT K
500       CLOSE #1
600       END
```

FIGURE 14.4

14.4 ADDING TO, UPDATING, AND CREATING FILES

```
100     ! ****************************************************
        ! P H O N E L I S T
        ! ****************************************************
           ! this displays the contents of the mapped file
           ! "PHONEDAT.DAT" at the terminal.

200        ON ERROR GOTO 19000

300        MAP (PHONE) L.NAM$=10 , F.NAM$=9, AREA$=3,       &
                   TELE$=8, INTEGER PRIORITY

400        OPEN "PHONEDAT.DAT" FOR INPUT AS FILE #1         &
                   ORGANIZATION SEQUENTIAL, MAP PHONE

500        WHILE 1
              GET #1
              PRINT  F.NAM$; L.NAM$; "(" ; AREA$; ") " ;    &
                      TELE$ ; PRIORITY
           NEXT

19000      IF ERR=11
              THEN RESUME 30000
              ELSE ON ERROR GOTO 0

30000 CLOSE #1
32000 END
```

FIGURE 14.5

the use of the `GET #1` statement to transfer a complete line from the file to the memory buffer. When a `GET` statement is carried out, the values of all the variables named in the `MAP` statement are transferred from one line of the file to the buffer, and the new values are immediately available for use in the program.

14.4 Adding to, Updating, and Creating Files

The method for adding information to an existing file is similar to that used to create the file. In this case, simply add the clause `ACCESS APPEND` to the `OPEN` statement (see Fig. 14.6). Note that neither `FOR INPUT` nor `FOR OUTPUT`

```
100  !*******************************************************
     ! P H O N E A D D
     !*******************************************************
        ! THIS SHOWS HOW TO ADD TO A MAPPED FILE
        !
200     MAP (PHONE) L.NAM$=10 , F.NAM$=9, AREA$=3,    &
            TELE$=8, INTEGER PRIORITY

300     OPEN "PHONEDAT.DAT" AS FILE  #1,              &
        ORGANIZATION SEQUENTIAL, ACCESS APPEND, MAP PHONE

400     INPUT "HOW MANY NAMES DO YOU WANT TO ADD";N
        FOR K = 1 TO N
           INPUT "LAST NAME"; L.NAM$
           INPUT "FIRST NAME"; F.NAM$
           INPUT "AREA CODE"; AREA$
           INPUT "PHONE NUMBER "; TELE$
           INPUT "PRIORITY"; PRIORITY
           PUT #1
        NEXT K

500     CLOSE #1
600     END
```

FIGURE 14.6

has been used in the OPEN statement. As a result, the computer will always open an existing file if there is one; if not, a new one is created.

The next example shows how to use the UPDATE statement to replace a line of the PHONEDAT.DAT file with new information. Updating a file is a three-step operation (Fig. 14.7):

1. Use the GET statement to read a line of the file into the MAP buffer.
2. Use program steps to replace the values of the variables to be updated.
3. Use the UPDATE statement to copy information into the file, replacing the original line.

The program in Figure 14.8 illustrates the process of updating a file.

Example: Improving Data Entry. The method used to update the file in the program of Fig. 14.8 is fairly crude. All of the information except for the name must be retyped, even if the information is correct.

14.4 ADDING TO, UPDATING, AND CREATING FILES

Consider the process of updating the area code:

```
PRINT "CURRENT AREA CODE: " ; AREA$
INPUT "NEW AREA CODE"; AREA$
```

This can be revised so that the user is asked if the information is to be changed. The following example has been written so that the user simply presses the return key if no change is to be made. However, a Y must be typed before a change is made.

```
PRINT "CURRENT AREA CODE: " ; AREA$
INPUT "CHANGE (Y)"; ANS$
IF ANS$="Y" OR ANS$="y"
   THEN
      INPUT "NEW AREA CODE"; AREA$
END IF
```

The next version is a little more complicated to write but easiest to use. The user types nothing unless a change is to be made, and if so, only the new information need be typed. This requires the use of an intermediate variable

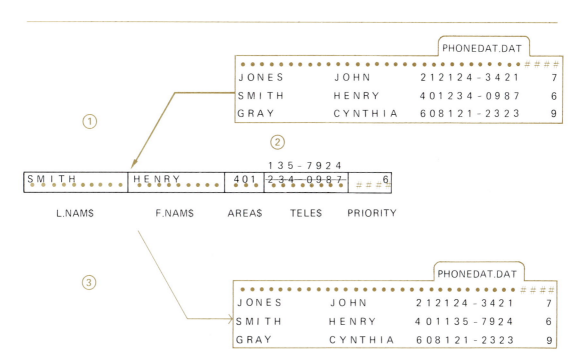

FIGURE 14.7 The process of updating a mapped file.

MAPPED AND INDEXED FILES

```
100  !**************************************************
     ! P H O N E C H N G
     !**************************************************
                ! THIS SHOWS HOW TO UPDATE A MAPPED FILE

200  ON ERROR GOTO 5000

300  MAP (PHONE) L.NAM$=10 , F.NAM$=9, AREA$=3,       &
         TELE$=8, INTEGER PRIORITY

400  OPEN "PHONEDAT.DAT" FOR INPUT AS FILE #1          &
         , ORGANIZATION SEQUENTIAL, MAP PHONE

500  INPUT "WHAT LAST NAME"; FIND.LAST$
     WHILE L.NAM$<> FIND.LAST$
        GET #1
     NEXT

600  PRINT F.NAM$;L.NAM$
     PRINT "CURRENT AREA CODE: " ; AREA$
     INPUT "NEW AREA CODE"; AREA$
     PRINT "CURRENT PHONE NUMBER: " ; TELE$
     INPUT "NEW PHONE NUMBER"; TELE$
     PRINT "CURRENT PRIORITY:"; PRIORITY
     INPUT "NEW PRIORITY"; PRIORITY

700  UPDATE #1

5000 IF ERR=11
        THEN PRINT "SEARCH FAILED"
             RESUME 6000
        ELSE ON ERROR GOTO 0
     END IF

6000 CLOSE #1
32000 END
```

FIGURE 14.8

14.4 ADDING TO, UPDATING, AND CREATING FILES

IN$ to record the response. If something is typed, then the value of AREA$ is updated; otherwise AREA$ is not changed.

```
PRINT "CURRENT AREA CODE:" ; AREA$
INPUT "NEW AREA CODE (<ret> IF NO CHANGE)"; IN$
IF IN$<>BLANK
  THEN AREA$=IN$
END IF
PRINT "UPDATED AREA CODE:" ; AREA$
```

The program of Fig. 14.9 incorporates this method of data entry and combines the features of the above programs using a menu and subroutines. This program also uses a string constant `BLANK` to denote an empty string.

The error trap is a little more complicated than the ones we have seen so far. It not only uses the predefined variable `ERR` to determine the type of error, but it also uses the predefined variable `ERL` to determine the line number on which the error took place. In particular, the error trap checks for an end-of-file error (`ERR = 11`) and then checks to see if the error happened while searching for a given name in line 1000 (`ERL = 1000`). If not, the end-of-file

FIGURE 14.9

```
100 !*******************************************************
    ! P H O N E M E N U
    !*******************************************************
    ! THIS SHOWS HOW TO CREATE AND USE A MAPPED FILE
    ! WITH TELEPHONE INFORMATION IN THE FORMAT:
    ! LAST    FIRST   AREA TELEPHONE
    ! NAME    NAME    CODE  NO.       PRIORITY
    ! |<-10->|<-9->|<-3->|<--8--->| integer   |
    !
    ! This program may be used to create a new file,
    ! add to an existing file, display the file, or
    ! update information in the file.
    ! -------------------------------------------
    !
200 ON ERROR GOTO error-cond

300 MAP (PHONE) L.NAM$=10 , F.NAM$=9, AREA$=3,   &
         TELE$=8, INTEGER PRIORITY

400 DECLARE INTEGER        SELECTION
    DECLARE STRING CONSTANT  BLANK = " "
```

(Continued)

FIGURE 14.9 Continued

```
         !
600    ! ----- begin main program loop ----------------
       !
    WHILE 1     ! ----  repeat:
       !
       GOSUB menu
       ON SELECTION GOSUB show_file , add_names , &
          update_info  OTHERWISE finish
    NEXT

700    ! ----- subroutine section --------------------
       !---------------------------------------------
       !     SUBROUTINE TO DISPLAY THE MENU
       !---------------------------------------------
             !
    menu:
       PRINT
       PRINT
       PRINT "                  M E N U"
       PRINT " ======================================="
       PRINT "   1 - DISPLAY THE INFORMATION IN THE FILE"
       PRINT "   2 - ADD INFORMATION TO THE FILE"
       PRINT "   3 - UPDATE INFORMATION IN THE FILE"
       PRINT "   4 - FINISH "
       PRINT " ======================================="
       PRINT
       INPUT " WHAT OPTION" ; SELECTION
    RETURN

       ! ---------------------------------------------
       !     SUBROUTINE TO DISPLAY THE FILE
       ! ---------------------------------------------
             !
    show_file:
       OPEN "PHONEDAT.DAT" AS FILE #1, &
          ORGANIZATION SEQUENTIAL, MAP PHONE
800    WHILE 1
         GET #1
         PRINT  F.NAM$; L.NAM$; "(" ; AREA$; ") " ;   &
                TELE$ ; PRIORITY
       NEXT
850    CLOSE #1
    RETURN
```

14.4 ADDING TO, UPDATING, AND CREATING FILES

```
900     !------------------------------------------------
        !       SUBROUTINE TO ADD TO THE FILE
        !------------------------------------------------
                  !
    add-names:
       OPEN "PHONEDAT.DAT" AS FILE #1       &
       , ORGANIZATION SEQUENTIAL, ACCESS APPEND, MAP PHONE
                  !
          GOSUB get-info
    RETURN


        !------------------------------------------------
        ! GET INFORMATION
        !------------------------------------------------
                  !
    get-info:
         PRINT 'TYPE THE INFORMATION AS REQUESTED'
         PRINT 'TYPE ALL BLANKS TO TERMINATE INPUT'
      in-block:
         WHILE 1
           INPUT 'LAST NAME:'; L.NAM$
           INPUT 'FIRST NAME:'; F.NAM$
           INPUT 'AREA CODE:'; AREA$
           INPUT 'TELEPHONE NO:'; TELE$
           INPUT 'PRIORITY:'; PRIORITY
           EXIT in-block IF L.NAM$+TELE$ = BLANK
           PUT #1
         NEXT
         CLOSE #1
    RETURN


        !------------------------------------------------
        ! SUBROUTINE TO UPDATE THE FILE
        !------------------------------------------------
    update-info:
         OPEN "PHONEDAT.DAT" FOR INPUT AS FILE #1       &
         , ORGANIZATION SEQUENTIAL, MAP PHONE
```

(Continued)

FIGURE 14.9 Continued

```
1000            !
                ! --- search file for specified name ---
      search:
        WHILE 1
          RESTORE #1
          PRINT "TYPE THE LAST NAME OF THE PERSON"
          PRINT "WITH A NEW PHONE NUMBER OR PRIORITY"
          PRINT "ENTER XXX WHEN FINISHED"
          INPUT "WHAT LAST NAME"; FIND.LAST$
          IF FIND.LAST$="XXX"
            THEN
              EXIT search
          END IF
          INPUT "WHAT FIRST NAME"; FIND.FIRST$
          GET #1
          WHILE L.NAM$<> FIND.LAST$ OR F.NAM$<>FIND.FIRST$
            GET #1
          NEXT

      !-- replace --
          PRINT "TYPE THE NEW INFORMATION WHERE REQUESTED"
          PRINT "PRESS THE RETURN KEY IF THERE IS NO CHANGE"

          PRINT
          PRINT F.NAM$; " " ; L.NAM$

          PRINT "CURRENT AREA CODE:" ; AREA$
          INPUT "NEW AREA CODE (<ret> IF NO CHANGE)"; IN$
          IF IN$<>BLANK
            THEN AREA$=IN$
          END IF
          PRINT "UPDATED AREA CODE:" ; AREA$

          PRINT "CURRENT TELEPHONE NO:" ; TELE$
          INPUT "NEW TELEPHONE NO (or <ret>)"; IN$
          IF IN$ <> BLANK
            THEN TELE$=IN$
          END IF
          PRINT "UPDATED TELEPHONE NO:"; TELE$

          PRINT "CURRENT PRIORITY:" ; PRIORITY
          INPUT "NEW PRIORITY (or <ret>)" ; PIN
          IF PIN<>0
            THEN PRIORITY=PIN
          END IF
          PRINT "UPDATED PRIORITY:" ; PRIORITY
```

```
            UPDATE #1
        NEXT
        CLOSE #1
     RETURN
   error-cond:
           IF ERR<>11
             THEN ON ERROR GOTO 0
           ELSE
             IF ERL=1000
               THEN PRINT "SEARCH FAILED"
               RESUME 1000
             ELSE
               INPUT "PRESS RETURN TO CONTINUE", IN$
               RESUME 850
             END IF
           END IF
                !
2000    ! -------------------------------------------------------
        ! END OF MAIN PROGRAM AND SUBROUTINES
        !-------------------------------------------------------
                     !
   finish:
   END
```

error happened while showing the file (line 800). In this case, the INPUT statement is used to create a pause in the program so that the user can read the display before the menu is printed again.

14.5 Indexed Files

If you use the previous program, one problem becomes apparent. The information is stored and displayed in the order that it was entered. This usually means that names are not in alphabetical order when you display the information.

An indexed file allows the information to be ordered in terms of one or more keys. A *key* may be an integer or a string. If the key is a string, then the file is alphabetically ordered using the key string in each line. If the key is an integer, then the ordering is from the smallest to the largest value of the key. (Real numbers cannot be used as keys.)

MAPPED AND INDEXED FILES

The key is specified in the OPEN statement:

```
300 MAP (PHONE) L.NAM$=10 , F.NAM$=9, AREA$=3, &
        TELE$=8, INTEGER PRIORITY

    OPEN "PHONEIND.DAT" AS FILE #1,   &
        ORGANIZATION INDEXED, MAP PHONE, &
        PRIMARY KEY L.NAM$
```

Once a key has been established, then GET statements access information in the order established by the key. Thus the following loop will display the last names in alphabetical order:

```
WHILE 1
  GET #1
  PRINT L.NAM$
NEXT
```

The key can also be used to find the line containing a particular last name. For example, if the desired last name is stored in FIND.LAST$, then the statement

```
GET #1 , KEY #0 EQ FIND.LAST$
```

will cause the computer to retrieve the line of the file in which the primary key (key #0) is equal to the value of FIND.LAST$.

Figure 14.10 shows how the program of Fig. 14.9 can be revised to incorporate an index that arranges the file alphabetically according to last name. This program uses another variation of the error trap to check for an unsuccessful key search (ERR = 155) before checking for an end-of-file error (ERR = 11).

FIGURE 14.10

```
100 REM *************************************************
        PROGRAM: P H O N I N D E X
        *************************************************
        This shows how to create and use an indexed file
        that contains information in the following format:

        LAST    FIRST  AREA TELEPHONE PRIORITY
        NAME    NAME   CODE  NO.
        |<-10->|<-9->|<-3->|<---8-->| integer  |

        This program may be used to create, add,
        or update information in the file: PHONEIND.DAT
        The file is indexed by last name and
        displayed in alphabetical order.
        -----------------------------------------
```

```
200     ON ERROR GOTO error-cond

300     MAP (PHONE) L.NAM$=10 , F.NAM$=9, AREA$=3, &
                TELE$=8, INTEGER PRIORITY

        OPEN "PHONEIND.DAT" AS FILE #1,    &
                ORGANIZATION INDEXED, MAP PHONE, &
                PRIMARY KEY L.NAM$

400     DECLARE INTEGER         SELECTION
        DECLARE STRING CONSTANT BLANK = ""

600     ! ----- begin main program loop ----------------
        !
    WHILE 1     ! ---- repeat:
        !
        GOSUB menu
        ON SELECTION GOSUB show-file , add-names , &
                update-info            &
                OTHERWISE close-file
    NEXT

        ! ----- subroutine section --------------------
        !---------------------------------------------
    menu:
        PRINT
        PRINT
        PRINT "                   M E N U"
        PRINT " ======================================="
        PRINT "   1 - DISPLAY THE INFORMATION IN THE FILE"
        PRINT "   2 - ADD INFORMATION TO THE FILE"
        PRINT "   3 - UPDATE INFORMATION IN THE FILE"
        PRINT "   4 - FINISH "
        PRINT " ======================================="
        PRINT
        INPUT "  WHAT OPTION" ; SELECTION
    RETURN

        ! ---------------------------------------------
        !       SUBROUTINE TO DISPLAY THE FILE
        ! ---------------------------------------------
    show-file:
        RESTORE #1
        WHILE 1
          GET #1
          PRINT F.NAM$; L.NAM$; "(" ; AREA$; ") " ; &
                TELE$ ; PRIORITY
        NEXT
```

(Continued)

MAPPED AND INDEXED FILES

FIGURE 14.10 Continued

```
        ! ----------------------------------------
        !       SUBROUTINE TO ADD TO THE FILE
        !-----------------------------------------
    add_names:
        PRINT 'TYPE THE INFORMATION AS REQUESTED'
        PRINT 'TYPE ALL BLANKS TO TERMINATE INPUT'
      in_block:
        WHILE 1
          INPUT 'LAST NAME:'; L.NAM$
          INPUT 'FIRST NAME:'; F.NAM$
          INPUT 'AREA CODE:'; AREA$
          INPUT 'TELEPHONE NO:'; TELE$
          INPUT 'PRIORITY:'; PRIORITY
          EXIT in_block IF L.NAM$+TELE$ = BLANK
          PUT #1
        NEXT
      RETURN

        ! ----------------------------------------
        ! SUBROUTINE TO UPDATE THE FILE
        ! ----------------------------------------
    update_info:
1000              !
              ! --- search file for specified name ---
      search:
        WHILE 1
          PRINT "TYPE THE LAST NAME OF THE PERSON"
          PRINT "WITH A NEW PHONE NUMBER OR PRIORITY"
          PRINT "YOU NEED ONLY ENTER THE FIRST FEW "
          PRINT "LETTERS OF THE LAST NAME"
          PRINT "ENTER XXX WHEN FINISHED"
          INPUT "WHAT LAST NAME"; FIND.LAST$
          IF FIND.LAST$="XXX"
            THEN
              EXIT search
          END IF

          GET #1 , KEY #0 EQ FIND.LAST$

    !-- replace --
        PRINT "TYPE THE NEW INFORMATION WHERE REQUESTED"
        PRINT "PRESS THE RETURN KEY IF THERE IS NO CHANGE"

        PRINT
        PRINT F.NAM$; " " ; L.NAM$
```

```
            PRINT "CURRENT AREA CODE:" ; AREA$
            INPUT "NEW AREA CODE (<ret> IF NO CHANGE)"; IN$
            IF IN$<>BLANK
              THEN AREA$=IN$
            END IF
            PRINT "UPDATED AREA CODE:" ; AREA$

            PRINT "CURRENT TELEPHONE NO:" ; TELE$
            INPUT "NEW TELEPHONE NO (or <ret>)"; IN$
            IF IN$ <> BLANK
              THEN TELE$=IN$
            END IF
            PRINT "UPDATED TELEPHONE NO:"; TELE$

            PRINT "CURRENT PRIORITY:" ; PRIORITY
            INPUT "NEW PRIORITY (or <ret>)" ; PIN
            IF PIN<>0
              THEN PRIORITY=PIN
            END IF
            PRINT "UPDATED PRIORITY:" ; PRIORITY

            UPDATE #1
          NEXT

       RETURN

    error-cond:
                   ! -- ERR=155: unsuccessful key search ---
           IF ERR = 155  AND ERL = 1000
              THEN PRINT "SEARCH FAILED"
                   RESUME 1000
              ELSE
                 IF ERR = 11
                    THEN
                       INPUT "PRESS RETURN TO CONTINUE", IN$
                       RESUME 600
                    ELSE
                       ON ERROR GOTO 0
                 END IF
           END IF

2000   ! ------------------------------------------------
       ! END OF MAIN PROGRAM AND SUBROUTINES
       !-------------------------------------------------

    close-file:
          CLOSE #1

    END
```

14.6 Using Compound Keys and Alternate Keys

Duplicate primary keys are not allowed in an indexed file. Therefore two people with the same last name cannot be included in the file created by the program of Fig. 14.10.

The program of Fig. 14.11 shows how to include the first name in the key. In addition, it uses an expanded map that contains space for the name, address, telephone number, birthday, and anniversary, and uses the Julian birthday and anniversary as alternate keys. Standard dates are converted to Julian dates using the FNJULIAN function of Fig. 10.40. The clause

```
ALTERNATE KEY BDAY DUPLICATES CHANGES
```

specifies that the integer BDAY is to be used as an alternate key; that duplicate values of BDAY are allowed (two people can have the same birthday); and that the value of BDAY can later be changed to allow for updating the file.

The program of Fig. 14.11 can be used to create or add to the expanded data file. Note that information written to the file is automatically ordered according to the primary key.

Example: Birthday List and Reminder Program. The program of Fig. 14.11 shows how to create an indexed file that contains, among other things, a name and a number BDAY, which gives the Julian birthday of each person listed.

The file has three keys: the name (key #0); the Julian birthday, BDAY (key #1); and another Julian date, OTHERDAY (key #2). When you specify a primary key (in this case, the name), the computer uses that key to establish an ordering for the lines of the file.

What about the secondary keys? Recall that index arrays were discussed in Section 9.8. They provide a means of establishing an ordering for a list without actually rearranging it. When you use a secondary key in an indexed file, the computer uses an index array to establish the ordering associated with that secondary key. For example, the secondary key BDAY is used to create an index array to specify an ordering for the file BLACKBOOK.DAT.

To begin with, the primary key is the active key. When a key number is used in a GET statement, that key becomes the active key. Thereafter, each GET operation will use the index for the active key. Thus you can display a list of names arranged according to birthday by specifying key #1 and executing successive GET statements. The program of Fig. 14.12 does this, displaying a list of dates and names in ascending order of birthday. The clause,

```
GET 1, KEY #1 GE TODAY
```

tells the computer to search for the first line of the file with a value of key #1

14.6 USING COMPOUND KEYS AND ALTERNATE KEYS

FIGURE 14.11

```
100     REM *************************************************
        PROGRAM: B L A C K B O O K
        -------------------------------------------------
            This program creates or adds to an indexed file
        that contains telephone numbers, addresses, and
        birthdays. The file may also contain another date
        such as an anniversary.

200     MAP (BBOOK) L.NAM$=10, F.NAM$=9, AREA$=3, TELE$=8, &
        STR.ADDR$=20 , APT-OR-BOX$=10, CITY-STATE-ZIP$=20,&
        WORD PRIORITY, BDAY , BYEAR , OTHERDAY, OTHERYEAR

300     OPEN "BLACKBOOK.DAT" AS FILE #1, INDEXED,          &
            MAP BBOOK, PRIMARY KEY (L.NAM$, F.NAM$),       &
            ALTERNATE KEY BDAY DUPLICATES CHANGES,         &
            ALTERNATE KEY OTHERDAY DUPLICATES CHANGES

        DECLARE STRING CONSTANT    BLANK = ""
        DECLARE WORD               D, Y

400
    get-data:
        WHILE 1
          INPUT "LAST NAME"; L.NAM$
          IF L.NAM$=BLANK
             THEN EXIT get-data
          END IF
          INPUT "FIRST NAME"; F.NAM$

          LINPUT "STREET ADDRESS"; STR.ADDR$
          LINPUT "APARTMENT OR BOX NUMBER"; APT-OR-BOX$
          LINPUT "CITY STATE AND ZIP CODE"; CITY-STATE-ZIP$

          INPUT "AREA CODE"; AREA$
          INPUT "TELEPHONE NUMBER"; TELE$

          INPUT "MONTH OF BIRTH (JAN, FEB, etc.)"; M$
          INPUT "DAY OF MONTH"; D
          INPUT "YEAR OF BIRTH (53, 56, etc., or 0 if unknown)"; BYEAR
          LET BDAY = FNJULIAN(D,M$)
```

(Continued)

FIGURE 14.11 Continued

```
            INPUT "MONTH OF ANNIVERSARY OR OTHER DATE (RETURN IF NONE)"; M$
            IF M$<>BLANK
              THEN
                INPUT "DAY OF MONTH FOR ANNIVERSARY"; D
                INPUT "YEAR OF ANNIVERSARY"; OTHERYEAR
                LET OTHERDAY = FNJULIAN(D,M$)
              ELSE
                LET OTHERDAY=0 \ OTHERYEAR=0
            END IF
            PUT #1
         NEXT

         !-------------------------------------------------------
1000     DEF FNJULIAN(DAY, MONTH$ )
1010       MON$ = EDIT$( SEG$(MONTH$,1,3) , 32 )
1100       SELECT MON$
              CASE = "JAN"
                    FNJULIAN = DAY
              CASE = "FEB"
                    FNJULIAN = DAY + 31
              CASE = "MAR"
                    FNJULIAN = DAY + 60
              CASE = "APR"
                    FNJULIAN = DAY + 91
              CASE = "MAY"
                    FNJULIAN = DAY + 121
              CASE = "JUN"
                    FNJULIAN = DAY + 152
              CASE = "JUL"
                    FNJULIAN = DAY + 182
              CASE = "AUG"
                    FNJULIAN = DAY + 213
              CASE = "SEP"
                    FNJULIAN = DAY + 244
              CASE = "OCT"
                    FNJULIAN = DAY + 274
              CASE = "NOV"
                    FNJULIAN = DAY + 305
              CASE = "DEC"
                    FNJULIAN = DAY + 335
              CASE  ELSE
                    FNJULIAN = -1
           END SELECT
1200     END DEF
2000  END
```

14.6 USING COMPOUND KEYS AND ALTERNATE KEYS

greater than or equal to (GE) the value of TODAY. In this case, the value of TODAY is zero so the computer switches to KEY #1 and obtains the "first" line of the file using the index array for BDAY. The GET #1 statements in the WHILE loop of line 400 will continue to use the BDAY index array.

```
100     REM ****************************************************
        PROGRAM:  B D A Y L I S T
        ----------------------------------------------------
            This program uses an indexed file that contains
        telephone numbers, addresses, and birthdays. The file
        may also contain another date, such as an anniversary.
        This program prints the list in ascending order of birthday.

150     DECLARE WORD TODAY
        ON ERROR GOTO error-handler

200     MAP (BBOOK) L.NAM$=10, F.NAM$=9, AREA$=3, TELE$=8, &
            STR.ADDR$=20 , APT-OR-BOX$=10, CITY-STATE-ZIP$=20,&
            WORD PRIORITY, BDAY , BYEAR , OTHERDAY, OTHERYEAR

300     OPEN "BLACKBOOK.DAT" AS FILE #1, INDEXED,          &
            MAP BBOOK, PRIMARY KEY (L.NAM$, F.NAM$),       &
            ALTERNATE KEY BDAY DUPLICATES CHANGES,         &
            ALTERNATE KEY OTHERDAY DUPLICATES CHANGES

400     TODAY = 0%
        GET #1, KEY #1 GE TODAY

   WHILE 1
        PRINT    SEG$(DATE$(2000+BDAY),1,6), F.NAM$; L.NAM$
        GET #1
   NEXT

   error-handler:
        IF ERR = 11
          THEN   CLOSE #1
                 RESUME 2000
        END IF

2000 END
```

FIGURE 14.12

MAPPED AND INDEXED FILES

```
100     REM ****************************************************
        PROGRAM:  B I R T H D A Y
        ----------------------------------------------------
          This program uses an indexed file that contains
        telephone numbers, addresses, and birthdays. The file
        may also contain another date, such as an anniversary.
          When the program is run, the file is checked to see
        who has the next listed birthday.
150     DECLARE WORD TODAY

200     MAP (BBOOK) L.NAM$=10, F.NAM$=9, AREA$=3, TELE$=8, &
        STR.ADDR$=20 , APT-OR-BOX$=10, CITY-STATE-ZIP$=20,&
        WORD PRIORITY, BDAY , BYEAR , OTHERDAY, OTHERYEAR

300     OPEN "BLACKBOOK.DAT" AS FILE #1, INDEXED,        &
            MAP BBOOK, PRIMARY KEY (L.NAM$, F.NAM$),     &
              ALTERNATE KEY BDAY DUPLICATES CHANGES,     &
              ALTERNATE KEY OTHERDAY DUPLICATES CHANGES

400     LET DSTR$=DATE$(0)
        LET D = VAL%(SEG$(DSTR$, 1, 2))
        LET M$ = SEG$(DSTR$, 4, 6)
        TODAY = FNJULIAN(D,M$)
        GET #1, KEY #1 GE TODAY
        PRINT "TODAY'S DATE IS: "; DSTR$
        PRINT "THE NEXT LISTED BIRTHDAY IS ON ";
        PRINT  SEG$(DATE$(2000+BDAY),1,6)
        PRINT "IT BELONGS TO "; F.NAM$; L.NAM$
        !----------------------------------------------
1000    DEF FNJULIAN(DAY, MONTH$ )
1010      MON$ = EDIT$( SEG$(MONTH$,1,3) , 32 )
1100      SELECT MON$
            CASE = "JAN"
                    .
                    . (as before)
                    .
            END SELECT
1200    END DEF
2000 END
```

FIGURE 14.13

The Julian date is converted to a standard date using the DATE$ function (see Exercise 10.8).

The example of Fig. 14.13 is a birthday reminder program that looks through the **BLACKBOOK.DAT** file to see whose birthday is coming up next. This program obtains the current date using **DATE$(0)** and converts it to a Julian date. Then it looks for the next larger value of **BDAY** (key #1) in the **BLACKBOOK.DAT** file and prints a reminder message giving the date and the name of the person with the next birthday.

This program will never let you forget a birthday—provided, of course, that you remember to run the program.

14.7 Exercises

14.1 Assume that you have a file **STUDAT.DAT**, which contains registration information. Each line is 80 characters long and is arranged as shown in Fig. 10.10. Write a program to read through the file and display a list of the names. Your program should use a map that defines a buffer with space for the string variables **SSN$**, **L.NAM$**, **F.NAM$**, and **THEREST$**.

14.2 Modify the program of Exercise 14.1 to create an indexed file **STUDAT2.DAT**, which contains the same information contained in **STUDAT.DAT**. The new file should use (**L.NAM$,F.NAM$**) as the key.

14.3 Write a program that uses the indexed file **STUDAT2.DAT** to print an alphabetical list of students.

14.4 Modify the program **PHONINDEX** of Fig. 14.10 to include **PRIORITY** as an alternate key. Include an option to list the names ranked according to **PRIORITY**.

14.5 Modify the **BIRTHDAY** program of Fig. 14.13 to also print the next anniversary (**OTHERDAY**).

14.6 Modify the **BIRTHDAY** program of Fig. 14.13 so that it computes the number of days until the next birthday. The modified program should display the next birthday only if the priority is greater than the number of days until the birthday. This version of the program reminds you of a birthday only when it is close at hand.

Other Features of VAX-BASIC

Until now, we have dealt with numeric variables almost without regard for the way in which these variables are stored in the computer. The computer stores numbers, carries out calculations, and prints the results with an accuracy that is adequate for most situations.

Occasionally, however, there are situations when more accuracy is required. For example, the usual methods give precise results for money calculations provided the numbers are not bigger than $9999.99. Larger numbers are either rounded or printed in scientific form using E format. This is not acceptable for calculating interest on a bank deposit of, say, several million dollars. In such situations, more accurate methods must be employed.

In addition, there are times when issues of data type are important if the output of one program is used for the input of another.

This chapter starts with a discussion of the data types that can be used in BASIC and then covers a number of special features of VAX-BASIC that relate to the process of compiling and linking program segments.

15.1 Standard Representation of Real Numbers

A real number can be represented as a decimal, such as 245.915 or 0.00538. Some real numbers, like PI or the square root of 2, can only be approximated by giving a decimal representation. Naturally, the more digits used, the better the approximation. For example, 3.1415926535 is a better approximation to PI than 3.1416. The first representation is said to have 11 significant digits, and the second, 5.

When you PRINT the value of a variable, the computer automatically converts the number into a form that is more suitable for display. It does this in such a way as to avoid displaying errors that might be present. For example, small errors can be introduced in the process of carrying out calculations, and so the computer might keep track of ten significant digits of each number involved in the calculation but display only six significant digits of the answer.

Using VAX-BASIC, the normal methods of storing and displaying numbers are accurate to six significant digits. This limitation is a result of the size of the storage block used for the numbers (normally 32 bits for real numbers or for integers). Greater accuracy can be obtained by using larger storage blocks. You can do this by using the options outlined in Table 15.1.

Two **BASIC** statements can be used to specify data types: the **DECLARE** statement and the **OPTION** statement. The **DECLARE** statement is used to spec-

Table 15.1 The size of the storage block associated with each data type available for VAX-BASIC and the decimal digits of accuracy available for calculations with real numbers. D indicates the default data type, which the computer uses unless you specify otherwise.

General Data Type	Specific Data Type	Number of Bits in Storage Block	Number of Decimal Digits of Accuracy
Real	Single (D)	32	6
	Double	64	16
	Gfloat	64	15
	Hfloat	128	33
	Decimal	0 to 368	31
Integer	Byte	8	
	Word	16	
	Long (D)	32	

ify a data type for one or more specific variables. The `OPTION` statement is used to prescribe a specific data type for all variables of a given general data type.

The DECLARE Statement

If you do not specify a data type in your program, a variable is automatically given the data type REAL unless you use a percent sign or a dollar sign at the end of the variable name. The `DECLARE` statement can be used to assign a specific data type or subtype to one or more variables. For example, N, M, I, J, and K can be specified as integer variables using the statements

```
200 DECLARE  WORD I, J, K
210 DECLARE  INTEGER N, M
```

The variables `I`, `J`, and `K` are given an explicit subtype WORD, and `N` and `M` are given the type INTEGER. Variables N and M will take on the default subtype LONG unless you specify otherwise (see the `OPTION` statement in Section 15.4).

A percent sign at the end of the variable name (I% or N%) can also be used to indicate an integer data type. In actuality, statement 210 above is equivalent to using variable names `N%` and `M%` without a `DECLARE` statement. Using the DECLARE statement for integer variables is preferable to using the percent sign because it prevents a common error that results when you forget to type the percent sign in your program. For example, without the `DECLARE` statement, it is easy to make a mistake like

```
100 FOR N% = 1 TO 10
200    PRINT X(N)
300 NEXT N%
```

Here, the variables `N%` and `N` are different, and therefore the same value `X(N)` will be printed ten times, where `N` is some unknown (fixed) value.

The `DECLARE` statement can also be used to create constants. Constants look exactly like variables but have values that cannot be changed in your program. For example:

```
230 DECLARE REAL CONSTANT EPSILON = 0.00001
240 DECLARE WORD CONSTANT YES=1, NO=0
```

The `DECLARE` statement must come at the beginning of the program, *before* the variable is used.

Data Types in the DIMENSION Statement

The data type of an array or matrix can be specified in a `DIMENSION` statement. The rules are similar to those used above for the `DECLARE` statement. For example, the statements

```
DIMENSION INTEGER INDX(20), K(3,5)
DIM STRING A(10), B(20)
```

illustrate the creation of the integer array INDX, the 3 by 5 integer matrix K, and string arrays A and B.

The OPTION Statement

The `OPTION` statement can be used to prescribe a specific data type or subtype for variables used in your program. The `OPTION` statement is normally used when the usual six digits of accuracy are not sufficient. The OPTION statement must be the first statement in a program, except possibly for `REM` statements. For example, consider the INTR program of Fig. 10.39. If we use a value of $200,000.00 for the principal at 10 percent interest, the output is as shown in Fig. 15.1.

MONTH	PRINCIPAL	INTEREST
1	$200000.00	$1666.67
2	$201667.00	$1680.56
3	$203347.00	$1694.56
4	$205042.00	$1708.68
5	$206750.00	$1722.92
6	$208473.00	$1737.28
7	$210211.00	$1751.76
8	$211962.00	$1766.35
9	$213729.00	$1781.07
10	$215510.00	$1795.92
11	$217306.00	$1810.88
12	$219117.00	$1825.97

FIGURE 15.1 The output of the INTR program of Fig. 10.39. Large numbers are displayed to six digits of accuracy.

15.1 STANDARD REPRESENTATION OF REAL NUMBERS

The principal amounts have been rounded to six significant digits, which is not acceptable for money calculations. This problem can be avoided by specifiying a data type of **DOUBLE** by using the **OPTION** statement. This will provide 16 decimal places of accuracy, as shown in Table 15.1.

Figure 15.2 shows how the **INTR** program can be modified to provide more accurate calculations. It uses an **OPTION** statement to specify double-precision arithmetic. In addition, the program has been revised to send output to a data file and restructured by removing some of the line numbers. Comment fields will cause an error message unless the **OPTION** statement precedes them, and so the ones at the beginning of the program have been removed and replaced by a remark statement.

FIGURE 15.2

```
1000 REM ****************************************************
          PROGRAM NAME: I N T R D B L
          ****************************************************
                   THIS COMPUTES INTEREST USING
                   DOUBLE-PRECISION CALCULATIONS.

                   LIST OF VARIABLES:
                   P- PRINCIPAL AMOUNT
                   R- ANNUAL INTEREST RATE
                   I- MONTHLY INTEREST
                   A$, B$ - FORMAT STRINGS

1100      OPTION SIZE = REAL DOUBLE
                   ! --- option must precede comment fields ---
          LET A$ = "######.##"
          LET B$ = "$$#####.##"


                   !--- get values of p and r -----------------
2000      INPUT "PRINCIPAL AMOUNT"; P
          INPUT "ANNUAL INTEREST RATE (AS A PERCENT)"; R
                   !
                   !--- open data file and print header ----
2400      OPEN "MONEY.DAT" FOR OUTPUT AS FILE #1
          PRINT #1,"TABLE OF VALUES FOR MONTHLY INTEREST ON ";&
            FORMAT$(P,B$)
          PRINT #1, " AT " ; R ; " PERCENT ANNUAL INTEREST"
```

(Continued)

FIGURE 15.2 Continued

```
                !--- set up header ------------------------
        PRINT   "MONTH        PRINCIPAL       INTEREST "
        PRINT #1, "MONTH        PRINCIPAL       INTEREST "
                !
3000            !--- compute interest to nearest cent
        FOR N = 1 TO 12
          LET I = P * R * .01 / 12
          PRINT     N , FORMAT$(P,B$) , FORMAT$(I,B$)
          PRINT #1, N , FORMAT$(P,B$) , FORMAT$(I,B$)
          LET P = P + VAL(FORMAT$(I,A$))
        NEXT N
                !--- close the file -----
3900    CLOSE #1
4000    END
```

OUTPUT

```
TABLE OF VALUES FOR MONTHLY INTEREST ON $200000.00 AT 10 PERCENT
ANNUAL INTEREST

MONTH      PRINCIPAL      INTEREST
1          $200000.00     $1666.67
2          $201666.67     $1680.56
3          $203347.23     $1694.56
4          $205041.79     $1708.68
5          $206750.47     $1722.92
6          $208473.39     $1737.28
7          $210210.67     $1751.76
8          $211962.43     $1766.35
9          $213728.78     $1781.07
10         $215509.85     $1795.92
11         $217305.77     $1810.88
12         $219116.65     $1825.97
```

DECIMAL Data Type

When a statement refers to DECIMAL data type, a special type of storage, called binary coded decimal, is set up in the computer. This allows the computer to store numbers of variable length and, with a sacrifice of speed, perform calculations to virtually any degree of accuracy. When you specify DECIMAL data type, you need to tell the computer the number of digits to use. For example, DECIMAL(12,2) tells the computer to allow 12 digits overall, with 2 digits after the decimal point.

Figure 15.3 shows the INTR program modified to use DECIMAL data.

FIGURE 15.3

```
1000   REM ********************************************************
              PROGRAM NAME: I N T D C M L
       ********************************************************
                    THIS COMPUTES INTEREST USING
                    DECIMAL DATA TYPE.

                         LIST OF VARIABLES:
                         P- PRINCIPAL AMOUNT
                         R- ANNUAL INTEREST RATE
                         I- MONTHLY INTEREST
                         A$, B$ - FORMAT STRINGS

1100   OPTION TYPE = DECIMAL, SIZE = DECIMAL(12,2) ,&
                         ACTIVE=DECIMAL ROUNDING
                    ! --- option must precede comment fields ---
                    !--- get values of p and r -----------------
2000   INPUT "PRINCIPAL AMOUNT"; P
       INPUT "ANNUAL INTEREST RATE (AS A PERCENT)"; R

                    !--- open data file and print header ----
2400   OPEN "MONEY.DAT" FOR OUTPUT AS FILE #1
       PRINT #1, "TABLE OF VALUES FOR MONTHLY INTEREST ON " ; P
       PRINT #1, " AT " ; R ; " PERCENT ANNUAL INTEREST"
                    !
                    !--- set up header ---------------------------
       PRINT     "MONTH      PRINCIPAL      INTEREST "
       PRINT #1, "MONTH      PRINCIPAL      INTEREST "
       LET F$ = "  ##        $$###,#####.##    $$#,#######.## "
```

(Continued)

FIGURE 15.3 Continued

```
3000              !--- compute interest to nearest cent
          FOR N = 1 TO 12
            LET I = P * R * .01 / 12
            PRINT    USING F$,    N , P , I
            PRINT #1 USING F$,    N , P , I
            LET P = P + I
          NEXT N
                  !--- close the file -----
3900      CLOSE #1
4000      END
```

OUTPUT

```
TABLE OF VALUES FOR MONTHLY INTEREST ON  1000000
AT  10  PERCENT ANNUAL INTEREST
MONTH         PRINCIPAL          INTEREST
  1         $1,000,000.00        $8,333.33
  2         $1,008,333.33        $8,402.77
  3         $1,016,736.10        $8,472.80
  4         $1,025,208.90        $8,543.40
  5         $1,033,752.30        $8,614.60
  6         $1,042,366.90        $8,686.39
  7         $1,051,053.29        $8,758.77
  8         $1,059,812.06        $8,831.76
  9         $1,068,643.82        $8,905.36
 10         $1,077,549.18        $8,979.57
 11         $1,086,528.75        $9,054.40
 12         $1,095,583.15        $9,129.86
```

15.2 Compiling Programs in DCL Mode

The process of translating a program from a high-level language, such as BASIC, to a form that the computer can understand proceeds in two steps:

1. The computer translates the source code (your program) into object code. *Object code* is an intermediate form that the computer can use to build a machine-language version of your program.

15.3 EXTERNAL FUNCTION PROGRAMS

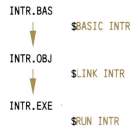

FIGURE 15.4 The process of compiling a BASIC program.

2. The object code is translated to a form that the computer can execute (that is, a machine language version of your program).

These steps are carried out automatically when you RUN a program in BASIC mode. You can carry out this process in DCL mode by using the `$BASIC`, `$LINK`, and `$RUN` commands.

For example, if you want to compile a program called `INTR.BAS` in DCL mode, first give the `$BASIC` command followed by the file name (that is, type $BASIC INTR). This translates the program file INTR.BAS to object code. Note that the presence of a file name changes the effect of the `$BASIC` command. This creates the file `INTR.OBJ`, which contains the object code (see Fig. 15.4). When you enter the command `$LINK INTR`, the computer creates the file `INTR.EXE`, which contains the instructions translated into machine code. Finally, the instructions contained in the file INTR.EXE are loaded into the computer's main memory and carried out when you type the command `$RUN INTR`.

15.3 External Function Programs

External function programs are similar to user defined functions except that they are defined outside the main program that uses them. The external function program is like a standard BASIC function definition except that it begins with a `FUNCTION` statement and ends with an `END FUNCTION` statement. The `FUNCTION` statement has the form

⟨line #⟩ FUNCTION ⟨data type⟩   ⟨function name⟩(arguments)

The ⟨data type⟩ is one of the key words `REAL`, `INTEGER`, `LONG`, and so on, that we discussed earlier. The key word describes the value that the function returns. The (arguments) section contains a list of the data types and local

OTHER FEATURES OF VAX-BASIC

```
100 FUNCTION REAL RUNWALK(D,T)
        ! external function to determine the
        ! exercise value of a run or walk

200 IF T=0
      THEN
          RUNWALK = -1
          EXIT FUNCTION
    END IF

300 LET RATE = D/T
    IF RATE < 6
      THEN
          LET EXVAL =10/3*( D*(RATE-1) -1 )
      ELSE
          LET EXVAL = 10/3*( D*(5+2/3*(RATE-6)) -1 )
    END IF

    IF EXVAL <0
      THEN EXVAL = 0
    END IF

    IF RATE > 15 OR EXVAL > 700
      THEN
           LET EXVAL = -1
    END IF

    RUNWALK = EXVAL
400 END FUNCTION
```

FIGURE 15.5

variables used in the function program to define the function. The program of Fig. 15.5 uses a function header of the form

    100 FUNCTION REAL RUNWALK(D,T)

The data type of the local variables D and T has not been specified, and they will take on the default type REAL unless otherwise specified in an OPTION statement. The data type could have been specified explicitly using the statement

    100 FUNCTION REAL RUNWALK(REAL D,REAL T)

A main program that makes use of an external function uses an EXTERNAL statement to inform the BASIC compiler that an external function

15.3 EXTERNAL FUNCTION PROGRAMS

```
100 REM !********************************
     AEROBIC2  showing the use of an
     external function.

200 EXTERNAL REAL FUNCTION RUNWALK(REAL,REAL)

300 INPUT 'HOW FAR DID YOU RUN'; DIST

400 INPUT 'HOW MANY HOURS'; TIME.HRS
    INPUT 'HOW MANY ADDITIONAL MINUTES';TIME.MIN
    LET TOT.TIME = TIME.HRS +TIME.MIN/60

500 LET EXVAL = RUNWALK(DIST,TOT.TIME)
    PRINT 'YOUR RUN HAD AN EXERCISE VALUE OF';EXVAL

600 END
```

FIGURE 15.6

program is to be used. The EXTERNAL statement has the form:

    EXTERNAL ⟨data type⟩ FUNCTION ⟨function name⟩(args)

The ⟨data type⟩ and ⟨function name⟩ are the same as in the function definition. The (args) clause is a list of the data types (only) of each of the arguments of the function. In particular, the EXTERNAL statement to reference the external function program of Fig. 15.5 would have the form,

    200 EXTERNAL REAL FUNCTION RUNWALK(REAL,REAL)

Figure 15.6 shows an example of a program that uses the external function program defined in Fig. 15.5.

A special procedure is required before running a program that uses an external function program (see Fig. 15.7). First, object files are created using the $BASIC AEROBIC2 and the $BASIC RUNWALK commands. Then these object files are linked by using the command $LINK AEROBIC2, RUNWALK. The

```
AEROBIC2.BAS           RUNWALK.BAS
       ↓ $BASIC AEROBIC2   ↓ $BASIC RUNWALK
AEROBIC2.OBJ           RUNWALK.OBJ
           ↘       ↙ $LINK AEROBIC2, RUNWALK
          AEROBIC2.EXE
```

FIGURE 15.7 The AEROBIC2 main program and the external function program RUNWALK are compiled separately and then linked to form the executable file AEROBIC2.EXE.

result is an executable file `AEROBIC2.EXE` which can then be loaded into the computer and carried out using the `$RUN AEROBIC2` command.

This procedure may seem long and hardly worth the effort. However, this method allows you to use function programs like the RUNWALK program in any number of different main programs. Each such function program thus becomes a building block that can be incorporated into larger programs.

The same type of procedure can be employed to use an external function written in a different language.

15.4 External Subprograms

External subprograms are independent program sections that are similar to external function programs except that they do not return a value to the main program. External subprograms begin with the `SUB` statement and end with the `END SUB` statement. The `SUB` statement has the form

<line #> SUB ⟨name⟩ (args)

Here again, the arguments are specified in terms of local variables. The data type of each argument may also be specified in the SUB statement.

The `CALL` statement is used in the main program to begin executing a subprogram. The `CALL` statement has the form

CALL ⟨name⟩ (args)

```
100 SUB GETWRD(IN$,W$,R$)
    ! This program separates the first word from
    ! a sentence that you type in.
    !  IN$ - the input string
    !  W$  - the first word of S$
    !  R$  - the remainder of S$
    !
200         ! --- convert to 'standard sentence'
    LET S$ = EDIT$(IN$,152)
300         ! --- split the sentence ----
    LET L = LEN(S$)
    LET F = POS(S$," ",1)
    LET W$ = SEG$(S$,1,F-1)
    LET R$ = SEG$(S$,F+1,L)
400 END SUB
```

FIGURE 15.8

```
100 !*****************************************
    ! PROGRAM: F I R S T W O R D
    !*****************************************
                !
    REM This program will separate the first
    word of a sentence.

200 INPUT 'TYPE A SENTENCE'; INP$
    CALL GETWRD(INP$,WW$,RR$)

300 PRINT WW$
    PRINT RR$

400 END
```

FIGURE 15.9

```
$BAS FIRSTWORD
$BAS GETWRD
$LINK FIRSTWORD, GETWRD
$RUN FIRSTWORD
```

FIGURE 15.10

where ⟨name⟩ is the name of the subprogram and ⟨args⟩ is a list of the actual arguments that are passed to the subprogram.

In the example of Fig. 15.8, the `GETWORD` program of Fig. 10.18 has been rewritten as a `BASIC` subprogram. This subprogram has three arguments, one that provides the input string `IN$` and two that return the split substring to the calling program. Thus, subprograms can return values much like function subprograms, except that the returned values must be arguments of the subprogram.

Figure 15.9 contains a program that calls the subprogram of Fig. 15.8. These programs can be compiled and linked separately and then run using a procedure similar to the one outlined above for an external function program (see Fig. 15.10).

15.5 Exercises

15.1 Write a short test program to illustrate that `N` and `N%` are different variables. What happens when you declare N to be an integer variable and use `N` and `N%` in your program? What happens when you try to declare N% as an integer variable?

15.2 Modify the AUTO program of Exercise 10.5 so that double-precision, real calculations are performed. Compare the output of the two versions of the program for base prices of $12,378.98 and $7678.23.

15.3 Rewrite the EXERCISE program (Fig. 12.3), so that a subprogram or external function program is used to calculate the exercise value of each different activity.

15.4 Write the `FNJULIAN` function of Fig. 10.40 as an external function program. Repeat Exercise 10.8, but this time use the external function program.

15.5 Modify the `BIRTHDAY` program of Fig. 14.13 so that it uses an external function program for the Julian date.

DEC Command Language Summary

Appendix A is a summary of the most useful DCL commands. In the following section, the term *filespec* is used as an abbreviation for file specification. On the VAX computer, a complete file specification has the form,

    _<node>::<disk>:[<username>]<filename.type>;<version #>

For example:

    _VAXA::DISKA1:[THISUSER]MYFILE.BAS;2

Except where noted, only the file name and type need to be specified for a filespec; the other information is supplied by the system.

All of the following commands may be abbreviated to the first three letters and in some cases to two letters if there is no possibility of confusion. For example LOGOUT, PRINT, and TYPE can be abbreviated to LO, PR, and TY, respectively.

APPENDIX A

APPEND   Copies the contents of the input file to the end of the target file. Format is

         APPEND <input filespec> <target filespec>

         After the APPEND command is carried out, the input file is unchanged and the target file contains the previous contents of both files.

BASIC   Enters BASIC mode when used alone. Compiles a BASIC program to produce an object file when used with a filespec (see Chapter 15).

COPY   Makes a second copy of an existing file. Format is

         COPY <existing filespec> <new filespec>

         Use the RENAME command if you do not want two copies of the same file.

DELETE   Erases a file from disk memory. Format is

         DELETE filename.type;version

         Note that the file version number is normally required. Use the form,

         DELETE filename.type;*

         to delete *all* versions of a file. Use the form,

         DELETE filename.type;

         to delete the *latest* version.

333

APPENDIX A

DIRECTORY	Types a list of your files.
EDIT	Enters EDIT mode (see Appendix H). Format is EDIT <filespec>
HELP	Calls the DCL help facility. Typing HELP alone will provide information about how to get help on DCL commands. Typing HELP followed by a command will provide information on that command.
LOGOUT	Ends a session.
MAIL	Enters MAIL mode. In MAIL mode, messages can be sent or received. Here is a brief description of the process: Type MAIL, and when you receive the mail prompt (MAIL>), press the RETURN key to read your new incoming mail or type SEND to send mail. You must know the USERNAME of the person to whom you are sending mail. Use the >EXIT command to return to DCL mode.
PHONE	Enters PHONE mode. In PHONE mode, two way communications between users can be established. Enter PHONE mode and type %HELP for more information.
PRINT	Causes the high-speed printer to print a copy of the named file. Format is PRINT <filespec>
PURGE	Deletes all but the highest-numbered version of files with the same name and type. Format is PURGE
RENAME	Gives a file a new name. Format is RENAME <old filespec> <new filespec>
SET PASSWORD	Enables you to change your password to one that is easier for you to remember. After you type the SET PAS command, you will be prompted to type your old password and then your new password. You will be asked to type the new password a second time to verify that there were no mistakes.
SHOW	Enables you to obtain information about the system. Some possible formats are, SHOW TIME SHOW DEFAULT SHOW USERS SHOW QUEUE <queue name>

SHOW TIME gives the current time; **SHOW DEFAULT** indicates the default user disk and user name in the form disk:[username], and **SHOW USERS** gives a list of users currently on the computer. See Section 1.11 for more about the **SHOW QUEUE** command.

TYPE   Displays the contents of a file. Format is

                  TYPE <filespec>

Summary of BASIC Commands

Appendix B is a summary of the most commonly used BASIC commands. Pointed brackets (⟨ ⟩) contain descriptions of parts of the BASIC command. Square brackets ([ ]) indicate that the enclosed parts are optional.

APPEND
: Brings a named program into main memory without deleting the current program. This can be used to combine programs (see Section 8.4.).

CONTINUE
: Resumes program execution after a STOP or an interruption using ⟨ctrl/c⟩.

DELETE
: Erases specified lines from the current program. Format is

    DELETE ⟨line #⟩

    to delete a single line, or

    DELETE ⟨first line #⟩ - ⟨ending line #⟩

    to delete a range of lines.

EDIT
: Enters EDIT mode (when typed alone) or changes program text (when typed with an argument). See Appendix H for more about EDIT mode. See Section 1.12 for more about using EDIT to change program lines. Format is

    EDIT /⟨old string⟩/new string⟩/ [⟨occurrence⟩] [,⟨sub-line⟩]

    If a slash (/) appears in either the old or the new string, substitute another delimiter like "?" or "@" that is not contained in either string.

EXIT
: Leaves BASIC mode and enters DCL mode.

HELP
: Displays information about BASIC commands or statements. Format is

    HELP [⟨topic⟩]

    Two common topics are COMMANDS (for help with BASIC commands) and STATEMENTS (for help with BASIC statements). Type HELP for a complete list of topics. Responses can be abbreviated.

LIST
: Displays the BASIC program currently in main memory. Displays a portion of the current program if line numbers are specified. Format is

    LIST [⟨start line #⟩ - ⟨end line #⟩]

APPENDIX B

APPENDIX B

LISTNH	Same as LIST, except the program header is not displayed.
NEW	Erases current program from main memory and names a new program. Format is NEW [<program name>]
OLD	Erases the current program from main memory and reads a copy of a specified program from disk memory into main memory. Format is OLD [<program name>]
RENAME	Gives the current program a new name. Format is RENAME <new name>
RESEQUENCE	Assigns new line numbers to the program in main memory. The program should be running properly before you resequence the lines. Typing RESEQUENCE will resequence all of the lines of the program, assigning new line numbers starting at 100 and using an increment, or STEP, of 10. You can also specify a range of line numbers, a starting value for the new line numbers, or a STEP value used to increment each line number. See Sections 1.7 and 8.4 for examples. Format is RESEQUENCE [<from #> - <to #> [<new start #> [STEP <val>]]]
RUN	Executes the current program. If a program name is specified, then that program will first be read into main memory. Format is RUN [<program name>]
RUNNH	Same as RUN, except the program header is not printed.
SAVE	Copies the current program into disk memory.
SEQUENCE	Starts the automatic generation of line numbers. Format is SEQUENCE [<start line # > [,<increment>]] See Section 1.12 for more about the SEQUENCE command.
UNSAVE	Deletes a previously saved file from disk memory. Format is UNSAVE <program name>

Summary of BASIC Statements

Appendix C is a summary of the most common BASIC statements.

CALL — Executes an external subprogram or library routine (see Section 15.8). Format is

CALL <name> [<method>] [(vbls)]

where ⟨name⟩ is the name of the subprogram or external library routine; ⟨method⟩ is the method by which parameter values are passed and is either BY REF, BY VALUE, or BY DESC; and (vbls) is a list of the actual variables passed.

CHANGE — Converts between a numeric array of ASCII values and a string of characters. Format is

CHANGE <string> TO <array>

or

CHANGE <array> TO <string>

For example, the statement

100 CHANGE "PLAN" TO A

will convert the word PLAN into the four ASCII values 80, 76, 65, and 78 and store the numbers in the array A. $A(1) = 80$, $A(2) = 76$, and so on. (See Appendix F for a list of ASCII values.)

CASE — See SELECT

CLOSE — Closes a file (see also OPEN in Appendix C). Format is

CLOSE #2

DATA — Supplies values for a READ statement. Data items are separated by commas. String data may be enclosed in quotes. DATA statements must begin with a line number and can contain only data (comments or other types of statements cannot be combined with a DATA statement). For example,

<line#> DATA 32, 456.789, 25%, TWO WORDS, " ONE AND, TWO"

DECLARE — Assigns an explicit data type (real, integer, or string) to a variable or creates user-defined constants. The format for

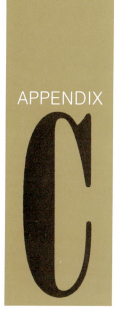

APPENDIX C

APPENDIX C

assigning a data type is

```
DECLARE <data type> <variable> [,<variable>...]
```

where the most common data types are REAL, INTEGER, and STRING (see Table 15.1 for a complete list of data types). Note that the variable names should not end with $ or %. Examples are

```
DECLARE INTEGER I, N, M
DECLARE STRING A, OUT, IN
DECLARE INTEGER K, STRING B, C, WORD L
```

Constants are declared as follows:

```
DECLARE REAL CONSTANT EPS=0.0001
DECLARE INTEGER CONSTANT MAX.N=10000
DECLARE STRING CONSTANT FORM1="######.##"
```

DEF   Used in conjunction with the FNEND or END DEF clause to create user-defined functions. Format is

```
DEF FN<name> ( <function parameters> )
   .
   .
   .
   <program statements defining the function value
   in terms of the function parameters>
   .
   .
   .
FNEND or END DEF
```

where FN⟨name⟩ is the function name—that is, it is a variable name starting with the letters FN. The function parameters are the local variables, separated by commas, that are used to define the function.

DELETE #⟨chnl⟩   Deletes the current line of the file that is open on channel number ⟨chnl⟩. See also the DELETE command in Appendix B.

DIM   Creates an array or matrix. A data type can also be declared as in the DECLARE statement above. Format is

```
DIM[ENSION] [<type>] <name>(<subscript sizes>) [,...]
```

Some examples are,

```
DIMENSION Y(3,2)
DIM OUT$(6), AA%(3,3)
DIM A(15), XX(2,3), N%(4), IN$(6)
```

SUMMARY OF BASIC STATEMENTS

```
DIMENSION INTEGER AA(3,3), B(2,5)
DIM STRING C(8)
DIM INTEGER D(12), STRING BW(6,16)
```

END   Marks the last statement of the program. The following forms are used as indicated:

     END DEF   Ends a user-defined function definition.
     END FUNCTION   Ends an external function program.
     END IF   Ends an IF-THEN or IF-THEN-ELSE block.
     END SELECT   Ends a SELECT/CASE block.
     END SUB   Ends an external subprogram.

EXIT   Leaves a function DEF block, an external function program, or an external subprogram. EXIT can also be used to leave a labeled FOR, IF, SELECT, UNTIL, or WHILE block. Format is

```
EXIT DEF
EXIT FUNCTION
EXIT SUB
EXIT <label>
```

EXTERNAL   This is used at the beginning of a program to indicate that an external function program will be used later in the program (see Chapter 15).

FNEND   Marks the last statement of a function definition. See also DEF and END DEF.

FOR   Begins a FOR Loop. FOR is used with the NEXT statement. Examples are,

```
FOR K = 1 TO 10            ( ... NEXT K)
FOR Y = 1 TO 9 STEP 2      ( ... NEXT Y)
FOR N = 11 TO 7 STEP -.5   ( . . NEXT N)
```

FUNCTION   Used at the beginning of an external function program. Format is

```
FUNCTION <data type> <name> [ (vbls) ]
```

where ⟨data type⟩ is the data type that the function returns (REAL, INTEGER, and so on), ⟨name⟩ is the function name, and (vbls) is a list of the dummy variables used in the function definition. The data type of each dummy variable can also be specified in (vbls).

APPENDIX C

GET Transfers a line from a mapped file to the map buffer in main memory. A key clause can also be specified to locate a record in an indexed file. Format is

GET #<chnl> [,key #<key number> <keyspec>]

where the ⟨keyspec⟩ uses one of the abbreviations EQ, GE, or GT (for equal to, greater than or equal to, and greater than, respectively) followed by a string or integer expression. For example,

GET #1

GET #1, KEY #1 GE N%

GET #1, KEY #0 EQ FIND.LAST$

GOSUB Transfers program execution to a specified subroutine. Format is

GOSUB <line number or label>

A RETURN statement at the end of the subroutine transfers control back to the statement following the GOSUB statement in the main program.

GOTO Transfers program control. Format is

GOTO <line number or label>

IF Used with THEN and ELSE to create decision-making constructs (see Chapter 4). Format is

<line #> IF <condition>
    THEN
        <statements>
    ELSE
        <statements>
    [END IF]

The first group of statements is carried out if the condition is true and the second group, if present, is carried out if the condition is false.

INPUT Assigns values to one or more variables from a terminal or a terminal format file. Examples are:

INPUT "A NAME", N$

INPUT "THREE NUMBERS"; X1, X2, X3

INPUT #1, A

INPUT #2, N%, AA1, S$

SUMMARY OF BASIC STATEMENTS

LET
Assigns values and can also perform calculations (see Sections 2.2 and 3.1). For example,
LET X = 7.56
LET X = Z**2 + SQR(W)
LET OUT$="ABCDEF"
LET X, Y, Z = 0

LINPUT
Assigns a value to a string variable from a terminal or a terminal format file. The LINPUT statement accepts the whole line, including commas and quotation marks, as input to the string variable. For example,
LINPUT "TYPE YOUR MESSAGE"; A$
LINPUT B$
LINPUT #1, C$

MAP
Associates a memory buffer with a sequential data file, and associates program variables with portions of the buffer. Format is
MAP (<name>) <map fields>

where ⟨name⟩ is the name of the MAP and ⟨map fields⟩ is one or more of the following items separated by commas:
<string variable name> = <string length>
[<data type>] <numerical variable name>
[<data type>] <numerical array name>(dimensions)

MARGIN
Sets the right margin for a terminal format file. Format is
MARGIN #<chnl>, <width>

MAT
Performs matrix operations (see Chapter 13). Used with one or more of the following special terms:
ZER   The zero matrix (all values equal to 0).
CON   The matrix with all values equal to 1.
IDN   The identity matrix (square matrices only).
NUL$ The null-string matrix (all values the empty string).
INV   Inverts a matrix (square, invertible matrices only).
TRN   Transposes a matrix (interchanges rows and columns).
Examples are:
MAT Z = CON   MAT A = B + C
MAT W = Z   MAT D = (3)*E
MAT X = Y*Z   MAT F = TRN G

APPENDIX C

MAT INPUT	Assigns values to array elements from a terminal or a terminal format file. For example,

MAT INPUT XX

MAT INPUT #1, YY

Values are assigned to the array row by row. Input from a file stops at the end of a line unless the last character on the line is an ampersand (&). Row and column zero are not assigned.

MAT LINPUT — Assigns values to a string array from a terminal or a terminal format file. For example,

MAT LINPUT AA$

MAT LINPUT #2, BB$

MAT PRINT — Displays the contents of an array on the terminal screen. For example,

MAT PRINT XX

MAT PRINT YY,

MAT PRINT ZZ;

Values in row and column zero are not displayed. The punctuation at the end of the statement determines the format of the output as follows:

- No punctuation: all values are displayed on separate lines.
- Comma: each row is displayed on one line with values printed in different tab zones.
- Semicolon: each row is displayed on one line with values separated by two spaces.

MAT READ — Assigns values to an array from a data list. For example,

MAT READ A

Values are assigned row by row beginning with row 1 and column 1. If the end of the data list is reached before all array elements are assigned, then the remaining array elements keep their original values. Row and column zero are not changed by a **MAT READ** statement.

ON ERROR — Traps certain errors within a program (see Section 11.4). For example,

ON ERROR GOTO 19000

will transfer program control to line 19000 if an error

SUMMARY OF BASIC STATEMENTS

occurs. The statement:

```
ON ERROR GOTO 0
```

returns to the usual system error handler. See also **RESUME**.

ON GOSUB — Transfers program control to one of a number of different subroutines (see Section 8.1). Format is

```
ON <cvbl> GOSUB <list of loc's> [ OTHERWISE <loc> ]
```

where 〈loc〉 is a location specified by a line number or a label and 〈cvbl〉 is an integer-valued control variable used to determine which line number is selected. For example,

```
ON K GOSUB 1000, 2000, 4000, 5000
ON L GOSUB show_file, add_names, &
update_info OTHERWISE close_file
```

ON GOTO — This is similar to the **ON GOSUB** except program control is transferred to the appropriate line. For example,

```
ON X GOTO 100, 300, 700
```

OPEN — Creates new data files or assigns existing ones. Terminal format files are opened using

```
OPEN "<filename.type>"[FOR OUTPUT or FOR INPUT] &
AS FILE #<chnl>
```

For example,

```
OPEN "NMBRS.DAT" FOR OUTPUT AS FILE #2
OPEN "BUSI.TXT" AS FILE #3
```

The OPEN statement can also be followed by one or more of the following clauses:

```
,[ORGANIZATION] SEQUENTIAL
,[ORGANIZATION] INDEXED
,ACCESS APPEND
,RECORDSIZE <size>
,MAP <name>
,PRIMARY KEY <key name> [DUPLICATES]
,ALTERNATE KEY <key name> [DUPLICATES] [CHANGES]
```

The **RECORDSIZE** clause is similar to the **MARGIN** statement. There are restrictions on the use of these clauses. See Chapter 14 for more information.

OPTION — Sets data types and other compile-time default conditions. The OPTION statement must be at the very beginning of the program (except for REM statements or the SUB or FUNCTION statement). The key word OPTION is followed by one or more of the following clauses, separated by commas:

TYPE = <data type>

SIZE = <subtype>

ACTIVE = <checks>

where ⟨data type⟩ is INTEGER or DECIMAL and specifies the data type of all variables in the program that are not explicitly given data types (REAL can also be specified, but this is the default); ⟨subtype⟩ is a data subtype specification for all variables of a given type and consists of a specification of a decimal size of the form DECIMAL(d,s), or a general and specific data-type pair of the form REAL DOUBLE or INTEGER WORD (see Table 15.1); and ⟨checks⟩ can be either DECIMAL ROUNDING or SUBSCRIPT CHECKING.

PRINT — Displays program data at the terminal or prints the data to a terminal format data file. Different expressions in a PRINT statement must be separated by a semicolon or a comma. A semicolon causes the next output to be printed immediately after the previous output. (Numbers are printed with a leading space or minus sign and a trailing space.) A comma causes the next output to be printed in the next tab zone. (Tab zones begin every 14 spaces.) An expression contained within quotes is printed literally. An expression containing variables is evaluated and the resulting value is printed. For example:

PRINT "THE AVERAGE IS "; SUM/N

PRINT #1, X, Y, Z

PRINT "X + Y = " ; X+Y

PRINT USING — Specifies how data is to be printed using a special format string. Examples are:

PRINT USING "ITEM:'LLLL " , A$

PRINT USING "PRICE:$$###.## " , X , Y

PRINT #1 USING "### , ###.## " , Z , W

PUT — Writes the contents of a MAP buffer to a mapped file (See Section 14.3). Format is

PUT #<chnl>

SUMMARY OF BASIC STATEMENTS

RANDOMIZE	Gives the RND function an unpredictable starting point. The RANDOMIZE statement is normally used only once in a program.
READ	Transfers values from a data list to one or more variables.
REM	Begins a remark statement. Everything from the REM key word to the next line number is ignored when the program is run.
RESTORE	Starts over at the beginning of a data list or a data file. That is, the next READ statement after a RESTORE statement reads the first entry in the DATA list, and the first INPUT # <chnl> statement after a RESTORE # <chnl> statement reads the first line of the data file open on that channel. For example, RESTORE RESTORE #2
RESUME	Used in the error handling section of a program to resume program execution at the point in the program where the error occurred or at a specified line number. A label cannot be used in the resume statement. For example, RESUME 350 RESUME
RETURN	Marks the end of a subroutine. The RETURN statement causes the program to resume at the statements immediately after the GOSUB or ON GOSUB statement that called the subroutine.

SELECT	Begins a select block that allows the computer to select one of a number of different options. The select block has the form,
	
	SELECT <test vbl>
	    CASE <condition>
	        <statements>
	    CASE <condition>
	        <statements>
	        .
	        .
	        .
	END SELECT
	
	where ⟨test vbl⟩ is the variable or expression to be tested and ⟨condition⟩ is the condition that ⟨test vbl⟩ is to satisfy.

APPENDIX C

The ⟨condition⟩ can be a standard relational or logical condition, such as

= 5
> 100
<= "Z"
<> X

or it can specify a range of values using TO,

X TO Y
3 TO 5
"A" TO "Z"

If the ⟨test vbl⟩ satisfies the ⟨condition⟩, then all of the statements after the CASE key word are carried out and the program continues with the next statement after the END SELECT. An optional CASE ELSE clause may be used as the last case item. The statements following this clause would be carried out if none of the other conditions were satisfied.

SLEEP — Causes a pause in program execution for up to 255 seconds. For example, the statement

SLEEP 10

causes a 10-second pause. Pressing the RETURN key ends the time delay.

STOP — Halts program execution and prints a message giving the line number where the STOP occurred. The program can be resumed by typing CONT. This is often useful in the debugging process.

SUB — Used as the first line of an external subprogram. Format is

SUB <name> [(vbls)]

where ⟨name⟩ is the name of the subprogram and (vbls) is a list of the dummy variables that represent parameters that are to be passed from the main program to the subprogram.

UNLESS — This is a modifier that can be placed after a statement:

<statement> UNLESS <condition>

The statement is executed unless the condition is true. For example, the following PRINT statement is not executed if X is negative:

100 PRINT "THE ROOT IS "; SQR(X)   UNLESS X < 0

SUMMARY OF BASIC STATEMENTS

UNTIL
: Marks the beginning of an UNTIL loop. (The end of the loop is indicated by the word NEXT.) Format is

    UNTIL <condition>

    The condition is first tested when the loop is started (that is, when the UNTIL statement is first executed), and tested again each time the NEXT statement at the end of the loop is executed. The statements in the loop are executed if the condition is found to be false. For example,

    UNTIL X < 0

    UNTIL A = 0 OR B > 20

UPDATE
: Replaces a record in a mapped file with the current contents of the map buffer. Format is

    UPDATE #<chnl>

WHILE
: Marks the beginning of a WHILE loop. (The word NEXT marks the end of the loop.) For example,

    WHILE X == 0

    WHILE (B/A)< 4

    The condition is tested when the loop starts and each time the NEXT statement is executed. The statements in the loop are executed if the condition is found to be true.

Numeric Functions and Constants

In Appendix D, we list most of the standard functions that are useful for calculations. This includes the SIN, COS, TAN and ATN (arctan) functions. All trigonometric functions use radian measure. An angle can be converted from degrees to radians by multiplying by `PI/180`. (`PI`, the constant 3.14159..., is always available for use in a BASIC program.)

ABS( )   Returns the absolute value of its argument. For example,

```
LET Y = ABS(6.7)
```

assigns the value 6.7 to Y, and

```
LET Z = ABS(-56.3)
```

assigns the value 56.3 to Z.

EXP( )   Returns the value of e raised to the power of the expression in the argument. (The symbol e represents a specific irrational number that is approximately equal to 2.71828) For example,

```
LET X = EXP(3.24)
```

assigns the value $e^{3.24}$ to X.

FIX( )   Returns a value that is the whole-number part of the argument. For example,

```
LET X =FIX(4.56)
```

assigns the value 4 to X, and

```
LET K = FIX(-5.78)
```

assigns the value -5 to K.

INT( )   Returns the value of the largest integer less than or equal to the argument. For example,

```
LET X =INT(4.56)
```

assigns the value 4 to X, and

```
LET K = INT(-5.78)
```

assigns the value -6 to K.

LOG( )   Returns the natural log of the argument.

LOG10( )   Returns the log to the base 10 of the argument.

PI   The constant 3.14159....

APPENDIX D

RND	Returns an unpredictable ("pseudo-random") number between 0 and 1 ($0 \leq \text{RND} < 1$).
SGN( )	Returns a number that represents the sign of its argument: +1 if the argument is positive, −1 if it is negative, and 0 if it is zero.
SQR( )	Returns the square root of its argument. The argument must be nonnegative.

In addition, there are the following trigonometric functions:

ATN( )	This is the inverse tangent or arc tangent function. It returns a value between -PI/2 and PI/2 that represents an angle (in radians) whose tangent is equal to the value of the argument.
SIN( ), COS( ), TAN( )	The argument of each of these functions must be specified in radians.

String Functions and Constants

`CHR$( )`	Converts a number into a string using the ASCII code. This function is useful in representing the nonprinting characters such as the "bell", `CHR$(7)`.
`DATE$( )`	Returns a date in the form DD-Mmm-YY. If the argument is 0, it returns the current date, otherwise a date is calculated, as described in Chapter 10.
`DIF$( , )`	Subtracts two numeric strings. For example, `DIF$(A$,B$)` subtracts the numeric string `B$` from the numeric string `A$` and returns a value that is a numeric string representing the difference.
`EDIT$( , )`	Edits the string specified in the first argument using instructions provided by the second argument. Some of the options for the second argument are as follows: 2 Discard all spaces and tabs. 8 Discard leading spaces and tabs. 16 Remove extra embedded spaces and tabs. 32 Convert lower- to uppercase letters. 128 Discard trailing spaces and tabs. More than one option can be specified by adding the numbers together. For example, 8 + 16 + 128 = 152 is used to convert to standard sentence format.
`ESC`	A string constant equal to the ASCII "escape" character. This is equivalent to `CHR$(27)`.
`FORMAT$( , )`	Converts a number into a string. The rules for conversion are the same as those for printing numbers with the `PRINT USING` statement. For example, `FORMAT$(X*Y , "$$###.##")`
`LEFT$( , )`	Duplicates the left part of a given string to create another string. For example, `100 LET B$ = LEFT$(A$,4)` forms the new string B$ by duplicating the first four characters of the string A$. The same thing can be accomplished using `SEG$(A$,1,4)`.

APPENDIX E

APPENDIX E

LEN( )   Returns a number giving the total length of a string. For example,

            LET N = LEN(D$)

MID$(, ,)   Duplicates part of a string to create another string. For example,

            LET B$ = MID$(A$,5,3)

creates a string of length 3 from string A$ starting at the fifth character. The same thing can be accomplished with SEG$(A$,5,7).

NUL$ The null or empty string array. This is used in the MAT statements.

NUM$( )   Converts a number into a string using the rules for printing numbers discussed in Chapter 3. The string includes a trailing space and a leading space or minus sign.

POS(, ,)   Searches a string for a given substring. It returns an integer giving the position of the first character of the substring. For example,

            LET N = POS(A$,"ER",4)

searches the string A$ beginning at character number 4 for the substring ER.

PROD$(, ,)   Multiplies numeric strings. See QUO$(, ,).

QUO$(, ,)   Divides numeric strings. For example,

            LET B$ = QUO$(N$,D$,3)

computes VAL(N$)/VAL(D$) and converts the answer to a string, rounding the result to three decimal places of accuracy. You may specify rounding from −5 up to 5 decimal places (−1 specifies rounding to the nearest tens, −2 to the nearest hundreds, and so on).

RIGHT$(,)   Duplicates the right portion of a given string to create a new string. For example,

            LET B$ = RIGHT$(A$,6)

creates a new string that duplicates the characters of string A$ starting from character 6. The same thing can be accomplished with

            LET B$ = SEG$(A$,6,LEN(A$))

STRING FUNCTIONS AND CONSTANTS

SEG$(, ,)	Duplicates a portion of a given string to create a new string. The original string is not changed in the process. For example, `LET B$ = SEG$(A$,5,7)` duplicates characters 5 through 7 of string A$ to create the new string B$.
SP	A string constant equal to the space character.
SPACE$( )	Creates a string consisting of a given number of spaces. For example, `LET B$ = SPACE$(12)` returns a string consisting of 12 spaces.
STRING$(,)	Returns a string with a given number of identical characters. For example, `LET B$ = STRING$(5,45)` returns a string of five hyphens or minus signs: "-----". The 45 is the ASCII decimal code for the minus sign.
STR$( )	Converts a number into a numeric string. This is identical to the NUM$ function, except that leading and trailing spaces are not added.
SUM$(,)	Calculates the sum of two numeric strings and converts the result into a string.
TAB( )	Used in a PRINT statement to move the print cursor to a specified column. For example, `PRINT A$; TAB(10) ; "*"` prints the asterisk in column 11 unless A$ has more than 10 characters. In this case, TAB(10) would have no effect and the asterisk would be printed immediately after the value of A$.
TIME$	This returns the current time of day as a string in the form 02:15 PM or 11:45 AM.
VAL( )	See VAL%( ).
VAL%( )	Converts a numeric string into a number. The string must be a valid representation of a number.
XLATE(,)	Translates a string using a look-up table that you provide. This may be used to convert from the EBCDIC code to ASCII code. (Also see Section 11.6.)

Table of ASCII Values

Number	Character	Number	Character
0	null (tape feed)	37	%
1	⟨ctrl/A⟩	38	&
2	⟨ctrl/B⟩	39	'
3	⟨ctrl/C⟩	40	(
4	⟨ctrl/D⟩	41	)
5	⟨ctrl/E⟩	42	*
6	⟨ctrl/F⟩	43	+
7	⟨ctrl/G⟩ (bell)	44	,
8	⟨ctrl/H⟩ (backspace)	45	−
9	⟨ctrl/I⟩ (tab)	46	.
10	⟨ctrl/J⟩ (line feed)	47	/
11	⟨ctrl/K⟩	48	0
12	⟨ctrl/L⟩ (form feed)	49	1
13	⟨ctrl/M⟩ (carriage return)	50	2
14	⟨ctrl/N⟩	51	3
15	⟨ctrl/O⟩	52	4
16	⟨ctrl/P⟩	53	5
17	⟨ctrl/Q⟩	54	6
18	⟨ctrl/R⟩	55	7
19	⟨ctrl/S⟩	56	8
20	⟨ctrl/T⟩	57	9
21	⟨ctrl/U⟩	58	:
22	⟨ctrl/V⟩	59	;
23	⟨ctrl/W⟩	60	⟨
24	⟨ctrl/X⟩	61	=
25	⟨ctrl/Y⟩	62	⟩
26	⟨ctrl/Z⟩	63	?
27	⟨esc⟩ (escape)	64	@
28	(file separator)	65	A
29	(group separator)	66	B
30	(record separator)	67	C
31	(unit separator)	68	D
32	⟨space⟩	69	E
33	!	70	F
34	"	71	G
35	#	72	H
36	$	73	I

APPENDIX F

Number	Character	Number	Character
74	J	101	e
75	K	102	f
76	L	103	g
77	M	104	h
78	N	105	i
79	O	106	j
80	P	107	k
81	Q	108	l
82	R	109	m
83	S	110	n
84	T	111	o
85	U	112	p
86	V	113	q
87	W	114	r
88	X	115	s
89	Y	116	t
90	Z	117	u
91	[	118	v
92	\	119	w
93	]	120	x
94	^	121	y
95	_	122	z
96	`	123	{
97	a	124	|
98	b	125	}
99	c	126	~
100	d	127	⟨del⟩ (delete)

Program Template

The program template of Appendix G gives a suggested layout for typing large programs.

```
        REM ***************************************************
                PROGRAM NAME:           AUTHOR AND DATE
        ***************************************************
           (brief description of program)
        LIST OF VARIABLES:
        LIST OF ARRAYS AND MATRICES:
        LIST OF CONSTANTS:
        LIST OF SUBROUTINES:
        LIST OF FUNCTIONS:
        LIST OF DATA FILES USED:
        !----- end of remark section ---------
200     OPTION clause must be first if used
        ON ERROR GOTO error-handler
        EXTERNAL function declarations
        DIMENSION arrays and matrices
        DECLARE variables
        DECLARE constant values
        MAP definitions
        OPEN files


1000    !--- main program logic -----------------



        GOTO finish
10000   !--- subroutines: ------------------------


15000   !--- functions: ------------------------
19000   !--- error handling: -------------------
        error-handler:


32000
         finish:
              END
```

APPENDIX G

The Text Editor

Text editing, or word processing, provides a convenient means of creating or changing text files. (A text file is often called an ASCII file because it contains information stored using the ASCII code of Appendix F.)

The text editor may be used from BASIC mode or from EDIT mode. While you are working in BASIC mode, you can use the text editor to make changes to the program list in main memory. After you have saved a BASIC program, you can use the text editor in DCL mode to make changes to the program file that contains a copy of the program on disk memory.

Appendix H contains a quick introduction to the EDT text editor. You must use a terminal that understands the standard cursor-control sequences in order to make full use of this editor. Before beginning you may wish to type the following version of the BOTTLES program:

```
100    PRINT "100 BOTTLES OF BEAR ON THE WALL"
110 PRINT "100 BOTTLES OF BEER BEER
120    PRINT "IF ONEOF THOSE BOTTLES SHOULD FALL"
130    PRINT     "99 BOTTES OF BEER ON THE WALL"
```

Enter BASIC mode, use the `NEW BOTTLES` command, and type the program exactly as you see it. Then `SAVE` the program to create a disk file to edit. You can `EXIT` from BASIC mode and use the editor to change the disk file or stay in BASIC mode and use the editor to change the program list in main memory.

H.1 Entering and Leaving EDIT Mode

Text editing is carried out in `EDIT` or in EDIT/CHANGE mode and uses special edit commands and function keys. Enter EDIT mode by typing the **EDIT** command in BASIC mode or in DCL mode (see Fig. H.1). The asterisk (*) is the EDIT command prompt.

Use the `EDIT` command from BASIC mode to edit the program stored in the program list of main memory. Use the `$EDIT` command (in DCL mode) to edit a specific disk file. The $EDIT command should be followed by the file specification of the disk file to be edited.

From BASIC mode:	From DCL mode:
`EDIT`	`$EDIT BOTTLES.BAS`

APPENDIX H

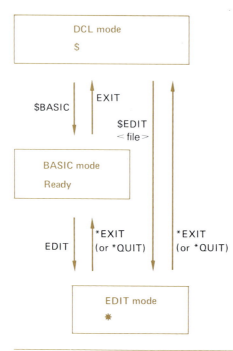

FIGURE H.1 Enter EDIT mode using the EDIT command from DCL mode or from BASIC mode. The asterisk (*) is the EDIT command prompt. Leave EDIT mode by typing the *EXIT command. Note that the *EXIT command causes a return to the mode from which the editor was called.

Normally, the editor will be used to make changes to an existing program or disk file. In this case the computer enters EDIT mode and displays the first line of the file followed by the EDIT command prompt.

```
1  100 PRINT "100 BOTTLES OF BEER ON THE WALL"
*
```

If the file you have specified is not in your directory, the editor creates a new (empty) file and displays the following response:

```
$EDIT BOTTOLES.BAS

Input file does not exist
[EOB]
*
```

The symbol [EOB] (end of buffer) marks the end of the file. The response shows that the end of the file marker is at the beginning of the file, and hence the file is empty.

If you wish, the editor can be used in this way to create a new file. However, it is recommended that you create BASIC program files from BASIC mode and use the editor only to make corrections.

If you have incorrectly typed the file specification and obtain the "Input file does not exist" response, recover from your mistake by typing the *QUIT command, and then retype the $EDIT command with the correct file specification. *QUIT is used instead of *EXIT to discard the newly created file. If you use *EXIT to leave edit mode, the system will save the empty file BOTTOLES.BAS.

```
*QUIT
$EDIT BOTTLES.BAS

1    100    PRINT "100 BOTTLES OF BEER ON THE WALL"
*
```

Review: Entering and Leaving EDIT Mode

- Use the `EDIT` command from BASIC mode to make changes on the program in main memory.
- Use the `$EDIT ⟨filespec⟩` command to make changes in a specific disk file.
- Use the `*EXIT` command to return to BASIC or DCL mode. Changes made while in EDIT mode will be incorporated in the new version of the program or file.
- Use the `*QUIT` command to return to BASIC or DCL mode. This returns you to where you were just before the EDIT command was entered. The changes made while in EDIT mode will not be incorporated into the program or file, and the previous version will be retained.

H.2 Entering and Leaving CHANGE Mode

Most corrections and changes will be carried out in EDIT/CHANGE mode. You can enter CHANGE mode from EDIT mode by typing the *C command (see Fig. H.2). You can return to EDIT mode by typing ⟨ctrl/Z⟩.

APPENDIX H

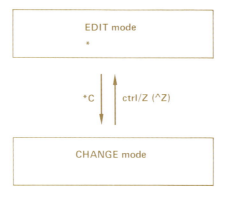

FIGURE H.2 Enter CHANGE mode from EDIT mode by typing the *C command. Return to EDIT mode by typing ⟨ctrl/Z⟩ (hold the control key down and type the letter z). There is no command prompt in CHANGE mode because commands are entered using special keys.

When the *C command is entered, the display screen will be erased and the file will be displayed. In CHANGE mode, the end of file marker, [EOB], is shown at the end of the file and the cursor is positioned at the beginning of the file.

```
100    PRINT "100 BOTTLES OF BEAR ON THE WALL"
110 PRINT "100 BOTTLES OF BEER BEER
120    PRINT "IF ONEOF THOSE BOTTLES SHOULD FALL"
130    PRINT    "99 BOTTES OF BEER ON THE WALL"
[EOB]
```

Review: Entering and Leaving CHANGE Mode

- Use the *C command to enter CHANGE mode from EDIT mode.
- Use ⟨ctrl/z⟩ to return to EDIT mode.

H.3 EDIT/CHANGE Command Keys

In EDIT/CHANGE mode, commands are entered using special command keys. There are 22 keys that have special uses in CHANGE mode (see Fig. H.3). These include the four arrow keys along the upper right edge of the keyboard and all of the keys on the numeric keypad to the right of the keyboard.

THE TEXT EDITOR

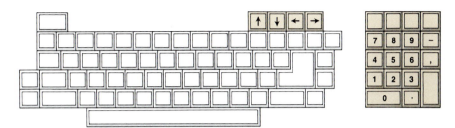

FIGURE H.3 The command keys used in EDIT/CHANGE mode.

H.4 An Easy Way to Make Changes

In EDIT/CHANGE mode, a portion of the file is displayed on the screen and the *cursor*, is shown as a blinking rectangle or underline character to indicate where new text may be entered in the file. To enter text, use the arrow keys to move the cursor to the position where the text is to be inserted and start typing.

As an illustration, consider the following version of the BOTTLES program:

```
100    PRINT "100 BOTTLES OF BEAR ON THE WALL"
110 PRINT "100 BOTTLES OF BEER BEER
120    PRINT "IF ONEOF THOSE BOTTLES SHOULD FALL"
130    PRINT    "99 BOTTES OF BEER ON THE WALL"
[EOB]
```

When you first enter EDIT/CHANGE mode the cursor is at the beginning of the file, and you can insert new text there; the existing text will be moved out of the way.

Try typing a couple of letters. As you type, the characters are inserted and the existing text is moved to the right. Notice that the cursor moves to the right as you type. Use the delete key to remove the text you have just entered. The cursor is moved to the left, and wipes out characters as it moves.

Next, use the right-arrow key (→) to move the cursor to the word ON in line 100. Use the left-arrow key (←) to move the cursor back to the letter R in BEAR. Notice that nothing happens to the text as the cursor moves past it. Correct the spelling error by pressing the ⟨delete⟩ key and typing the letter 'E' (see Fig. H.4).

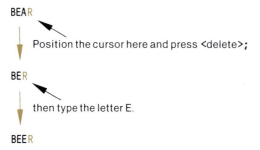

FIGURE H.4 Move the cursor to a position immediately after the spot where a correction is to be made. Use the ⟨delete⟩ key to remove unwanted text and then type in the correct text.

Now press the right-arrow key several times to move the cursor past the end of the line. Notice that the cursor goes off the end of line 100 and appears at the beginning of line 110. Continue to press the key until the cursor is positioned after the line number but before the word **PRINT**. Correct the spacing by pressing the space bar. This inserts space characters and moves the text to the right (see Fig. H.5).

As an exercise, move the cursor to the end of line 110, remove the extra word **BEER**, and insert a quotation mark. The program should end up as follows:

```
100    PRINT "100 BOTTLES OF BEER ON THE WALL"
110    PRINT "100 BOTTLES OF BEER"
120    PRINT "IF ONEOF THOSE BOTTLES SHOULD FALL"
130    PRINT    "99 BOTTES OF BEER ON THE WALL"
[EOB]
```

Next, use the down-arrow key to move to line 120. Position the cursor to the second O in ONEOF and insert a space. Then use the arrow keys to move to the letter E in BOTTES on line 130, and insert the letter L.

FIGURE H.5 Insert spaces to move text to the right. This technique can be used to correct spacing.

THE TEXT EDITOR

Review: Quick Corrections

- Use EDIT/CHANGE mode to insert text at the position of the cursor.
- Use the four arrow keys to move the cursor UP, DOWN, LEFT, or RIGHT to a position immediately to the right of the spot where the change is to be made.
- Use the ⟨delete⟩ key to remove unwanted text to the left of the cursor.

H.5 Splitting and Joining Lines

The ⟨return⟩ key can be used to split a line of text into two lines. As an illustration, position the cursor at the letter S in the word SHOULD on line 120, and press the ⟨return⟩ key. Line 120 will be split into two lines, and line 130 will be moved down to allow space (see Fig. H.6). The cursor remains at the letter S and moves to the beginning of the new line.

Next, rejoin the line by pressing the ⟨delete⟩ key. The cursor was positioned at the beginning of the line, and so the ⟨delete⟩ key removed the "line separator," thus joining the lines together.

The ⟨return⟩ key can also be used to make room for the insertion of new lines. Position the cursor at the end of a line and press the ⟨return⟩ key, or position the cursor at the beginning of a line and press the ⟨return⟩ key. This opens up a blank line for the insertion of new text.

Review: Splitting and Joining Lines

- A line can be split by positioning the cursor at the point where the new line is to begin and pressing the ⟨return⟩ key.
- A line can be joined to the previous one by positioning the cursor at the beginning of the line and pressing the ⟨return⟩ key.

```
120 PRINT "IF ONE OF THOSE BOTTLES SHOULD FALL"
```

Position the cursor here, and press the \<return\> key.

```
120 PRINT "IF ONE OF THOSE BOTTLES
SHOULD FALL"
```

FIGURE H.6 Use the ⟨return⟩ key to split a line.

■ A blank line can be created for the insertion of text by positioning the cursor at the end of the previous line or at the beginning of the following line and pressing the ⟨return⟩ key.

H.6 Some Additional Features of EDT

In Section H.5, we outlined an easy way to make changes in EDIT mode. Just about any kind of change can be made using that procedure.

The EDT editor has other features that make it easier to accomplish the same type of change. This section will go over some of these features.

Generally speaking, the additional features make it possible to move through the file more rapidly and permit deletion of larger chunks of the file. These require the use of commands entered through the keypad to the right of the terminal keyboard (see Fig. H.7).

The advance and backup commands (keypad keys 4 and 5) tell the computer the direction to move the cursor when the word and line com-

PF1 GOLD	PF2 HELP	PF3	PF4 DEL L (UND L)
7	8	9	— DEL W (UND W)
4 ADVANCE	5 BACKUP	6 CUT (PASTE)	,
1 WORD	2 EOL	3	ENTER
0 LINE		• SELECT	

FIGURE H.7 Some of the special EDIT/CHANGE-mode commands that can be entered through the terminal keypad. All of the keys have special functions. We will discuss only the ones shown here.

mands are entered (keypad keys 1 and 0). The delete line (key PF4) and the delete word (the minus key on the keypad) delete text a chunk at a time. The PF4 and minus keys can be used with the GOLD key (PF1) to undelete a line or undelete a word.

To become familiar with these commands, press the advance command (key 4) and press the word command (key 1). The cursor should advance to the beginning of the next word. Continue to press key 1 to advance the cursor to the end of the program. Now press the backup command (key 5) and press the word key several times to move the cursor back to the beginning of the program. Press the advance command and the line command (key 0) to move the cursor to the beginning of the next line. Press the end-of-line command (key 2) to move the cursor to the end of the line. Continue to use keys 0, 1, 2, 4, and 5 to move through the file until you feel comfortable using them.

Next, position the cursor at the beginning of the word SHOULD in line 120. Press the delete-word command (the minus key) twice to delete the last two words of the line. You can always undo the last deletion by pressing the GOLD command (key PF1) followed by the delete-word command (the minus key). The GOLD command changes the delete-word command to the undelete-word command, and so the last word deleted (FALL") is restored.

Finally, move the cursor to the beginning of line 110 and press the delete-line command (key PF4). Restore this line by using the GOLD command (key PF1) followed by the delete-line command (key PF4). Once again, the GOLD key has changed the delete-line command to the undelete-line command.

You can ask the computer to give you help on any of these commands by pressing the help command (key PF2) and following directions.

H.7 Cut-and-Paste Operations

Cut-and-paste operations are useful when you wish to move blocks of your program around. Cut and paste is a three-step process:

- SELECT the text to be moved.
- CUT the selected text out of the program.
- PASTE the text back into the program at the desired location.

TO SELECT THE TEXT

1. Move the cursor to the beginning of the text.
2. Press the select command (the decimal point key).
3. Move the cursor to the end of the text to be selected.

While selecting text, you may use any of the usual methods to move the cursor (arrow keys or keys 0, 1, 2, 4, or 5). Selected text will be outlined in reverse video.

TO CUT THE SELECTED TEXT
1. Press the CUT command (key 6).

TO PASTE THE SELECTED TEXT
1. Move the cursor to the place where the text is to be inserted. Text will be inserted immediately before the cursor.
2. Enter the PASTE command by pressing the GOLD key (key PF1) followed by the CUT command (key 6). Here the GOLD key changes the CUT command to the PASTE command.

Effective Use of the Video Terminal

The video terminal used with the VAX computer has a number of special features that can be employed to enhance your programs or make them easier to use. This appendix outlines some of these features. This information applies to the standard VT 100 series of terminals as well as the newer VT 200 series (see Fig. I.1). However the special color graphics capabilities of the VT 240 series of terminals are not discussed here.

FIGURE I.1 Graphics terminals like the VT241 can be used to display color graphs and charts. Most applications use custom software to create graphics displays. Special graphs may be created using BASIC programs.

I.1 Communications

The terminal is essentially a communications device that sends and receives information in the form of characters (see Fig. I.2). When you press a letter key, a signal is sent to the VAX computer, and the VAX sends a confirmation signal back to the terminal. This confirmation signal normally causes the letter to be displayed. For example, if you press the L key, the L character is sent to the VAX computer, and it sends back, or "echoes," the same charac-

APPENDIX
I

ter. As a result, the letter L is displayed on the terminal screen. Thus the terminal depends on the VAX computer to display the characters that you type.

You can conduct a short experiment to illustrate the communications aspect of the terminal. Beginning in DCL mode, press the NO SCROLL key and type one or more commands. For example,

BASIC <ret> HELP <ret> STATEMENT <ret> SLEEP <ret>

You will not see anything on the screen because the NO SCROLL key has temporarily stopped the computer from echoing your commands. The commands have nevertheless been entered into the computer. You can verify this by pressing the NO SCROLL key again. The computer has stored your commands and will carry them out at the appropriate time.

The receiver of the video terminal normally takes the characters sent to it from the VAX and displays the appropriate letter or symbol. However, there are some special characters that serve as commands to the terminal. These commands begin with the escape character (character number 27 in the ASCII code). The internal logic of the terminal will recognize these command sequences and carry out special operations in response. For example, the special sequence ⟨esc⟩[2J will cause the terminal screen to be erased. That is, if the terminal is sent this sequence of characters, it will interpret them as the special command to erase the screen (see Fig. I.3).

Here is a short program to erase the screen:

```
100 LET ERAS$ = ESC + "[2J"
110 PRINT ERAS$
120 END
```

The string variable ERAS$ stores the special character sequence for erasing the screen. When ERAS$ is "printed," the value of ERAS$ is sent to the terminal for display, but the internal logic recognizes it as a special command and erases the screen instead. A list of some of the special command sequences is given in Table I.1.

TABLE I.1 Escape sequences that can be used to perform the indicated operations. There is nothing special about the choice of names for the string variables ERAS$, ERAL$, and so on. The ones shown here have been used in some of the example programs.

ERAS$=ESC+"[2J"	Erases the screen.
ERAL$=ESC+"[K"	Erases the rest of the line.
GRA$=ESC+"(0"	Shifts to graphics characters.
STD$=ESC+"(B"	Returns to standard characters.
REV$=ESC+"[7m"	Turns on reverse video.
NOR$=ESC+"[0m"	Turns off reverse video.

EFFECTIVE USE OF THE VIDEO TERMINAL

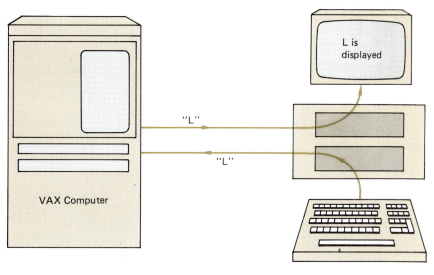

FIGURE I.2

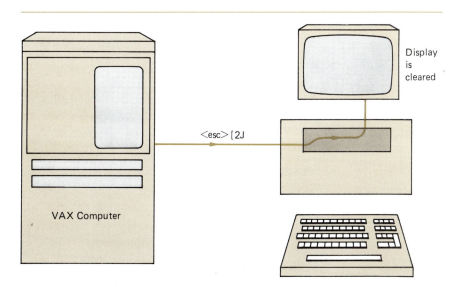

FIGURE I.3 The terminal receiver reroutes special escape sequences to internal logic circuits that perform display operations.

I.2 Double-Size Displays

The video terminal can display oversize characters using the sequences

<esc>#3
<esc>#4

The first sequence is used for the upper half of the display, and the second, for the lower half. Here is an example:

```
100 PRINT ESC; "#3"; " H E L L O"
110 PRINT ESC; "#4"; " H E L L O"
```

and one a little more sophisticated:

```
100 LET DBL.U$= ESC+"#3"
    LET DBL.L$= ESC+"#4"
    LET ERAS$= ESC+"[2J"
200 INPUT 'WHAT MESSAGE'; M$
    PRINT ERAS$
    PRINT DBL.U$; M$
    PRINT DBL.L$; M$
300 END
```

I.3 Moving the Cursor

The typical terminal display consists of 24 lines of 80 columns. When characters are received by the terminal, they are displayed at the bottom of the existing text. If the screen is full, the existing lines are moved up or "scrolled" to make room for new text. If the cursor is moved to a new position on the screen, text will be displayed from that position, thus overwriting part of the existing display.

The simplest way to move the cursor is to use the sequence

<esc>[23A

This particular command will move the cursor up 23 lines from its current position. Other numbers can be used in the command to move the cursor a different number of lines. This is a relatively primitive method of moving the cursor. It is also possible to move the cursor to a prescribed location on the screen. For example, the sequence

<esc>[3;5H

will move the cursor to row 3 and column 5. The function

```
DEF FNPOS$(R,C) = ESC + "[" + STR$(R) + ";" + STR$(C) + "H"
```

can be used in a program to locate the cursor at row R and column C. Once this function has been defined, the cursor can be moved to the appropriate spot using

```
PRINT FNPOS$(R,C);
```

This method of cursor positioning has been used in some of the more advanced examples in the text.

INDEX

! comment delimiter, 56–57
& used for line continuation, 84, 240, 268

Abbreviating DCL commands, 8
ABS function, 72, 351
Absolute value function, 71
ACCESS APPEND clause in OPEN statement, 299–300
Accessing a file. *See* File
Adding to a data file, 299–300
Algebraic expression, 65–70
Algebraic expressions in a PRINT statement, 66
Algebraic operations, 66–70
   priority, 67
   symbols and meanings, 67
Algorithm, 4–5, 128–130
American National Standards Institute. *See* ANSI
American Standard Code for Information Interchange. *See* ASCII
Ampersand (&) for multiline statement, 84, 240, 268
AND, 81
ANSI standard BASIC, 1
APPEND command (Basic), 337
   to combine programs, 153–160
   DCL command, 333
Argument
   for external modules, 327–330
   for a function, 71–74
   for user-defined function, 148–150
Arithmetic expression, 65–70
Arithmetic logic unit (ALU), 5
Arithmetic operations, 66–70
Array. *See also* Matrix, 163
   rectangular, 262–263
   specifying data type, 322
   string, 164
Arrow keys, use in EDIT mode, 365–367
ASCII, 118
ASCII table, 357–358

Assignment statement, 65–66
ATN function, 352
Average, 100–101, 113

Backspace key, 10–11
Bar graph, 106–109
BASIC, ANSI standard, 1
BASIC command (DCL), 13–15, 333
BASIC mode, 13
BDAYLIST program, 315
BIRTHDAY program, 316
BLACKBOOK program, 313–314
Boolean variable,
   used in bubble sort, 175–177
BOTTLES program, 16
Bubble sort, 172–177
Buffer for a mapped file, 296–297
Bugs, 131
Building a program, 150–160
Built-in function, 71–75
   ABS, 71
   INT, 72
   RANDOM, 73
   RND, 73
   SQR, 71
BUSINESS program, 270–278
Byte, 118
   data type, 320

Calculations
   in LET or PRINT statement, 65–70
   with matrices, 268–270
CALL statement, 330, 339
Calling an external program, 329–331
Caps lock key, 10
CASE statement, 93
   CASE ELSE, 93
Cathode ray tube (crt), 8
Centering text, 193–194
Central processor, 5–7
Change mode (for editing), 363–364
CHANGE statement, 339
Channel, 220, 223
Character string. *See* String
CHR$ function, 185–187, 353

INDEX

CLOSE statement, 221, 339
Column of a matrix, 262–263
Combining programs, 151–160
Comma
   in MAT PRINT statement, 265
   in PRINT statement, 48
   in PRINT USING statement, 204
Comment field, 56–57
Comments, wise use of, 133
Comparisons, string, 124
Compiling a program, 326–327
Compound interest (example programs), 207–209, 325–326
Computer notation, 68
CON matrix, 270, 343
Concatenation, 188–190
Condition, logical, 80
Conditional execution
   IF-THEN, 80
Conditional statements, 79
Constant, declaring, 321
Continuation lines, 84, 240, 268
CONTINUE command, 132, 337
Control key, 10
Control variable, 99
Conversions
   number to string, 197–198
   string to number, 200–202
Correcting program errors, 15–21
   using the text (EDT) editor, 361–370
COPY command (DCL), 333
COS function, 352
CRYPTO program, 233
Cursor, 365–368
Cursor control, 289, 374–375
   in LIFE program, 284–286
   in LINEQ2 program, 288–291
Cut and paste editing, 369–370

Data
   improved entry method, 300–307
   running out of, 131
Data file, 219–230, 295–312
   for matrix, 266–268
   updating, 299–307
Data list, 3–4, 51
DATA statement, 50–53, 339
   for string, 120
DATE$ function, 187, 353
DCL commands, 333–335
   abbreviating, 8
   from BASIC mode, 29–31
Decimal data type, 320, 325–326

Decision-making construct, 79–86
DECLARE statement, 321, 339
   in HANGMAN program, 213
   used in example, 313, 315, 316
DECODE program, 234
DECwriter, 33
DEF statement, 148–150, 340
Default values, 22
DELETE command (Basic), 154–155, 337
DELETE command (DCL), 27–29, 333
Delete key, 10–11
DELETE statement, 340
Deleting a program, 26–29
Delimiters, for string, 119
DIF$ function, 353
Dimension of an array, 165
DIMENSION statement (DIM), 165–166, 261, 340–341
   using data types in, 322
DIRECTORY command (DCL), 22, 25, 334
   from BASIC mode, 30
Discriminant, 86–87
Disk storage, 5
Double dollar sign ($$) in PRINT USING, 204
Dummy variables. *See* Local variables

E format, 71
Economic indicators (BUSINESS program), 272
ECOUNT program, 229
ECOUNT2 program, 240–242
EDIT command (Basic), 36–37, 337, 361
EDIT command (DCL), 334, 361
EDIT mode, 6–7, 361–370
EDIT$ function, 187–188, 353
EDIT/CHANGE mode, 363–367
Empty string, 119
END DEF (same as FNEND), 148–150, 341
END FUNCTION, 327–330, 341
END IF statement, 83, 90, 94
End of file error, testing for, 226
END SELECT statement, 92, 341
END statement, 58, 341
END SUB statement, 330, 341
EOB symbol, 363
Equal sign in an assignment statement, 65–66
Erasing the terminal screen, 372
   ERAS$, ERAL$ used in LINEQ2, 289
ERR system variable, 227
Error
   logical, 132
   messages, 226
   trap, 227
ESC constant, 353

Exercise calculation, 88
EXERCISE program, 242–247
EXIT command (Basic), 14, 337
EXIT command (Edit), 362–363
EXIT statement, 240–242, 341
EXP function, 351
Exponential notation, 70–71
Expression, 44–45
External program modules, 326–330
EXTERNAL statement, 328–330, 341
EXVAL calculation for run, 88
EXVAL program, 158

File
    adding to or appending, 227, 299–300
    creating, 225
    indexed, 307–317
    INPUT or LINPUT from, 223–224
    input to a matrix, 266–268
    mapped, 295–307
    terminal format, 219–228
    testing for end, 226
File name, 22–23
File specification, 21–23
File type, 22
FIRSTWORD program, 330
FIX function, 351
FNEND statement (same as END DEF), 148–150, 341
FNJULIAN function in BIRTHDAY program, 312–317
FNPLOT function for graphs, 273, 278
FNPOS$(R,C) function, 375
    used in LINEQ2, 289
FOR loop, 98–101
    nested, 104–106
FOR statement, 98–100, 341
FORMAT$ function, 198–200, 353
Formatting output (PRINT USING), 202–207
FORMTXT program, 247–257
FUNCTION statement, 327–330, 341
Functions, 75, 148–150
    CHR$, 185–187
    DATE$, 187
    EDIT$, 187–188
    FNJULIAN, 312–317
    FORMAT$, 198–200
    Julian date, 211
    NUM$, 197
    POS, 194–195
    STR$, 198
    string, 185–202
    user-defined, 141, 148–150

G.P.A. Example, 92
Game of life, 278–286
Game simulations (RND), 74
Geometric patterns, 109
GET statement, 298–299, 342
GETWORD program, 196
GFLOAT data type, 320
GOSUB statement, 142–143, 342
    with label, 239–242
GOTO statement, 58, 342
    avoiding use of, 58, 129
    before a subroutine, 142
    with label, 239–242
Graph
    age line, 59
    bar, 106–109
    in BUSINESS program, 272–273

HANGMAN program, 213
HELP command, 37–38, 334, 337
HFLOAT data type, 320
High speed printer, 32–33

IDN matrix, 270, 343
IF-THEN, 80
    multi-line, 82
IF-THEN-ELSE, 80, 84–86, 90, 342
    nested, 93
Immediate mode, 69
Index arrays, 179–182
Indexed file, 307–317
Indexing, 179–182
Input
    from a file, 223
    improved method, 300–307
    for a matrix, 266–268
    for string, 120
Input device, 5–7
INPUT statement, 53–56, 342
    FOR A MATRIX, 266–268
    FORMAT ERROR, 131
INT function, 72, 351
INTDCML program, 325–326
Integer data type, 320–321
INTR program, 209
INTRAMT program, 208
INTRDBL program, 323–324
INV matrix operator, 270, 286, 343
Inverting a matrix, 286
IRA program, 103
IRAGRAPH program, 108

Julian date, 210
    in BIRTHDAY program, 312–317

INDEX

Key, 295, 307–331
   compound, 312–317
Key word, 41
Keyboard, 9–11, 365–368

Labels, 240–242
Largest number, 166
LEFT$ function, 353
LEN function, 192–194, 354
LET statement, 41, 43–45, 65–66, 343
   for a matrix, 264–265
   for string, 119
LIFE program, 278–284
LIFEPLOT program, 284–286
Line continuation while using SEQUENCE, 83
Line numbers, 2, 14–20
   omitting, 239–240
   renumbering, 19–21
Linear equation solving, 286–291
LINEQ program, 286–288
LINEQ2 program, 288–291
Linking a program, 326–330
LINPUT statement, 122, 224, 343
LIST command, 17, 21, 337
Listing a program, 17–21
Lists and arrays, 166
Local variables, 149
LOG function, 351
LOG10 function, 351
Logging in, 11–12
Logging out, 14–15
Logical conditions, 80–82
Logical errors, 132
Logical operators, 81–82
   AND, OR, XOR, 81
LOGOUT command (DCL), 15, 334
LONG data type, 320
Loop, 97–114
   control variable, 99
   UNTIL, 111–114
   WHILE, 111–114

MAIL command (DCL), 334
Mail mode, 6–7
MAP statement, 295–297, 343
MARGIN statement, 221–222, 343
Mass storage, 5–7
MAT INPUT statement, 266–268, 344
MAT LINPUT statement, 344
MAT PRINT statement, 265, 344
MAT READ statement, 265, 344
MAT statements, 263–270, 343–344

Matrix
   calculations, 268–270
   inversion, 286, 291
   specifying data type, 322
   subscripts, 261–263
Menu, 145–148
   in EXERCISE program, 243
   in EXVAL program, 158
   in PHONEMENU program, 304
   in PHONINDEX program, 309
MID$ function, 354
Minus sign, 67
   in PRINT USING statement, 204
Mode, 6–7
   EDIT, 6–7
   MAIL, 6–7
   PHONE, 6–7
Monetary calculations, 199
Multiline IF-THEN statement, 82–83
Multiple alternatives, 91
Multiplication, 69

Naming variables, 42–43, 87
Nested IF-THEN-ELSE statement, 93
NEW command, 13, 15, 338
NEXT statement, 98–99
No scroll key, 10–11
NOR$ as used in LINEQ2, 289
NUL$ matrix, 264, 354
Null string, 119
NUM$ function, 197, 354
NUMBER program, 85, 138
Numeric functions, 71
Numerical accuracy, 320

Object code, 326–327
OLD command, 24, 26, 338
ON-ERROR statement, 226–227, 344–345
ON-GOSUB statement, 145–146, 345
ON-GOTO statement, 345
OPEN statement, 220–225, 345
   to append to a file, 299–300
Operator
   logical, 81
   relational, 81
   STRING, 124
OPTION statement, 322–323, 345–346
OR, 81
Outline of a program, 128
Output to a file, 220
Output device, 5–7

INDEX

PFILE program, 228
PHONE command (DCL), 334
Phone mode, 6-7
PHONEADD program, 300
PHONECHNG program, 302
PHONELIST program, 299
PHONEMAP program, 298
PHONEMENU program, 303-307
PHONINDEX program, 308-311
PI constant, 351
Pointer, 51
POS function, 194-195, 354
Pound sign (#)
   in PRINT USING statement, 204
Present-worth factor, 70
PRINT command, 31-33, 334
Print queue, 33
PRINT statement, 46-49, 65-66, 346
   for a matrix, 263-265
   for string, 119
   tabbing over, 48-50
   two-part, 47
PRINT USING statement, 202-207, 346
   special format symbols, 204
Printing at a terminal, 33
Printing files, 31-35
   using a data file, 222-223
Problem solving, 127-132
PROD$ function, 354
Program, 2-5
   block, 128, 141
   bugs, 131
   corrections, 15-21, 361-370
   external, 327-331
   list, 2-4
   planning, 127-129
   template, 359
   test run, 131
Program examples
   BDAYLIST, 315
   BIRTHDAY, 316
   BLACKBOOK, 313-314
   BUSINESS, 270-278
   CRYPTO, 233
   DECODE, 234
   ECOUNT, 229
   ECOUNT2, 240-242
   EXERCISE, 242-247
   EXVAL, 158
   FIRSTWORD, 330
   FORMTXT, 247-257
   GETWORD, 196
   HANGMAN, 213
   INTDCML, 325-326
   INTR, 209
   INTRAMT, 208
   INTRDBL, 323-324
   IRA, 103
   IRAGRAPH, 108
   LIFE, 278-284
   LIFEPLOT, 284-286
   LINEQ, 286-288
   LINEQ2, 288-291
   NUMBER, 138
   OUTLINE, 128
   PFILE, 228
   PHONEADD, 300
   PHONECHNG, 302
   PHONELIST, 299
   PHONEMAP, 298
   PHONEMENU, 303-307
   PHONINDEX, 308-311
   QUADRA, 89
   RUNVAL, 91
   SROOT, 221
Prohibited words, 43
PURGE command (DCL), 26, 334
PUT statement, 298-299, 346

QUADRA program, 89
Quadratic equation, 74, 86
Queue, 33
QUO$ function, 354
Quotation sign, 119
Quoted string, 119

Random number table, 73
RANDOMIZE, 74-75, 347
READ statement, 50-53, 347
   for a matrix, 263-266
   for string, 120
READ/DATA pair, 50-53
Real numbers
   double precision, 320, 323-324
Rectangular array, 262
Recursive subroutine, 247
Relational operator
   meanings, 81
   string, 124
REMARK statement and !, 56-57, 347
   using REM without line numbers, 240
RENAME command, 26-29, 334, 338
Renaming a program, 26-29
Repeating program steps, 98

INDEX

RESEQUENCE command, 88, 338
RESTORE statement, 52–53, 347
   for data file, 230
RESUME statement, 226–228, 347
   line number required for, 239
Retirement graph, 108
Retirement table, 102
Return key, 10–12, 367–368
RETURN statement in a subroutine, 142–143
REV$ used in LINEQ2, 289
RIGHT$ function, 354
RND function, 72, 352
   game simulations, 74
Row of a matrix, 262–263
RUN command, 14, 54, 338
Running a program, 17
RUNVAL program, 91

SAVE command, 14–15, 25, 338
Scientific notation, 71
SEG$ function, 191–192, 355
SELECT statement, 91–94, 347–348
Selection sort, 169–172
Semicolon
   in MAT PRINT statement, 265
   in PRINT statement, 46
SEQUENCE command, 35–36, 61, 338
   and line continuations, 83–84
   used to align statements, 130
SET PASSWORD command (DCL), 334
SGN function, 352
Shift key, 10
SHOW DEFAULT command (DCL), 22, 334–335
SHOW QUEUE command (DCL), 33, 334
Significant digits, 70–71
Simulation, 278–281
SIN function, 352
SLEEP statement, 110, 348
Solving a linear equation, 286–291
Sort
   bubble, 172–177
   selection, 169–172
   tandem, 178–179
Sorting a list, 169–182
Source code, 326–327
SP constant, 355
SPACE$ function, 235, 355
SQR function, 73, 352
Square root, 72
Squared expressions, 70
SROOT program, 221

Start value in FOR loop, 99
Statement, 41
   CASE, 93
   conditional, 79
   DATA, 50–53
   DECLARE, 321
   DIMENSION, 165, 261, 322
   FOR, 98
   GET, 298–299
   GOSUB, 142–143
   GOTO, 58
   IF-THEN-ELSE, 84
   INPUT, 53–56
   LET, 41, 43–45
   MAP, 295–297
   ON-GOSUB, 145–146
   OPEN, 297
   OPTION, 322–323
   PRINT, 46–49
   PRINT USING, 202–207
   PUT, 298–299
   READ, 50–53
   REMARK, 56–57
   RETURN, 142–143
   SELECT, 91
Step size in FOR loop, 99
STOP statement, 132, 348
Storage block, 42
   for a matrix, 262–263
   for string, 118
STR$ function, 198, 355
String
   comparisons, 124
   concatenation, 188–190
   functions, 185–202
   null or empty, 119
   segmenting (SEG$), 190–192
   variables, 117–123
STRING$ function, 355
SUB statement, 330–331, 348
Subroutine, 141
   calling itself, 247
   use in program, 150–153
   used at beginning of program, 243
Subscript out of range, 131
Subscripted variable, 163
SUM$ function, 355
Swapping numbers, 170
Swimming calculation, 149
Syntax errors in LET statement, 44–45
Syntax rules, 41
System commands, 8

INDEX

TAB function, 49–50, 355
Tab zones, 48
Table, retirement, 60
TAN function, 352
Tandem sort, 178–179
Template, program, 359
Terminal, 8–11
   keys, 9–11
Terminal-format files, 219–228
Test program, 130
Text re-formatting, 250–257
Time delays, 110
TIME$ function, 355
Trailing minus sign in PRINT USING, 204
TRN operator to transpose a matrix, 270, 343
TYPE command (DCL), 23–24, 335
Typing mistakes, 8–11

UNLESS statement, 348
UNSAVE command, 28–29, 338
UNTIL loop, 111–114
UNTIL statement, 111, 349
UPDATE statement, 300–302, 349
Updating a data file, 299–300

User-defined function, 141, 148–150
Using statements, 59–61

VAL% and VAL function, 201, 355
Variable, 41–42
   matrix, 261
   setting the initial value, 130
   subscripted, 163–165, 261
Variable list, 128
VAX-Basic, 1–2
VAX computer, 1, 5–8
Version number, 22
Video terminal, 8–11, 371–375

WHILE loop, 111–114
WHILE statement, 111, 349
Window to DCL, 29–31
Word data type, 320–321
Word processing, 249–251

XLATE function, 232, 355
XOR, 81

ZER matrix, 264, 270, 343